stews, casseroles & one pot

stews, casseroles & one pot

igloo

Published by Igloo Books Limited
Henson Way
Kettering
Northants
NN16 8PX
info@igloo-books.com

This edition printed in 2005

Copyright © 2005, Arcturus Publishing Limited
26/27 Bickels Yard, 151–153 Bermondsey Street, London SE1 3HA

ISBN 1-84193-313-9

Printed in China

Author: Victoria Chow
With thanks to Yew Yuan Chow and James Mitchell

Project management by Metro Media Limited

Contents

Introduction

There is something immediately comforting about a hot bowlful of stew or casserole. Whether it is to warm you up on a winter's afternoon, or to feed the family in the evening, this book will provide you with many recipes to suit your tastes. Also included are one-pot dishes, such as Beef stroganoff and Rice verde one-pot – delicious dishes that are easy to prepare.

Meat is frequently the main ingredient for stews, and so that is the chapter to open this book. Whether it is lamb, beef, pork, goat or veal that takes your fancy, you will find the recipe here. Recipes include Beef & mushroom stew, Sausage & egg casserole, Lamb & white bean stew and Baked bean & bacon casserole. These are perfect to warm you up on the coldest of days.

If you prefer poultry, then turn to the second chapter which includes delightful chicken, turkey and duck dishes, such as Turkey & tomato one-pot, Duck stew with turnips & onions, Tortilla chicken casserole and One-pot Cajun chicken gumbo. Recipes range from the simple and comfy to the more unusual and complex.

The vegetable chapter is perfect for those who are staying away from meat or just fancy a change. Here you can find Turnip, potato & onion stew, Mushroom hot-pot, Pasta & bean casserole and Brown rice & lentil stew. Vegetables are given a new lease of life in these exciting dishes.

If you are a fish and seafood lover, then dishes such as Trout stew, Monkfish & prawn casserole, Spicy scallop & cauliflower stew and Tuna noodle casserole may inspire you. From snappers to scallops, trout to tuna and cod to clams, you will find fish and seafood recipes from far and wide in this chapter.

Whatever the occasion and the preference, you are bound to find something here to set your taste buds alight.

Meat

Used as a basic ingredient for stews and casseroles through the ages, meat is still regarded by many as a vital part of any dish. Here there are beef, pork and lamb recipes, with inspiration coming from around the world. Irish lamb stew, Tuscan veal stew, Southeast Asian hot pot and Mexican nacho casserole are just a few examples of the variety of tastes ahead.

Lamb & leek stew

SERVES 4

INGREDIENTS:

8 small lamb cutlets (trimmed of all fat, cut into cubes)
450g/1lb leeks (thickly sliced)
3 carrots (thickly sliced)
2 turnips (cut into chunks)

900ml/1½pt lamb stock
Salt and pepper
450g/1lb potatoes (cut into large chunks)
2 tablespoons chopped fresh parsley

- Put all the ingredients except the potatoes and parsley in a large saucepan.
- Bring to the boil and skim the surface. Reduce the heat, part-cover and simmer gently for 1 hour.
- Add the potatoes and a little more seasoning and simmer for a further 30 minutes, or until the potatoes and meat are tender. Serve hot.

Beef & stout casserole

SERVES 4

INGREDIENTS:

700g/1½lb beef
175g/6oz lean bacon (cubed)
1 tablespoon vegetable oil
15g/½oz butter
2 tablespoons plain flour
1 bottle of stout

450g/1lb shallots
Salt and pepper
3 garlic cloves (crushed)
1 tablespoon sugar
1 tablespoon wine or cider vinegar

- Preheat the oven to 150°C/300°F/Gas mark 2.
- Sauté the beef and bacon in the oil. Drain off the excess liquid. Remove the meat and set aside.
- Add the butter to the pan and melt. Stir in the flour to make a roux. Gradually stir in the stout. Place the meat and the shallots in a deep casserole dish and season with the salt and pepper. Add the garlic. Sprinkle the sugar on top, and pour in the sauce. Cover and place in the oven. Cook very gently for up to 3 hours.
- Remove from the oven and mix in the vinegar. Serve with boiled potatoes.

Liver & macaroni casserole

SERVES 4

INGREDIENTS:

350g/12oz pigs' livers (thinly sliced)
25g/1oz butter
2 onions (thinly sliced)
3 tablespoons plain flour
400g/14oz canned chopped tomatoes

150ml/5fl oz chicken stock
2 teaspoons chopped fresh sage
Salt and pepper
100g/4oz macaroni

- Preheat the oven to 180°C/350°F/Gas mark 4.
- Brown the liver in half the butter in a flameproof casserole dish for 1 minute on each side. Remove from the pan with a slotted spoon.
- Add the remaining butter and sauté the onions for 3 minutes until softened and lightly golden. Add the flour and cook, stirring, for 1 minute. Blend in the can of tomatoes and stock. Bring to the boil, stirring, for 1 minute.
- Return the liver to the pan and add the sage and a little salt and pepper. Cover and cook in the oven for 1 hour.
- Cook the macaroni according to the directions on the packet. Drain and stir into the casserole. Serve hot.

Beef hotpot

SERVES 4

INGREDIENTS:

900g/2lb rump steak (cubed)
Salt and pepper
350g/12oz carrots (thickly sliced)

2 onions (thickly sliced)
700g/1½lb potatoes (thickly sliced)
500ml/18fl oz beef stock

- Preheat the oven to 170°C/325°F/Gas mark 3.
- Arrange a layer of beef in a casserole dish. Sprinkle over a little salt and pepper, then top with a layer of carrots, onions and potatoes. Pour in the stock.
- Cover and bake for 2 to 2½ hours or until the meat is tender. Increase the oven temperature to 200°C/400°F/Gas mark 6 and cook for another 30 minutes or until potatoes are brown.

French beef stew

SERVES 6–8

INGREDIENTS:

225g/8oz unsmoked streaky bacon (cubed)
3 tablespoons olive oil
2 large onions (sliced)
1.4kg/3lb rump steak (cut into 2.5cm/1in cubes)
3 large carrots (sliced)

700g/1½lb tomatoes (roughly chopped)
1 tablespoon tomato purée
3 garlic cloves (crushed)
Salt and pepper
100g/4oz pork rinds (diced)
600ml/1pt red wine
50ml/2fl oz brandy

- Preheat the oven to 150°C/300°F/Gas mark 2.
- Fry the bacon in the olive oil until lightly browned. Scoop out and spread over the base of an ovenproof casserole dish.
- Fry the onions in the same fat, until golden, and add to the casserole.
- Brown the beef in the fat, over a high heat, in batches. Arrange on top of the onions. Add the carrots, tomatoes, tomato purée, garlic, salt and pepper. Cover with the pork rinds.
- Pour the excess fat out of the frying pan and pour in the wine. Bring to the boil and pour over the contents of the casserole.
- Add the brandy to the pan, warm quickly and set alight at arm's length. When the flames die down, pour the brandy into the casserole. Add enough water to almost cover the casserole dish's content. Cover tightly and cook in the oven for 3 to 4 hours, stirring once or twice. Serve hot.

Irish hotpot

SERVES 6

INGREDIENTS:

6 potatoes (thinly sliced)
2 onions (thinly sliced)
3 carrots (thinly sliced)
Salt and pepper
75g/3oz cooked long-grain rice

400g/14oz canned peas
600g/1lb 5oz pork and herb sausages
425g/15oz canned condensed tomato soup (diluted)

- Preheat the oven to 190°C/375°F/Gas mark 5.
- Layer the potatoes, onions and carrots in a large casserole dish, seasoning as you

go with salt and pepper. Sprinkle with the rice and peas and top with the sausages. Pour the diluted soup over all.

● Bake, covered, for 1 hour. Remove the cover, turn the sausages and bake for a further 1 hour, uncovered.

Sweet lamb hotpot & dumplings

SERVES 4-6

INGREDIENTS:

700g/1½lb neck of lamb (chopped)
2 teaspoons redcurrant jelly
2 onions (chopped)
3 carrots (chopped)
1 turnip (chopped)
175g/6oz mushrooms (sliced)
1 parsnip (chopped and blanched)
Salt and pepper

1 tablespoon tomato purée
600ml/1pt vegetable stock

For the dumplings:
100g/4oz self-raising flour
50g/2oz suet (shredded)
1 teaspoon chopped fresh parsley

● Set oven to 190°C/375°F/Gas mark 5.
● Put the pieces of meat in the bottom of a large casserole dish. Spread them with the redcurrant jelly and place in the oven for 15 minutes. Remove and add the vegetables and a little salt and pepper. Stir the tomato puree into the stock or water. Pour over the meat and vegetables. Return to the oven. Reduce the heat to 180°C/350°F/Gas mark 4 and cook for about 1½ hours until the meat is tender.
● To make the dumplings, mix together the flour, suet, parsley and seasoning with enough water to form a stiff dough. This should make about 6 small dumplings.
● Add the dumplings to the hotpot for the last 30 minutes of cooking.

Biscuit-topped Italian casserole

SERVES 6-8

INGREDIENTS:

450g/1lb minced beef
150g/5oz onion (chopped)
50ml/2fl oz water
¼ teaspoon ground black pepper
225g/8oz tomato sauce

175g/6oz tomato purée
250g/9oz frozen mixed vegetables (thawed)
225g/8oz mozzarella cheese (grated)
275g/10oz digestive biscuits (crushed)

- Preheat the oven to 190°C/375°F/Gas mark 3. Grease a 30 x 20cm/12 x 8in baking dish.
- In a large frying pan, brown the beef and onion, then pour off the fat. Stir in the water, pepper, tomato sauce and tomato purée and simmer for 15 minutes, stirring occasionally. Remove from the heat and stir in the vegetables and 200g/7oz mozzarella. Spoon the mixture into the prepared baking dish.
- Sprinkle the biscuits over the top of the meat mixture, then sprinkle the remaining cheese over the top. Bake in the oven for 20 to 25 minutes, until the biscuits are browned.

Beef pot roast

SERVES 4-6

INGREDIENTS:

2 green peppers (chopped)
1 large tomato (finely chopped)
3 spring onions (finely chopped)
3 garlic cloves (finely chopped)
3 sprigs fresh parsley (finely chopped)
3 sprigs fresh thyme (finely chopped)
1.8kg/4lb topside beef
2 tablespoons malt vinegar
2 tablespoons soy sauce

4 teaspoons brown sugar
600ml/1pt beef stock
1 medium onion (finely chopped)
3 carrots (sliced)
225g/8oz yellow yam (peeled and diced)
225g/8oz potatoes (peeled and diced)
Salt and pepper

- Mix 1 pepper with the tomato, spring onions, garlic, parsley and thyme to create

a seasoning mixture. Cut deep slits in the beef and stuff with the seasoning, rubbing any excess over the meat. Place in a deep dish, pour over the vinegar and soy sauce and leave at room temperature for 4 hours, basting frequently.
- Drain the meat, pat dry and rub in the sugar.
- Brown the meat in a casserole dish or cast iron pot, then add the stock, onion, remaining pepper and any left-over marinade.
- Bring to the boil, then cover and simmer for 3 hours or until meat is tender. Add the carrots, yam and potatoes for the last 20 minutes of the cooking time.
- Serve hot.

Spanish-style pork stew with saffron rice

SERVES 4

INGREDIENTS:

2 tablespoons olive oil
900g/2lb boneless pork shoulder (diced)
1 large onion (sliced)
2 garlic cloves (finely chopped)
1 tablespoon plain flour
450g/1lb canned chopped plum tomatoes
175ml/6fl oz red wine
1 tablespoon chopped fresh basil
1 green pepper (sliced)

50g/2oz olives (halved and pitted)
Salt and pepper

For the saffron rice:
1 tablespoon olive oil
25g/1oz butter
1 small onion (finely chopped)
Few strands of saffron (crushed)
250g/9oz long-grain white rice
600ml/1pt chicken stock

- Preheat the oven to 150°C/300°F/Gas mark 2.
- Heat the oil in a large flameproof casserole dish and add the pork in batches. Fry over a high heat until browned. When browned remove and place on a plate.
- Lower the heat and add the onion to the casserole. Cook for 5 minutes, until soft and starting to brown. Add the garlic and stir briefly before returning the pork to the casserole. Add the flour and stir.
- Add the tomatoes. Gradually stir in the red wine and add the basil. Bring to simmering point and cover. Transfer the casserole to the lower part of the oven and cook for 1½ hours. Stir in the green pepper and cook for 30 minutes.
- Season to taste with salt and pepper.
- To make the saffron rice, heat the oil with the butter in a saucepan. Add the onion and cook for 5 minutes over a medium heat until softened. Add the

→

←

saffron and rice and stir well. Add the stock, bring to the boil, cover and reduce the heat as low as possible. Cook for 15 minutes, covered, until the rice is tender and the stock is absorbed. Adjust the seasoning and serve with the stew.

Pot roast

SERVES 6

INGREDIENTS:

1 teaspoon dried thyme
1 teaspoon dried rosemary
1 teaspoon paprika
1 tablespoon salt
½ teaspoon freshly ground
black pepper
1.8kg/4lb fillet steak
2 tablespoons vegetable oil
2 large onions (sliced)
6 garlic cloves (chopped)
50ml/2fl oz red wine

300ml/½pt beef stock
2 bay leaves
450g/1lb carrots (cut into 2.5cm/1in
chunks)
450g/1lb small potatoes
450g/1lb turnips (quartered)
6 celery sticks (cut into 2.5cm/1in
chunks)
25g/1oz plain flour
15g/½oz butter (softened)
2 tablespoons chopped fresh parsley

- Combine the thyme, rosemary, paprika, salt and pepper and rub the meat thoroughly with the mixture. Marinate at room temperature for 1 hour.
- Preheat the oven to 180°C/350°F/Gas mark 4.
- Heat the oil in a flameproof casserole dish and brown the meat well on all sides. Remove the meat with a slotted spoon. Add the onion and garlic and cook just until lightly browned. Add the wine and stock. Bring to the boil over a high heat, scraping any bits from the bottom of the pot with a wooden spoon. Return the meat to the pot.
- Add the bay leaves, cover and bake in the oven for 1 hour.
- Uncover, turn the meat over and add the carrots, potatoes, turnips and celery.
- Cover and cook another 1½ to 2 hours, or until the meat can easily be pierced by a fork and the vegetables are tender.
- Use a fork to incorporate the flour into the butter in a small bowl.
- Remove the meat and vegetables to a plate. Put the pot over a medium heat.
- Whisk in the flour and butter and bring to a boil. While the sauce thickens, cut the meat into thick slices. Spoon the sauce over the meat and serve with the vegetables.

Lamb & white bean stew

SERVES 6-8

INGREDIENTS:

75ml/3fl oz olive oil
1.3kg/3lb boneless stewing lamb
(trimmed)
100g/4oz onions (diced)
1 carrot (sliced)
1 tablespoon minced garlic
400g/14oz canned chopped tomatoes

½ teaspoon dried thyme
½ teaspoon dried rosemary
Salt and pepper
2 tablespoons chopped fresh parsley
225ml/8fl oz red wine
450ml/³/₄pt beef stock
350g/12oz cooked haricot beans

Preheat the oven to 180°C/350°F/Gas mark 4.

- Heat 3 tablespoons oil in a frying pan over a medium-high heat. Add the lamb and brown on all sides, in batches. Remove the lamb with a slotted spoon and place it in an flameproof casserole dish.
- Add the remaining fat to the pan and sauté the onions, carrot and garlic for about 5 minutes, stirring frequently, until the onion is translucent. Scrape the mixture into the casserole dish with the lamb.
- Add the tomatoes, thyme, rosemary, seasoning, parsley, wine and stock to the pan, and bring to a boil over a medium-high heat.
- Place the casserole dish in the centre of the oven and bake for 2½ hours, or until the lamb is beginning to become tender. Add the beans, and bake for a further 30 to 40 minutes. Serve hot.

Sausage & sweet pepper casserole

SERVES 4-6

INGREDIENTS:

2 tablespoons olive oil
450g/1lb spicy sausages (cut into
5cm/2in slices)
700g/1½lb green peppers (sliced)

225g/8oz tomatoes (skinned and
quartered)
1 teaspoon chopped fresh parsley
Salt and pepper

- Heat the oil in a pan and gently fry the sausages until lightly browned. Add the

→

←

peppers and fry for a further 3 minutes, stirring continuously.
- Add the tomatoes, parsley and seasoning to the pan, then cover and cook gently for about 10 minutes until the sausages are cooked through. Serve hot.

New Orleans beef stew

SERVES 6-8

INGREDIENTS:

2 tablespoons olive oil
1 large onion (cut into wedges)
2 celery sticks (chopped)
1 green pepper (chopped)
1kg/2½lb lean braising steak (cubed)
50g/2oz plain flour (seasoned with salt and pepper)
600ml/1pt beef stock

2 garlic cloves (crushed)
150ml/5fl oz red wine
2 tablespoons red wine vinegar
2 tablespoons tomato purée
½ teaspoon Tabasco sauce
1 teaspoon chopped fresh thyme
2 bay leaves
½ teaspoon Cajun spice mix

- Preheat the oven to 150°C/300°F/Gas mark 2.
- Heat the oil in a large heavy-based, flameproof casserole dish. Add the onion wedges and cook until browned on all sides. Remove with a slotted spoon and set aside.
- Add the celery and pepper to the pan and cook until softened. Remove with a slotted spoon and set aside.
- Coat the meat in the seasoned flour, add to the pan and sauté until browned on all sides.
- Add the stock, garlic, wine, vinegar, tomato purée, Tabasco sauce and thyme and heat gently.
- Return the onions, celery and pepper to the pan. Tuck in the bay leaves and sprinkle with Cajun seasoning.
- Bring to the boil, transfer to the oven and cook for 2½ to 3 hours or until the meat and vegetables are tender.

Brown veal stew with tomatoes & mushrooms

SERVES 6

INGREDIENTS:

1.3kg/3lb stewing veal (cut into 5cm/2in pieces)
3 tablespoons olive oil
150g/5oz onions (minced)
Salt and pepper
25g/1oz plain flour
300ml/¹/₂pt dry white wine
450g/1lb tomatoes (skinned, deseeded, juiced and roughly chopped)

¹/₂ teaspoon dried basil
¹/₂ teaspoon thyme
7cm/3in strip of orange zest
2 garlic cloves (crushed)
Salt and pepper
225g/8oz button mushrooms
¹/₂ tablespoon cornflour (mixed with 1 tablespoon water to form a paste)

- Preheat the oven to 170°C/325°F/Gas mark 3.
- Dry the veal on kitchen paper. Heat the oil in a frying pan until almost smoking. Brown the meat, a few pieces at a time, then arrange in a casserole dish.
- Lower the heat to moderate. Pour all but 1 tablespoon oil out of the pan, then brown the onions lightly for 5 to 6 minutes.
- While the onions are browning, toss the meat in the casserole dish with salt and pepper, then with the flour. Toss and stir over moderate heat for 3 to 4 minutes to brown the flour lightly. Remove from the heat.
- Add the wine to the frying pan with the onions. Boil for 1 minute, scraping up the sauté juices. Pour the wine and onions into the casserole and bring to a simmer, stirring to mix the liquid and flour.
- Stir the tomatoes into the casserole dish, then add the herbs, orange zest and garlic. Bring to a simmer and season lightly to taste. Cover and bake in the oven for 1¹/₄ to 1¹/₂ hours, or until the meat is almost tender when pierced with a fork.
- Add the mushrooms to the casserole dish and baste them with the sauce. Bring to a simmer on top of the stove, then cover and return to the oven for a further 15 minutes.
- Remove the casserole from the oven, then pour the contents into a sieve placed over a saucepan. Remove the orange zest and return the meat and vegetables to the casserole dish. Skim the fat off the sauce in the saucepan and boil the sauce down rapidly until it has reduced to about 450ml/³/₄pt. Blend in the cornflour paste and simmer for 2 minutes. Pour the sauce over the veal and serve.

One-pot beef dinner

SERVES 6

INGREDIENTS:

3 tablespoons vegetable oil
1 small onion (chopped)
1 large egg (lightly beaten)
450g/1lb minced beef
50ml/2fl oz water

50g/2oz plain breadcrumbs
1½ teaspoons onion powder
1½ teaspoons garlic salt
4 medium potatoes (sliced)
450g/1lb frozen carrots

- Heat the oil in a frying pan over a medium-high heat. Reduce the heat to medium once the oil is hot. Add the onion to the pan.
- In a large bowl, mix the egg, beef, water, breadcrumbs, onion powder and garlic salt. Press the meat into the bottom of the bowl to form a rounded loaf. Invert the bowl to remove and place the loaf on top of the onion. Place the sliced potatoes around the loaf and the carrots on top of the potatoes.
- Sprinkle with additional seasonings if desired. Cover and cook for about 1 hour.
- After 30 minutes turn the meatloaf over and stir the vegetables.

Southeast Asian hotpot

SERVES 6

INGREDIENTS:

700ml/1¼pt chicken stock
700ml/1¼pt water
450g/1lb sirloin steak (thinly sliced)
450g/1lb straw mushrooms
675g/1½lb medium prawns (shelled and deveined)
225g/8oz meatballs

450g/1lb beansprouts
225ml/8fl oz fish sauce
1 head green lettuce (shredded)
3 tablespoons white wine vinegar
200g/7oz rice vermicelli

- Combine all the ingredients, except the vinegar and vermicelli, in a large casserole dish and bring to the boil. Add the vinegar and reduce the heat to medium.
- Simmer for 1 hour, or until the meat is tender and cooked.
- Cook the rice vermicelli in boiling water for 5 minutes. Drain and immediately rinse in cold water. Drain and add to the casserole, simmer all the ingredients for 30 minutes. Serve hot.

Potato, mushroom & ham casserole

SERVES 8

INGREDIENTS:

50g/2oz butter
200g/7oz new red potatoes (boiled and quartered)
200g/7oz cooked ham (cut into 2.5cm/1in cubes)
50ml/2fl oz olive oil
175g/6oz mushrooms (quartered)
1/4 teaspoon paprika
1/4 teaspoon dried thyme

1/8 teaspoon cayenne pepper
1/8 teaspoon garlic powder
Salt and pepper
18 eggs
125ml/4fl oz milk
2 tomatoes (sliced)
100g/4oz Cheddar cheese (grated)
1 tablespoon chopped fresh parsley

- Preheat the oven to 180°C/350°F/Gas mark 4.
- Melt the butter in very hot frying pan and sauté the potatoes until brown.
- Reduce the heat to medium, add the ham and sauté for a further 1 minute.
- Heat the oil in another, medium-hot, frying pan, add the mushrooms and sauté until soft. Season with paprika, thyme, cayenne, garlic powder, salt and pepper. Add the mushrooms to the ham mixture and toss lightly to combine.
- Pour the ham-mushroom mixture into a casserole dish.
- Beat the eggs in a mixing bowl with milk until frothy and season well with salt and pepper. Pour the eggs over the ham-mushroom mixture, then bake in the oven for 30 minutes.
- Arrange the tomato slices around the top and sprinkle with grated cheese. Return the casserole to the oven and bake until the eggs are set, the cheese is melted and the top is brown. Sprinkle with parsley.

One-pot sausage jambalaya

SERVES 4

INGREDIENTS:

2 Italian sausages (coarsely chopped)
500g/1lb 2oz canned chopped tomatoes
550ml/18fl oz water

200g/7oz long-grain rice
1 teaspoon dried basil
1 red pepper (chopped)

→

←

- In large wide non-stick saucepan over a medium-high heat, brown the sausages for 8 minutes, then drain off any fat.
- Add the tomatoes, then stir in the water, rice and basil.
- Cover and bring to the boil, then reduce the heat to low and simmer for 20 minutes, stirring once. Stir in the pepper, cover, and simmer for 5 minutes.

Green chilli & meat stew

SERVES 5

INGREDIENTS

2½lb stewing beef (cubed)
1.2 litres/2pt water
100g/4oz green chillies (roasted, peeled and chopped)

Salt and pepper
2 teaspoons garlic powder
1 teaspoon cornflour
2 teaspoons cold water

- Cover the meat with water in a large pan, bring to the boil, simmer for 4 hours.
- Add the chillies, seasoning and garlic powder. Mix the cornflour in the water and stir in rapidly. When the mixture has thickened, simmer for about 45 minutes.

One-pot ham & rice

SERVES 6

INGREDIENTS:

250g/9oz cooked ham (diced)
50g/2oz butter
75g/3oz onions (chopped)
200g/7oz long-grain white rice
225ml/8fl oz chicken stock

225ml/8fl oz water
1 sweet potato (peeled and diced)
50g/2oz Parmesan cheese (grated)
Salt and pepper

- In a flameproof casserole dish, fry the ham without any fat over a medium heat for about 4 minutes, stirring, until golden. Transfer to a plate. In the same dish, melt half the butter.
- Add the onion and cook for about 5 minutes, until softened.
- Add the rice, stock and water and bring to a simmer. Stir in the sweet potato and ham. Cover, reduce the heat to very low and steam (still covered) for 18 minutes.
- Remove the pan from the heat. Stir in the remaining butter, the onions and cheese. Season and serve.

Tuscan veal broth

SERVES 4

INGREDIENTS:

50g/2oz dried peas (soaked for 2 hours and drained)
900g/2lb boned neck of veal (diced)
1.2 litres/2pt beef stock
600ml/1pt water
50g/2oz barley
Salt and pepper

1 carrot (diced)
1 turnip (diced)
1 leek (thinly sliced)
1 red onion (finely chopped)
100g/4oz tomatoes (chopped)
1 basil sprig
100g/4oz dried vermicelli

- Put the peas, veal, stock and water into a large pan and bring to the boil over a low heat. Using a slotted spoon, skim off any scum that rises to the surface.
- When all of the scum has been removed, add the barley and a pinch of salt to the mixture. Simmer gently over a low heat for 25 minutes.
- Add the carrot, turnip, leek, onion, tomatoes and basil to the pan and season with salt and pepper to taste. Leave to simmer for about 2 hours, skimming the surface from time to time to remove any scum. Remove the pan from the heat and set aside for 2 hours.
- Set the pan over a medium heat and bring to the boil. Add the vermicelli and cook for 12 minutes. Season with salt and pepper to taste, then remove and discard the basil. Serve immediately.

One-pot spaghetti

SERVES 2

INGREDIENTS:

100g/4oz minced beef
1 tablespoon chopped onion
225g/8oz tomato sauce

400ml/14fl oz water
75g/3oz spaghetti
100g/4oz Parmesan cheese (grated)

- Crumble the beef into a microwave-proof casserole dish and add the onion.
- Microwave on high for 2½ minutes or until no longer pink, stirring once. Drain and stir to break the meat into smaller pieces. Add the tomato sauce, water and spaghetti. Cover with the casserole lid. Microwave for a further 10 to 11 minutes or until the spaghetti is tender, stirring twice. Serve with the cheese sprinkled over.

Korean hotpot

SERVES 6

INGREDIENTS:

225g/8oz calves' liver (thinly sliced)
2 tablespoons vegetable oil
Salt and pepper
225g/8oz prepared tripe
100g/4oz lean rump steak
100g/4oz lean minced beef
1 egg
1 tablespoon soy sauce
1 small carrot (sliced)

6 dried Chinese black mushrooms
(soaked and sliced)
1.2 litres/2pt beef stock
75g/3oz canned bamboo shoots
(drained)
18 canned gingko nuts (drained)
1 red chilli (shredded)
3 onions (shredded)

- Sprinkle the liver with salt and pepper and fry lightly in 1 tablespoon vegetable oil until coloured and sealed on the surface. Set aside.
- Boil the tripe for 8 minutes in lightly salted water, drain and cut into narrow strips. Cut the steak into thin slices. Pound with a meat mallet and cut into small squares. Mix the minced beef with the egg, adding salt, pepper and a few drops of soy sauce. Form small meatballs with wet hands. Fry in the remaining vegetable oil until lightly browned.
- Bring the stock to the boil in a casserole dish. Add the meat, vegetables and nuts and simmer gently for about 15 minutes. Spoon straight from the pot into small bowls. When the meat and vegetables have been eaten, add the finely shredded chilli and green onions to the remaining stock and serve in soup bowls.

Beef & red chilli stew

SERVES 5

INGREDIENTS:

700g/1½lb stewing beef (cubed)
1.2 litres/2pt water
450g/1lb potatoes (cubed)
1 teaspoon red chilli powder

1 teaspoon cornflour
1½ tablespoons water
Salt and pepper

- Cover the meat with water and bring to the boil in a large casserole dish. Reduce the heat to a simmer. Add the potatoes and cook until both meat and potatoes are tender.

- Mix the chilli powder and cornflour in a bowl with the water to make a paste. Stir slowly into the stew and mix well to thicken. Simmer for 30 minutes. Season to taste and serve.

Sausage & bean casserole

SERVES 4

INGREDIENTS:

8 Italian sausages
1 tablespoon olive oil
1 large onion (chopped)
2 garlic cloves (chopped)

1 green pepper (chopped)
400g/14oz canned chopped tomatoes
2 tablespoons tomato purée
400g/14oz canned cannellini beans

- Prick the sausages all over with a fork. Cook the sausages under a preheated grill for 10 to 12 minutes, turning occasionally, until brown all over. Set aside and keep warm.
- Heat the oil in a large frying pan. Add the onion, garlic and pepper to the frying pan and cook for 5 minutes, stirring occasionally, or until slightly reduced and thickened.
- Stir the tomatoes, tomato purée, beans and sausages into the mixture in the frying pan.
- Cook for 5 minutes, or until the mixture is piping hot. Serve immediately.

Irish lamb stew

SERVES 6

INGREDIENTS:

2kg/4½lb lamb shoulder
3 onions (thickly sliced)
700g/1½lb carrots (thickly sliced)
900g/2lb potatoes (peeled and halved)

1 bay leaf
2 teaspoon Worcestershire sauce
Salt and pepper

- Trim a fair amount of the fat off the meat and reserve. Cut the meat into large cubes. In a heavy-based pan, render down the fat over a low heat. Brown the meat in the fat then set aside and brown the onions and carrots. Drain off any excess fat.
- Return the meat to the pan with the potatoes, bay leaf, Worcestershire sauce,

→

←

seasoning and water to cover. Simmer for 2 to 3 hours until the meat is tender and the potatoes are soft and melting. Skin off the fat and serve hot.

Beef stroganoff

SERVES 4

INGREDIENTS:

15g/¹/₂oz dried ceps
2 tablespoons olive oil
100g/4oz shallots (sliced)
175g/6oz chestnut mushrooms
350g/12oz beef fillet (cut into
5mm/¹/₄in slices)

Salt and pepper
¹/₂ teaspoon Dijon mustard
75ml/3fl oz double cream

- Put the ceps in a bowl,cover with hot water and leave to soak for 20 minutes. Drain, reserving the soaking liquid, and chop. Sieve the soaking liquid through a fine-mesh sieve and reserve.
- Heat half the oil in a large frying pan. Add the shallots and cook over a low heat, stirring occasionally, for 5 minutes, or until softened. Add the ceps, reserved soaking water and chestnut mushrooms. Cook, stirring frequently, for 10 minutes, or until almost all of the liquid has evaporated, then transfer to a plate.
- Heat the remaining oil in the frying pan, add the beef and cook, stirring frequently, for 4 minutes, or until browned all over. You may need to do this in batches. Return the mushroom mixture to the frying pan and season to taste. Put the mustard and cream in a small bowl and stir to mix, then fold into the mixture. Heat through and serve.

Oxtail stew

SERVES 4-6

INGREDIENTS:

2 oxtails, about 1.5kg/3lb (jointed)
Plain flour (seasoned), for dusting
3 tablespoons olive oil
2 onions (sliced)
3 garlic cloves (sliced)
450g/1lb carrots (thickly sliced)
4 wide strips orange zest

5cm/2in cinnamon stick
3 cloves
350ml/12fl oz red wine
2 thyme sprigs
2 bay leaves
1 rosemary sprig
Salt and pepper

Coat the oxtail in the flour and brown in the oil in a flameproof casserole dish over a high heat. Lift out the oxtail and set aside. Reduce the heat and add the onions and garlic. Fry gently, without browning, until the onions are tender.

Return the oxtail to the pan with all the remaining ingredients and enough water to cover. Bring to the boil, skim any scum from the surface, then cover and simmer for 3 hours. Uncover and continue simmering for a further 1 to 2 hours, stirring occasionally, until the meat falls easily from the bone and the sauce has thickened.

Skim the fat from the surface, then taste and adjust the seasoning. Serve immediately.

Chilli meat loaf & potato casserole

SERVES 6

INGREDIENTS:

For the meat loaf:
675g/1½lb minced beef
175g/6oz onion (finely chopped)
75g/3oz Ritz crackers (crumbled)
1 egg (beaten)
3 tablespoons milk
1 teaspoon chilli powder
½ teaspoon salt

For the topping:
300g/11oz potatoes (boiled and mashed)
300g/11oz canned sweetcorn (drained)
75g/3oz onions (thinly sliced)
200g/7oz Cheddar cheese (grated)

Preheat the oven to 190°C/375°F/Gas mark 5.

In a large bowl, combine the meat loaf ingredients, mixing thoroughly, then gently press into the bottom of a baking dish.

Bake in the oven for 20 to 25 minutes, or until the juices run clear. Carefully pour off the drippings.

Meanwhile, in a medium bowl, combine all the topping ingredients, except the cheese. Spread over the meat loaf to the edges of the dish, then sprinkle with cheese. Grill 10cm/4in from the heat for 3 to 5 minutes or until the top is lightly browned.

Low-calorie beef stew

SERVES 8

INGREDIENTS:

550g/1lb 4oz boneless beef steak (cut
into 2.5cm/1in cubes)
350ml/12fl oz water
1 teaspoon Worcestershire sauce
2 bay leaves
1 garlic clove (minced)
1/4 teaspoon pepper
8 medium carrots (quartered)

4 small potatoes (quartered)
2 courgettes (sliced)
2 small onions (quartered)
100g/4oz button mushrooms
1 tablespoon cornflour
50ml/2fl oz cold water
125ml/4fl oz red wine
Salt and peppeer

- In a large casserole dish, brown the beef frying in its own fat over a medium-high heat.
- Add the water, Worcestershire sauce, bay leaves, garlic and pepper. Cook, covered, for 1 1/4 hours, stirring frequently.
- Remove the bay leaves and add the vegetables. Cook, covered, for a further 30 minutes.
- Drain, reserving the liquid, and skim any scum from the surface. Add enough water to the liquid to bring it up to 300ml/1/2pt and return to the casserole dish.
- Combine the cornflour and the cold water and stir into the liquid. Add the red wine and bring to the boil. Simmer, stirring, for 2 minutes. Add the beef and vegetables and heat through. Season to taste. Serve hot.

Lamb & apple casserole

SERVES 4

INGREDIENTS:

450g/1lb potatoes (thinly sliced)
225g/8oz onion (thinly sliced)
1 large cooking apple (peeled, cored
and sliced)
25g/1oz raisins
900g/2lb middle neck of lamb
(trimmed and chopped)

1/2 teaspoon dried mixed herbs
Salt and pepper
2 teaspoons Marmite
300ml/1/2pt hot water
15g/1/2oz butter

- Preheat the oven to 180°C/350°F/Gas mark 4.

- Cover the base of a large casserole dish with a layer of half the potato, followed by half the onions and half the apple. Add the raisins and meat, then sprinkle with herbs and a shake of salt and pepper. Top with the remaining apple and onions then lastly with remaining potato slices.
- Dissolve the Marmite in the hot water and pour over the vegetables and meat. Dot the top with small pieces of butter then cover with a lid. Bake in the centre of the oven for 1½ hours. Uncover and continue to cook for further 20 to 30 minutes or until the potatoes are golden.

Ballymaloe Irish stew

SERVES 4-6

INGREDIENTS:

*1.5kg/3lb lamb chops, at least
2.5cm/1in thick
5 onions (roughly chopped)
5 carrots (roughly chopped)
Salt and pepper*

*600ml/1pt lamb stock
8 potatoes (roughly chopped)
1 sprig thyme
1 tablespoon chopped fresh parsley
1 tablespoon chopped fresh chives*

- Preheat the oven to 180°C/350°F/Gas mark 4.
- Cut the chops in half and trim off some of the excess fat. Heat the fat in a heavy-based pan and cook over a gentle heat. Toss the meat in the hot fat until slightly brown. Transfer the meat to a casserole dish and toss the onion and carrot in the fat quickly.
- Build up the meat, onion and carrot in layers in the casserole dish, seasoning each layer well with salt and pepper.
- Pour the stock into the pan and stir well, then add to the casserole dish. Place the potatoes in the casserole dish and season well. Add the thyme and bring to the boil over a high heat. Cover and transfer to the oven for 1 to 1½ hours, until the lamb is cooked.
- When the stew is cooked, pour off and reserve the cooking liquid and skim off the fat. Reheat the liquid in another saucepan. Check the seasoning, then add the parsley and chives and pour it back into the casserole dish. Bring it up to boiling point and serve immediately.

Mexican nacho casserole

SERVES 4

INGREDIENTS:

450g/1lb minced beef
1 tablespoon dried mixed herbs
100g/4oz canned refried beans
50g/2oz onions (chopped)

200g/7oz nacho chips
1 green pepper (diced)
100g/4oz Cheddar cheese (grated)

- Preheat the oven to 200°C/400°F/Gas mark 6.
- Cook the minced beef and herbs in a frying pan, mixing well.
- Spread the refried beans in the bottom of a medium-sized casserole dish, then sprinkle with onions. Place the meat over the beans. Bake in the oven for 15 minutes. Tuck the nacho chips around edge of the casserole, then top with the pepper and cheese and bake for a further 5 minutes. Serve hot.

Lamb hotpot

SERVES 4

INGREDIENTS:

675g/1½lb lean lamb neck cutlets
2 lamb's kidneys
675g/1½lb potatoes (thinly sliced)
1 large onion (thinly sliced)

2 tablespoons chopped fresh thyme
150ml/¼pt lamb stock
Salt and pepper
25g/1oz butter (melted)

- Preheat the oven to 180°C/350°F/Gas mark 4.
- Remove any excess fat from the lamb. Skin and core the kidneys and cut them into slices. Arrange a layer of potatoes in the base of a 1.8 litre/3pt ovenproof dish.
- Arrange the lamb neck cutlets on top of the potatoes and cover with the kidneys, onion and thyme. Pour the stock over the meat and season to taste with salt and pepper.
- Layer the remaining potato slices on top, overlapping to completely cover the meat and onion.
- Brush the potato slices with the butter, cover the dish and cook in the oven for 1½ hours.
- Remove the lid and cook for a further 30 minutes, until golden brown on top.
- Serve hot.

Lamb & cabbage casserole

SERVES 6

INGREDIENTS:

Salt and pepper
4 lamb chops (trimmed)
Vegetable oil for greasing
100g/4oz plain flour
450g/1lb white cabbage (cored and
thinly sliced)

25g/1oz butter
125ml/4fl oz hot water
3 tablespoons whole black peppercorns

Lightly salt the chops, preferably an hour before you plan to cook them. Grease
a heavy casserole dish and put in 2 chops and sprinkle them with half the flour.
Place a layer of cabbage over them, sprinkle with seasoning and flou and dot
with butter. Continue making layers, ending with cabbage and a little butter.
Pour on the hot water. Tie the peppercorns securely in muslin and lightly
bruise them with a rolling pin. Bury the peppercorns in the casserole.
Cover and bring to the boil. Immediately lower the heat and simmer very gently
for about 1½ hours, until the meat is very tender and the cabbage almost melted.
Remove the peppercorns. Serve with boiled potatoes.

Beef & celery stew

SERVES 6

INGREDIENTS:

1 teaspoon saffron
1 teaspoon granulated sugar
800ml/1pt 7fl oz hot water
50ml/2fl oz olive oil
6 garlic cloves (finely chopped)
2 onions (roughly chopped)
1½ teaspoons ground turmeric
1 teaspoon sweet paprika
450g/1lb beef fillet (cut into 2.5cm/1in
pieces)

Salt and pepper
4 celery sticks (cut into 2.5cm/1in
pieces)
50g/2oz chopped flat-leaf parsley
50g/2oz chopped mint
Juice of 1 lime
1 tablespoon tomato purée

Using a mortar and pestle, grind the saffron and sugar and combine with
50ml/2fl oz hot water in a small bowl, set aside.

→

←

- In a large shallow saucepan, heat 2 tablespoons oil over a medium heat. Add the garlic and onions. Cook for about 10 minutes, until golden brown. Stir in 1 teaspoon turmeric and paprika. Add the beef, salt, and pepper. Cook for about 10 minutes, until the meat is browned. Add 250ml/9fl oz hot water and stir to combine. Cover, and cook for 20 minutes.
- In a large frying pan, heat the remaining oil over a medium heat. Add the celery and cook for 20 minutes, stirring occasionally. Add the parsley and mint to the celery. Stir in seasoning and the remaining turmeric and cook for 2 minutes.
- Add the celery mixture, lime juice, tomato purée and 500ml/16fl oz hot water to the beef and stir to combine. Cover, and cook over a low heat for 1 hour.
- Add the safron and sugar liquidand serve.

Pork hotpot

SERVES 6

INGREDIENTS:

450g/1lb lean diced lamb
4 teaspoons plain flour
Salt and pepper
¼ teaspoon ground cinnamon
2 onions (chopped)
3 carrots (chopped)
15g/½oz butter
Grated rind of 1 lemon
1 teaspoon lemon juice
50g/2oz raisins
150ml/¼pt cider
150ml/¼pt lamb stock

½ teaspoon dried mixed herbs1.5kg/3½lb belly pork (cut into chunks)
600ml/1pt pork stock
10 spring onions (thinly sliced)
125ml/4fl oz soy sauce
75ml/3fl oz Chinese rice wine
25ml/1fl oz rice wine vinegar
2 tablespoons demerera sugar
3 star anise
10cm/4in piece of fresh root ginger (peeled and sliced)

- Place the pork in a large saucepan and pour over enough boiling water to just cover, then bring to the boil. Simmer gently for about 5 minutes, skimming the scum off the surface, then drain. Bring the stock to the boil in a separate pan.
- Return the pork to the pan and pour over enough stock to cover it.
- Add half the spring onions to the pan with the soy sauce, rice wine, vinegar, sugar, star anise and ginger. Cover and simmer for 2 hours, turning the meat occasionally, until the pork is tender.
- Remove the pork with a slotted spoon and set aside. Strain the cooking liquid into a clean pan. Skim off any fat, then boil the stock to reduce until syrupy.
- Return the pork to the sauce and heat through. Scatter with the remaining spring onions before serving.

Veal & mushroom stew

SERVES 6

INGREDIENTS:

*900g/2lb breast of veal (cut into
5cm/2in chunks)*
*450g/1lb boned shoulder of veal (cut
into 5cm/2in chunks)*
1 onion (quartered)
4 cloves
1 carrot (quartered)
1 celery stick (quartered)
1 garlic clove
300ml/½pt dry white wine

1 bouquet garni
Salt and pepper
24 pearl onions
225g/8oz button mushrooms
50g/2oz butter
1½ tablespoons plain flour
2 egg yolks
150ml/¼pt crème fraîche
Squeeze of lemon juice

- Put the meat into a large pan and add enough water to cover. Bring slowly to the boil, skimming off any scum as it rises. Stud each quarter of the onion with a clove and add to the pan with the carrot, celery, garlic, wine and bouquet garni. Season with salt and pepper.
- Cover and leave to simmer for 1¼ to 1½ hours until the meat is tender. Pick out the onion, carrot, celery, garlic and bouquet garni and discard.
- Add the pearl onions and the mushrooms and continue to simmer, uncovered, for a further 15 to 20 minutes, until the onions and mushrooms are tender.
- Transfer the solids into a bowl and strain the cooking juices.
- Melt the butter in a large pan and sprinkle the flour into it. Stir for 1 minute.
- Gradually whisk in the reserved cooking liquid. Bring to the boil and simmer for about 20 minutes until the sauce is reduced to a rich, creamy consistency.
- Return the veal and vegetables to the sauce and simmer for a few more minutes to heat through. Reduce the heat to low.
- Beat the egg yolks lightly into the crème fraîche, then gradually whisk in a few spoonfuls of the hot sauce, one at a time. Tip this back into the pan and stir for 2 minutes, without letting it boil, until the sauce thickens slightly. Remove from the heat and add the lemon juice. Serve immediately.

Fruity lamb stew

SERVES 4

INGREDIENTS:

450g/1lb lean diced lamb
4 teaspoons plain flour
Salt and pepper
¼ teaspoon ground cinnamon
2 onions (chopped)
3 carrots (chopped)
15g/½oz butter

Grated zest of 1 lemon
1 teaspoon lemon juice
50g/2oz raisins
150ml/¼pt cider
150ml/¼pt lamb stock
½ teaspoon dried mixed herbs

- Toss the meat in the flour and season with salt, pepper and cinnamon.
- Fry the onions and carrots in the butter for 2 minutes in a flameproof casserole dish. Add the meat and continue frying until golden brown. Stir in half the lemon zest, the lemon juice, raisins, cider, stock and herbs. Bring to the boil, stirring. Reduce the heat, cover and simmer gently for 1 hour or until the meat and vegetables are tender. Taste and adjust the seasoning if necessary. Garnish with the remaining lemon zest and serve.

Beef goulash one-pot

SERVES 6

INGREDIENTS:

1 tablespoon vegetable oil
250g/9oz onion (chopped)
900g/2lb lean stewing beef
Salt and pepper
2 teaspoons paprika

½ green pepper (sliced)
4 carrots (sliced)
4 potatoes (cut into 2.5cm/1in cubes)
225ml/8fl oz water

- Add the oil and onions to a large casserole dish and brown over a medium-high heat for 5 minutes. Stir in the beef, salt, pepper and paprika. Place half the pepper on top of the meat mixture. Heat through and reduce the heat to low, then simmer for 1½ hours.
- Add the remaining vegetables and 225ml/8fl oz water and bring to the boil.
- Reduce the heat to medium-low and simmer for a further 20 to 30 minutes, until the vegetables are tender.

One-pot pork chop supper

SERVES 4

INGREDIENTS:

1 tablespoon vegetable oil
4 pork chops
400g/14oz canned tomato soup
125ml/4fl oz water
1 teaspoon Worcestershire sauce

½ teaspoon salt
½ teaspoon caraway seeds
3 medium potatoes (quartered)
4 carrots (cut into 5cm/2in pieces)

- In a large frying pan, brown the chops in the oil. Pour off any fat, then add the soup, water, Worcestershire sauce, salt, caraway, potatoes and carrots.
- Cover and simmer for 45 minutes or until tender.

International beef pot

SERVES 4

INGREDIENTS:

550g/1lb 4oz braising steak (trimmed and cubed)
3 large onions (sliced)
450ml/¾pt beef stock
1 bay leaf
Salt and pepper

175g/6oz button mushrooms
225g/8oz canned water chestnuts (drained and sliced)
450g/1lb potatoes (thinly sliced)
300g/11oz canned condensed mushroom soup

- Place the meat in a saucepan with the onions, stock, bay leaf and a little salt and pepper. Bring to the boil and skim the surface.
- Reduce the heat, part-cover and simmer very gently for 2 hours or until the meat is really tender. Add the mushrooms for the last 15 minutes. Taste and adjust the seasoning if necessary.
- Preheat the oven to 160°C/325°F/Gas mark 3.
- Remove the bay leaf. Drain off the stock and reserve. Put half the meat and mushroom mixture into a large shallow ovenproof dish. Top with the water chestnuts and the remaining meat mixture. Arrange the potatoes, overlapping, on top.
- Spoon the mushroom soup over the top then pour the stock over to moisten thoroughly. Bake in the oven for 2 hours, until the top is golden and the potatoes are cooked.

Swedish meatball stew

SERVES 4-5

INGREDIENTS:

100g/4oz Ritz crackers (crumbled)
225ml/8fl oz full-fat milk
1 large egg
450g/1lb minced beef
Salt and pepper

25g/1oz butter
700g/1½lb potatoes (cubed)
700ml/1¼pt beef stock
1 teaspoon paprika
2 tablespoons chopped fresh parsley

- Soak the crackers for 10 minutes in the milk in a small bowl. Squeeze the milk out of the crackers.
- Place the egg in a blender or food processor and run for 15 seconds. Add the crackers, beef, salt and pepper and process until the consistency is of paste. Make as many meatballs, 2.5cm/1in in diameter, as you can. Set aside.
- In a large casserole dish, melt the butter over a medium-high heat. Brown the meatballs with the potatoes for about 4 minutes, until golden on all sides. Pour in the stock and season to taste and add the paprika. Reduce the heat to low, cover and cook for 30 minutes. Uncover, raise the heat to medium and cook until the potatoes are tender, about 30 minutes.
- Sprinkle with parsley 5 minutes before the stew is done and serve hot.

Persian lamb & rhubarb stew

SERVES 4-6

INGREDIENTS:

50g/2oz butter
1 tablespoon sunflower oil
2 large onions (sliced)
675g/1½lb boned shoulder of lamb
(cut into 5cm/2in cubes)
1 teaspoon ground coriander

3 tablespoons chopped fresh parsley
3 tablespoons chopped fresh mint
450g/1lb rhubarb (trimmed and cut into 5cm/2in lengths)
Salt and pepper

- Melt half the butter with the oil in a frying pan and fry the onions until golden.

- Raise the heat, add half the meat and fry until browned. Remove the onions and meat and reserve, then brown the remaining meat. Transfer all the meat and onions to a flameproof casserole dish and add the coriander. Add just enough water to cover and simmer, covered, for 1 hour. Season.
- Fry the parsley and mint in the remaining butter, stirring constantly, for 5 to 10 minutes. Add to the stew and continue simmering, half covered, for a further 30 minutes, stirring occasionally.
- Shortly before serving, add the rhubarb. Stir to mix and simmer for 6 to 8 minutes.
- Taste and adjust the seasoning and serve hot.

Pork & pepper stew with oranges

SERVES 6-8

INGREDIENTS:

1.5kg/3½lb boneless pork shoulder
Salt and black pepper
4 tablespoons olive oil
900g/2lb onions (halved and thickly sliced)
2 garlic cloves (thickly sliced)
2 celery sticks (thickly sliced)
3 red chillies (deseeded and thickly sliced)
1 red pepper (thinly sliced)

¾ teaspoon fennel seed
2 teaspoons dried oregano
400g/14oz canned chopped tomatoes
1.2 litres/2pt chicken stock
300ml/½pt white wine
2 tablespoons chilli powder
2 tablespoon raisins
2 tablespoon chopped fresh coriander
Orange segments, to garnish

- Season the pork liberally with salt and pepper. In a heavy casserole dish, heat 2 tablespoons oil and quickly brown the pork, in batches if necessary. Remove and set aside.
- Add the remaining oil to the casserole dish and sauté the onions, garlic, celery, chillies and pepper over a moderate heat until just beginning to colour. Add the fennel seed, oregano, tomatoes, stock, wine and chilli powder and bring to the boil.
- Add the pork and raisins, reduce the heat, cover, and simmer gently until the pork is tender, about 35 to 40 minutes. Remove from the heat and skim any fat from the top.
- Just before serving, stir in the coriander.
- Serve garnished with orange segments.

Danish beef stew

SERVES 4

INGREDIENTS:

50g/2oz butter
1 large onion (chopped)
450g/1lb fillet steak (cut into
2.5cm/1in cubes)
600ml/1pt beef stock
Salt and pepper

3 bay leaves
6 peppercorns
700g/1½lb potatoes (cut into
2.5cm/1in cubes)
2 tablespoons chopped spring onions

- Melt the butter in a large flameproof casserole dish and add the onion and meat.
- Cook gently, stirring, until the onion is tender, but not browned.
- Add the stock, seasoning, bay leaves and peppercorns. Bring to the boil, cover and simmer for 1½ hours. Add the potatoes and continue simmering, half-covered, for a further 45 minutes, stirring, until the potatoes disintegrate. Adjust the seasoning and sprinkle with the spring onions to serve.

Beef & mushroom stew

SERVES 4

INGREDIENTS:

1 tablespoon vegetable oil
450g/1lb stewing beef (cut into
2.5cm/1in cubes)
150g/5oz onion (chopped)
25g/1oz tablespoon plain flour
Salt and pepper
200g/7oz button mushrooms (halved)

225ml/8fl oz dry vermouth
225ml/8fl oz chicken stock
3 tablespoons orange juice
1 teaspoon dried basil
½ teaspoon dried thyme
3 garlic cloves (crushed)
400g/14oz canned chopped tomatoes

- Heat the vegetable oil in a large frying pan over a medium-high heat until hot.
- Add the beef and onion and sauté for 5 minutes.
- Combine the flour and seasoning and sprinkle over the beef mixture. Cook for 1 minute, stirring constantly. Add the remaining ingredients and bring to the boil.
- Reduce the heat and simmer, uncovered, for 40 minutes or until the beef is tender, stirring occasionally. Serve hot.

Goat stew

SERVES 6

INGREDIENTS:

225g/8oz salt beef
900g/2lb leg of goat (cubed)
3 tablespoons vegetable oil
1 large onion (finely chopped)
2 red chillies (deseeded and chopped)
3 garlic cloves (crushed)

3 tablespoons annatto oil
4 small tomatoes (skinned and chopped)
1 tablespoon lime juice
Salt and pepper
4 potatoes (diced)

- Soak the salt beef in water for 1 hour, using enough water to cover completely. Drain, then cut into cubes.
- Fry the beef and goat together in a little vegetable oil until brown. Transfer to a large saucepan, cover with cold water and bring to the boil, then simmer for 1¼ hours. When the meat is tender, drain and reserve the stock.
- Heat the remaining vegetable oil in a large saucepan, add the onion and chillies and sauté over a medium heat until the onion is tender but not brown. Add the garlic and sauté for a further 1 minute. Add the meat, annatto oil, tomatoes, lime juice and seasoning and simmer for 20 minutes. Add the stock and potatoes and bring to the boil, then cover and simmer for 40 minutes. Serve hot.

Pork & beetroot casserole

SERVES 2

INGREDIENTS:

500g/1lb 2oz loin of pork (cubed)
50g/2oz streaky bacon
2 onions
400ml/14fl oz beetroot liquid (from jar of beetroot)

1 tablespoon granulated sugar
Salt
6 black peppercorns
3 allspice berries
2 tablespoons pearl barley

- Preheat the oven to 180°C/350°F/Gas mark 4.
- In a large frying pan, brown the pork with the bacon. Remove the pork and bacon from the pan and lightly brown the onions in the remaining fat. Transfer the pork, onions and bacon to a casserole dish.
- Add the beetroot liquid, sugar, salt, peppercorns, allspice berries and barley and cook, covered, for 1 hour.

Ham & cheese casserole

SERVES 8

INGREDIENTS:

100g/4oz plain flour
Salt and pepper
75g/3oz butter
600ml/1pt milk
300g/11oz ham (chopped)

600g/1lb 5oz potatoes (thinly sliced)
250g/9oz Cheddar cheese (grated)
1 onion (chopped)
1 green pepper (chopped)

- Preheat the oven to 180°C/350°F/Gas mark 4.
- Mix the flour, salt and pepper. Melt the butter in a saucepan, then add the flour mixture. Cook over a medium heat for 1 minute, stirring constantly. Remove from the heat and stir in the milk. Return to the heat and cook until thick.
- In a very large bowl, mix the remaining ingredients with the sauce. Bake in a casserole dish for 1½ hours, covered for the first 30 minutes. Allow to cool for 15 minutes before serving.

Rich beef stew

SERVES 4

INGREDIENTS:

1 tablespoon vegetable oil
15g/½oz butter
225g/8oz baby onions (halved)
600g/1lb 5oz stewing steak (diced into large chunks)
300ml/½pt beef stock
150ml/¼pt red wine

4 tablespoons chopped fresh oregano
1 tablespoon granulated sugar
1 orange
25g/1oz porcini
4 tablespoons warm water
225g/8oz plum tomatoes

- Preheat the oven to 180°/350°F/Gas mark 4.
- Heat the oil and butter in a large frying pan. Add the onions and sauté for 5 minutes or until golden. Remove the onions with a slotted spoon and set aside.
- Add the beef to the pan and cook, stirring, for 5 minutes, or until browned all over.
- Return the onions to the frying pan and add the stock, wine, oregano and sugar, stirring to mix well. Transfer the mixture to an ovenproof casserole dish.
- Pare the zest from the orange and cut it into strips. Slice the orange flesh into

rings. Add the flesh and zest to the casserole. Cook in the oven for 1¼ hours.
- Soak the mushrooms for 30 minutes in a small bowl with the warm water.
- Peel and halve the tomatoes. Add the tomatoes, mushrooms and their soaking liquid to the casserole dish. Cook for a further 20 minutes until the beef is tender. Serve hot.

Bean & beef casserole

SERVES 4

INGREDIENTS:

450g/1lb minced meat
1 garlic clove (minced)
½ onion (minced)
2 green peppers (finely chopped)
250g/9oz cooked haricot beans

200g/7oz tomatoes (finely chopped)
1 teaspoon salt
1 teaspoon granulated sugar
1½ teaspoon chilli powder

- Preheat the oven to 180°C/350°F/Gas mark 4.
- Put the hamburger meat, garlic, onion and green peppers in a frying pan over a medium-high heat, until starting to brown, stirring often. Pour off any fat and transfer to a large casserole dish.
- Add the other ingredients to the casserole dish and bake in the oven for 30 minutes.

Pork & apricot casserole

SERVES 4

INGREDIENTS:

4 lean pork loin chops
1 medium onion (finely chopped)
2 yellow peppers (sliced)
2 teaspoons medium curry powder
1 tablespoon plain flour

250ml/9fl oz chicken stock
100g/4oz dried apricots
2 tablespoons wholegrain mustard
Salt and pepper

- Trim the excess fat from the pork and fry without fat in a large, heavy-based pan until lightly browned. Add the onion and peppers and stir over a moderate heat for 5 minutes. Stir in the curry powder and the flour.
- Add the stock, stirring, then add the apricots and mustard. Cover and simmer for 25 to 30 minutes, until tender. Adjust the seasoning and serve hot.

Beef & walnut stew

SERVES 4

INGREDIENTS:

25g/1oz butter
2 tablespoons vegetable oil
900g/2lb fillet steak (sliced into
5cm/2in strips)
1 garlic clove (crushed)
1 red pepper (cut into strips)

1 large onion (cut into strips)
200g/7oz walnuts (chopped)
225ml/8fl oz tomato juice
Salt and pepper
700g/1½lb mushrooms (sliced)

- In a large pan, melt the butter in half the oil over a medium heat. Cook the meat until browned on all sides and remove with a slotted spoon to a warmed dish.
- Place the garlic, pepper and onion in the remaining oil and lightly fry until the onion is soft.
- Return the meat to the pan and lightly mix together. Stir in the walnuts and cook for 1 minute. Stir in the tomato juice and season to taste.
- Cover and bring to a boil. Reduce the heat and simmer for 1½ hours. Stir in the mushrooms and cook for a further 20 minutes.

Irish stew pie

SERVES 6-8

INGREDIENTS:

For the pastry:
225g/8oz plain flour
Pinch of salt
75g/3oz butter
50g/2oz suet (minced)
150ml/¼pt water
1 egg (beaten), to glaze

For the filling:
900g/2lb leg of lamb (cut into
2.5cm/1in cubes)
900g/2lb potatoes (thinly sliced)
Salt and pepper
450g/1lb onion (sliced)
600ml/1pt chicken stock

- To make the pastry, put the flour into a bowl with the salt and add enough water to make a firm dough. Cover and refrigerate. Cream the butter lightly with the suet.
- Roll out the pastry to a 5mm/¼in thick rectangle. Cover two-thirds of the pastry with flakes of half of the suet and half of the butter mixture. Fold into 3, so there is a layer of fat between each layer of pastry. Seal the ends, then cover and chill for 10 minutes.

- Roll out the pastry again and repeat the process with the remaining suet and butter mixture. Cover and chill while you prepare the filling.
- Preheat the oven 180°C/350°F/Gas mark 4.
- Place the lamb, potatoes and onion in layers in a pie dish, seasoning well. Add the stock and cover with the pastry. Bake in the oven for 1 hour and serve hot.

Kidney & sausage casserole

SERVES 6

INGREDIENTS:

25g/1oz butter
12 pearl onions
100g/4oz button mushrooms
6 lamb kidneys
25g/1oz plain flour
1 tablespoon tomato purée

250ml/9fl oz beef stock
2 tablespoons dry sherry
Salt and pepper
100g/4oz peas
225g/8oz cocktail sausages

- Preheat the oven to 160°C/325°F/Gas mark 3.
- Heat the butter in a frying pan and cook the onions and mushrooms for 5 minutes, then place in a casserole dish.
- Skin the kidneys, cut in half and remove the core. Dredge the kidneys in the flour and sauté gently for a few minutes Add the tomato purée, stock, sherry and seasoning and mix well.
- Pour into the casserole dish. Cover and bake for about 20 minutes
- Add the peas and bake for another 25 minutes until kidneys are tender.
- Meanwhile, sauté the sausages until they are golden brown and add to the dish when cooked. Serve hot.

Calves' kidney stew

SERVES 6-8

INGREDIENTS:

350g/12oz calves' kidney (peeled and diced)
Salt and pepper
Plain flour (seasoned), for coating
50g/2oz butter

100g/4oz onions (chopped)
175g/6oz carrots (chopped)
1 turnip (finely chopped)
3 celery sticks (finely chopped)
1.7 litres/3pt beef stock

→

←

- Place the kidney in a bowl and cover with cold water and a good pinch of salt.
- Leave to soak while you prepare the vegetables, then drain and dry with kitchen paper and toss in the flour.
- Melt the butter in a saucepan, add the kidney and vegetables and toss for 1 to 2 minutes in the butter. Season with salt and pepper and add the stock. Bring to the boil and simmer for 45 to 60 minutes, until tender.
- Place the stew in a blender or food processor and blend for 2 minutes, then reheat and serve hot.

One-pot pork

SERVES 4-6

INGREDIENTS:

2 tablespoons vegetable oil
2 large sweet potatoes (sliced)
1 large aubergine (sliced)
25g/1oz cornflour
3 teaspoons garlic salt
3 teaspoons paprika
8 lean pork chops (trimmed)
50ml/2fl oz hot water

1 red onion (sliced into rings)
450g/1lb canned chopped tomatoes
250ml/9fl oz sweet white wine
1 large cooking apple (peeled, cored and sliced)
2 teaspoons brown sugar
1 tablespoon chopped fresh oregano
Salt and pepper

- Heat the oil in a heavy-based frying pan and quickly brown the sweet potato and aubergine. Remove and set aside.
- Mix the cornflour, garlic salt and paprika together. Dredge each pork chop in this mixture to coat all sides, then fry in the hot oil until lightly browned. Drain off any excess oil and transfer the pork to a large heavy-based cooking pot.
- Deglaze the frying pan with the hot water and pour this over the chops. Arrange the onion on top of the chops and add the tomatoes. Mix the remaining cornflour mixture with the wine and add to the pot. Simmer slowly over a low heat.
- Add the apple to the pot and sprinkle with the sugar, oregano and seasoning to taste. Part-cover the pan and continue to simmer for about 20 to 30 minutes until the chops are tender and the sauce has thickened. Serve hot.

Corn casserole with hot dogs

SERVES 6

INGREDIENTS:

75g/3oz butter, plus extra for greasing
25g/1oz plain flour
1 teaspoon salt
1/4 teaspoon pepper
300ml/1/2pt hot milk

200g/7oz canned sweetcorn
3 eggs (beaten)
75g/3oz dried breadcrumbs
6 hot dogs

- Preheat the oven to 180°C/350°F/Gas mark 4. Lightly grease a deep baking dish with butter.
- Heat 40g/1 1/2oz butter in a saucepan over a medium-low heat. Blend in the flour then add the salt and pepper. Gradually stir in the hot milk. Continue cooking and stirring until thickened and smooth.
- Remove from heat, add the corn and slowly stir in the eggs. Pour the mixture into the prepared baking dish. Top with breadcrumbs and dot with the remaining butter.
- Bake in the oven for 30 minutes. Score each hot dog several times on the diagonal and arrange on top of the casserole, then bake for an additional 15 to 20 minutes.

Fruity lamb casserole

SERVES 4

INGREDIENTS:

450g/1lb lean lamb (trimmed and cut into 2.5cm/1in cubes)
1 teaspoon ground cinnamon
1 teaspoon ground coriander
1 teaspoon ground cumin
2 teaspoons olive oil
1 medium red onion (finely chopped)
1 garlic clove (crushed)

400g/14oz canned chopped tomatoes
2 tablespoons tomato purée
100g/4oz dried apricots
1 teaspoon caster sugar
300ml/1/2pt vegetable stock
Salt and pepper

→

←

- Preheat the oven to 180°C/350°F/Gas mark 4.
- Place the lamb in a mixing bowl and add the spices and oil. Mix thoroughly, so that the lamb is well coated.
- Heat a non-stick frying pan for a few seconds, until it is hot, then add the spiced lamb. Reduce the heat and cook for 5 minutes, stirring, until browned all over.
- Using a slotted spoon, remove the lamb and transfer to a large, ovenproof casserole dish.
- In the same frying pan, cook the onion, garlic, tomatoes and tomato purée for 5 minutes. Season to taste. Stir in the apricots and sugar, add the stock and bring to the boil.
- Spoon the sauce over the lamb and mix well. Cover and cook in the oven for 1 hour, removing the lid for the last 10 minutes. Serve hot.

Savoury hotpot with mash

SERVES 4

INGREDIENTS:

1½ tablespoon vegetable oil
500g/1lb 2oz rump steak (diced)
1 onion (finely diced)
200g/7oz button mushrooms (sliced)
525ml/17fl oz water
425g/15oz canned chopped tomatoes

500g/1lb 2oz sweet potato (peeled and cut into 2.5cm/1in pieces)
500g/1lb 2oz potato (peeled and cut into 2.5cm/1in pieces)
2 tablespoons milk
50g/2oz mayonnaise

- Heat 2 teaspoons oil in a large saucepan over a high heat. Add half the beef and cook for 2 to 3 minutes or until brown. Remove and repeat with 2 teaspoons of oil and the remaining beef. Set aside.
- Heat the remaining oil over a medium heat. Add the onion and cook for 1 to 2 minutes or until the onion is soft. Add the mushrooms, water and tomatoes and return the meat to the pan. Bring to the boil, reduce heat and cook, covered, for 10 minutes or until the meat is tender.
- Meanwhile, cook the sweet potato and potatoes in a large saucepan of water over medium heat. Bring to the boil and cook, covered, for 10 to 12 minutes or until soft.
- Drain the potatoes and sweet potato and place in a large mixing bowl. Add the milk and mayonnaise and mash until smooth. Serve the hotpot with the mash.

Breakfast casserole

SERVES 4

INGREDIENTS:

Butter, for greasing
4 slices white bread
450g/1lb rindless back bacon
200g/7oz Cheddar cheese (grated)

6 eggs (beaten)
350ml/12fl oz milk
1 teaspoon dry mustard

- Preheat the oven to 180°C/350°F/Gas mark 4. Grease the bottom of a casserole dish.
- Tear up the bread and place in the bottom of the dish. Dry-fry the bacon in a frying pan, then drain and crumble over the bread pieces.
- Sprinkle the cheese over the meat. Mix the eggs, milk and mustard together and pour over the casserole. Bake in the oven for 35 to 40 minutes.

Veal & tomato stew

SERVES 4

INGREDIENTS:

4 slices of shin of veal, 5cm/2in thick
Salt and pepper
Plain flour (seasoned), for dusting
50g/2oz butter
1 garlic clove (quartered)
150ml/¼pt dry white wine

350g/12oz tomatoes (skinned and chopped)
150ml/¼pt chicken stock
Finely grated zest of 1 lemon
3 tablespoons chopped fresh parsley
2 garlic cloves (chopped)

- Dust the veal with flour and fry in the butter in a wide frying pan over a brisk heat until browned on both sides. Add the garlic when the meat is half done.
- Discard the garlic when the veal is browned.
- Reduce the heat and add the wine to the pan. Leave to simmer gently for 10 minutes, then add the tomatoes and cook for another 10 minutes. Add enough stock to cover the meat and season with salt and pepper. Bring to a quiet simmer, cover tightly and leave to simmer for 1½ to 2 hours or until the meat is very tender. Taste and adjust the seasoning.
- Mix the lemon zest with the parsley and garlic, then chop the whole lot together very finely. Once the stew is done, sprinkle this mixture over the top and serve immediately.

Baked bean &
bacon casserole

SERVES 3

INGREDIENTS:

6 rashers rindless back bacon
450g/1lb canned baked beans
2 tablespoons minced onion

2 tablespoons ketchup
1 teaspoon prepared mustard
2 tablespoons demerara sugar

- Preheat the oven to 190°C/375°F/Gas mark 5.
- Dry-fry the bacon in a frying pan until very crisp. In a deep casserole dish, combine the beans, onion, ketchup, mustard and demerara sugar. Mix thoroughly.
- Crumble the bacon and sprinkle over the baked bean mixture. Heat, uncovered, in the oven for 10 minutes or until the sauce is bubbly.

Pork chop &
apple casserole

SERVES 4

INGREDIENTS:

4 thick pork chops
25g/1oz butter
1 small onion (chopped)
2 medium tart apples (chopped)
25g/1oz granulated sugar

1 tablespoon crystallized ginger (finely chopped)
100g/4oz fresh breadcrumbs
Salt and pepper
50ml/2fl oz water

- Preheat the oven to 180°C/350°F/Gas mark 4.
- In a frying pan, sear the chops on both sides then remove from the pan. Add the butter to the drippings and sauté the onion until clear.
- Drain the onion and mix with the apples, sugar, ginger, breadcrumbs, seasoning and water. Spread this mixture in the bottom of a shallow casserole dish, then arrange the pork chops on top and bake, covered, for 1 hour.
- Remove the lid for the last 10 minutes to brown the top.

Turkish lamb stew

SERVES 2

INGREDIENTS:

*350g/12oz lean boneless lamb
(trimmed and cut into 2.5cm/1in
cubes)
1 large onion (cut into 8 wedges)
1 garlic clove (crushed)
1/2 red pepper (diced)
300ml/1/2pt lamb stock
1 tablespoon balsamic vinegar
2 tomatoes (peeled and roughly
chopped)*

*1 1/2 teaspoons tomato purée
1 bay leaf
1/2 teaspoon dried sage
Salt and pepper
350g/12oz potatoes (cut into
2.5cm/1in cubes)
7 black olives (halved and pitted)*

- Place the lamb in a non-stick saucepan with no extra fat and heat gently until the fat runs and the meat begins to seal. Add the onion and garlic and fry for a further 4 minutes.
- Add the pepper, stock, vinegar, tomatoes, tomato purée, bay leaf, sage and seasoning. Cover and simmer gently for 30 minutes.
- Add the potatoes to the stew and stir well. Cover the pan again and simmer for a further 25 to 30 minutes, or until tender. Add the olives and adjust the seasoning.
- Simmer for a further 5 minutes and serve.

Veal & spinach stew

SERVES 4

INGREDIENTS:

*900g/2lb loin of veal (chopped into
2.5cm/1in cubes)
900g/2lb spinach
2 onions (chopped)*

*25g/1oz butter
225ml/8fl oz water
Salt and pepper*

- Put all the ingredients in a large casserole dish. Cover and cook over a high heat for about 35 minutes.
- Serve hot.

Rustic pork casserole

SERVES 4

INGREDIENTS:

4 lean pork chops (trimmed)
50g/2oz butter
450g/1lb potatoes (cut into 2.5cm/1in cubes)
100g/4oz button mushrooms (sliced)
425g/15oz canned butter beans (drained)

1 garlic clove (chopped)
300ml/½pt pork stock
Salt and pepper
1 tablespoon cornflour
1 tablespoon water
2 tablespoons chopped fresh parsley

- Preheat the oven to 180°C/350°F/Gas mark 4.
- Fry the chops in half the butter on both sides to brown in a flameproof casserole dish. Remove from the dish and set aside. Add the remaining butter and fry the potatoes quickly for about 3 minutes until golden all over. Add the mushrooms and stir well.
- Return the meat to the casserole dish and add the butter beans and garlic. Pour in the stock and season well. Cover with a lid and cook in the oven for 1½ hours until the potatoes and pork are really tender. Transfer the meat and vegetables to warmed serving plates.
- Blend the cornflour with the water and stir into the juices in the casserole dish.
- Bring to the boil and cook, stirring, for 1 minute. Taste and adjust the seasoning if necessary. Spoon over the pork and vegetables and sprinkle with parsley.

Honeyed pork stew

SERVES 4-6

INGREDIENTS:

225g/8oz dried haricot beans
450g/1lb pork chops (boned, trimmed and cubed)
300ml/½pt cider
600ml/1pt chicken stock
1 onion (studded with 4 cloves)
1 tablespoon clear honey

1 bouquet garni
3 carrots (sliced)
2 leeks (sliced)
2 celery sticks (sliced)
2 tablespoons Worcestershire sauce
1 tablespoon tomato purée

- Soak the beans overnight in cold water.

- Place the pork in a frying pan over a high heat and fry until the fat runs.
- Drain the beans and add to the pork. Add the cider, stock, onion, honey and bouquet garni.
- Gently bring to the boil, cover and simmer for 1 hour or until the beans are just tender. Add the carrots, leeks, celery, Worcestershire sauce and tomato purée.
- Continue simmering for a further 20 to 30 minutes or until the beans are very tender. Remove the bouquet garni. Serve immediately.

Hotpot lamb curry

SERVES 4

INGREDIENTS:

450g/1lb neck of lamb (cubed)
1 tablespoon vegetable oil
2 star anise
6 cloves
5cm/2in piece cinnamon stick (chopped)
4 cardamoms (smashed)
3 stalks curry leaves
2 pandan leaves (shredded and knotted)
1 onion (chopped)
2 garlic cloves (crushed)
10cm/4cm piece root ginger (peeled and chopped)
10cm/4cm piece galangal (peeled and chopped)

2 stalks lemon grass (chopped)
1 teaspoon ground black pepper
2 tablespoons curry powder
1 tablespoon chilli paste
2 tomatoes (cubed)
2 potatoes (cubed)
Salt and pepper

For the marinade:
1 tablespoon soy sauce
1 teaspoon curry powder
3/4 coconut (grated, and mixed with 600ml/1pt water)
4 tablespoons vegetable oil

- Mix together the marinade ingredients and marinate the lamb for 15 to 20 minutes. Reserve the marinade.
- Heat the oil in a frying pan and sauté the star anise, cloves, cinnamon, cardamoms, curry leaves and pandan leaves. Add the sliced onion and fry until soft.
- Add the garlic, ginger, galangal, lemon grass, black pepper, curry powder and chilli paste. Fry for 1 to 2 minutes then add in the lamb and tomatoes. Fry until heated through and pour in the reserved marinade. Bring to a low simmering boil. After about 25 to 30 minutes, add in the potatoes and continue to cook until meat is tender and the gravy turns thick. Season to taste and serve hot.

Hunter's stew

SERVES 8-10

INGREDIENTS:

25g/1oz porcini mushrooms
1.2kg/2½lb sauerkraut
700g/1½lb white cabbage (shredded)
300ml/½pt water
225g/8oz smoked streaky bacon (diced)
25g/1oz butter
1 large onion (chopped)

450g/1lb boneless pork chops (cubed)
8 prunes (pitted and chopped)
300ml/½pt chicken stock
300ml/½pt red wine
1 bay leaf
1 tablespoon granulated sugar
Salt and pepper

- Cover the porcini with hot water and soak for 30 minutes. Pick out the porcini and chop, then strain and reserve the soaking liquid. Rinse the sauerkraut in cold water, place in a large pan with the cabbage and add the water. Bring to boil then simmer for 40 minutes.
- Cook the bacon in a large frying pan, adding some of the butter if needed.
- Remove from the pan and reserve. Fry the onion in the fat, adding the remaining butter, until tender but not browned. Add the pork and cook gently until lightly coloured. Add the porcini and their soaking liquid, the bacon, onion, meat and all the remaining ingredients to the sauerkraut and cabbage. Simmer, covered, for 40 minutes. Taste and adjust the seasonings, then serve.

Beef enchilada casserole

SERVES 4

INGREDIENTS:

Butter for greasing
450g/1lb minced beef
150g/5oz onion (chopped)
275g/10oz canned red enchilada sauce
275g/10oz canned condensed
mushroom soup
275g/10oz canned chicken soup

100g/4oz canned chopped green
chillies
225ml/8fl oz milk
1 garlic clove (minced)
200g/7oz tortilla chips (crumbled)
225g/8oz Cheddar cheese (grated)
100g/4oz pitted black olives

- Preheat the oven to 190°C/375°F/Gas mark 5. Lightly grease a deep roasting tin with butter.
- In a large frying pan, brown the beef with the onion, then remove from the heat

and drain off any excess fat. Add the chilli sauce, soups, chillies, milk and garlic and mix well.

- In the prepared roasting tin, place a layer of half the tortilla chips and top with half the beef mixture, then repeat the layers. Sprinkle the cheese and olives over the top. Bake in the oven for 35 to 40 minutes. Leave to stand for 10 minutes before serving.

One-pot sausage paella

SERVES 4

INGREDIENTS:

1 tablespoon vegetable oil
350g/12oz hot Italian sausage (cut into thick slices)
1 onion (finely chopped)
3 garlic cloves (crushed)
450ml/³/₄pt chicken stock
200g/7oz long-grain rice
2 tomatoes (chopped)

1 green pepper (sliced)
2 bay leaves
¼ teaspoon ground turmeric
½ teaspoon hot pepper sauce
200g/7oz frozen peas (thawed)
Salt and pepper
200g/7oz Cheddar cheese (grated)

- Fry the sausage with the vegetable oil in a large frying pan over a medium-low heat for 10 minutes, or until it is no longer pink. Pour off any fat. Add the onion and garlic and cook until softened.
- Stir in the stock, rice, tomatoes, green pepper, bay leaves, turmeric and hot pepper sauce. Cover and simmer for 25 minutes or until rice is tender. Stir in the peas and seasoning to taste. Cook for 3 minutes. Spread the cheese on top and place under a hot grill for a few minutes to melt it.

Lancashire hotpot

SERVES 6

INGREDIENTS:

12 lamb cutlets
6 lambs' kidneys (halved)
50g/2oz butter (melted)
1.1kg/2½lb potatoes (thinly sliced)
3 large onions (sliced)

225g/8oz flat-cap mushrooms (thickly sliced)
Salt and pepper
300ml/½pt water

→

- Preheat the oven to 220°C/425°F/Gas mark 7.
- Brown the cutlets and kidneys in a pan, using half the butter, over a high heat.
- Layer the potatoes, cutlets, kidneys, onions and mushrooms in a deep casserole, seasoning well between each layer. End with a layer of potatoes, neatly overlapping and covering the surface of the dish.
- Pour the water over. Brush the remaining butter on the top potato layer and season.
- Cover the casserole dish and place in the oven. Give it 20 to 25 minutes to heat through, then reduce the oven temperature to 150°C/300°F/Gas mark 2 and leave to cook for a further 2 hours.
- Remove the lid, raise the oven temperature back to 220°C/425°F/Gas mark 7 and cook for a final 20 to 30 minutes until the top layer of potatoes is browned.

Warwickshire stew

SERVES 6

INGREDIENTS:

700g/1½lb stewing beef (cubed)
25g/1oz plain flour
1 tablespoon vegetable oil
150ml/¼pt beef stock
6 potatoes (cubed)
4 carrots (chopped)

2 medium onions (chopped)
350g/12oz tomatoes(chopped)
100g/4oz mushrooms (sliced)
2 garlic cloves (crushed)
1 tablespoon chopped fresh parsley
Salt and pepper

- Preheat the oven to 140°C/275°F/Gas mark 1.
- Lightly dust the beef with the flour. Heat the oil in a frying pan and sauté the beef to seal and lightly colour. Remove the meat and place in a casserole dish.
- Add the stock to the pan and heat gently, while scraping the bottom of the pan.
- Add all the ingredients to the casserole dish, cover and cook for 3 hours.

One-pot beef & vegetables

SERVES 8

INGREDIENTS:

1.3kg/3lb rump steak
1½ teaspoons salt
1 teaspoon ground black pepper
1 teaspoon onion powder

1 teaspoon garlic powder
400g/14oz beef stock
6 potatoes (quartered)
6 carrots (cut into 2.5cm/1in chunks)

- Preheat the oven to 160°C/325°F/Gas mark 3.
- Sprinkle the beef with salt, pepper, onion powder and garlic powder and place in a casserole dish. Add the stock and bake in the oven, covered, for 1 hour.
- Add the potatoes and carrots and cook for a further 30 minutes, or until tender.
- Serve hot.

St Lucian pork stew

SERVES 8-10

INGREDIENTS:

25g/1oz vegetable oil
225g/8oz butter
1 leek (chopped)
1 sprig thyme
1 celery stick (finely chopped)
450g/1lb onions (chopped)
1.8kg/4lb pork shoulder (cubed)
4 garlic cloves (chopped)

225g/8oz tomatoes (skinned and chopped)
100g/4oz green cabbage (shredded)
25g/1oz carrots (chopped)
Salt and pepper
450g/1lb cucumbers (diced)
3 cloves (crushed)
2 sprigs parsley (chopped)

- Heat the oil and butter in a large stew pot, add the leek, thyme, celery and onions and sauté until tender. Then add the pork, garlic, tomatoes, cabbage, carrots and seasoning and simmer for about 1½ hours, until the pork is tender.
- Add the cucumbers and cloves and simmer for a further 15 to 20 minutes. When cooked, sprinkle with parsley and serve hot.

Nacho beef casserole

SERVES 4

INGREDIENTS:

450g/1lb minced beef
150g/5oz onion (chopped)
Salt and pepper to
450g/1lb refried beans
100g/4oz canned chopped green chillies

250g/9oz Cheddar cheese (grated)
200g/7oz salsa
50g/2oz green onion (sliced)
100g/4oz pitted black olives
1 tomato (chopped)

- Preheat the oven to 200°C/400°F/Gas mark 6.

→

←

- In a heavy-based frying pan, brown the beef and onion, then drain well. Season to taste with salt and pepper.
- Spread the refried beans in a casserole dish, then top with the meat mixture and sprinkle with the chillies, then the cheese. Drizzle the salsa evenly over all. Bake in the oven for 20 minutes.
- Remove from the oven and sprinkle with the green onions, olives and tomato.

Chinese potato & pork stew

SERVES 3

INGREDIENTS:

900ml/1½pt chicken stock
2 large potatoes (diced)
2 tablespoons rice wine vinegar
2 tablespoons cornflour
4 tablespoons water
100g/4oz pork fillet (sliced)
1 tablespoon soy sauce

1 teaspoon sesame oil
1 carrot (cut into matchsticks)
1 teaspoon chopped root ginger
3 spring onions (thinly sliced)
1 red pepper (sliced)
225g/8oz bamboo shoots (drained)

- Put the stock, potatoes and 1 tablespoon vinegar in a saucepan and bring to the boil. Reduce the heat until the stock is just simmering. Mix the cornflour into the water and then stir into the stock.
- Bring the stock back to the boil, stirring until thickened, then reduce the heat until it is just simmering again.
- Place the pork in a dish and season with the remaining vinegar, the soy sauce and sesame oil.
- Add the pork, carrot and ginger to the stock and cook for 10 minutes. Stir in the spring onions, red pepper and bamboo shoots. Cook for a further 5 minutes.

Bacon & egg casserole

SERVES 6

INGREDIENTS:

10 rashers unsmoked back bacon
150g/5oz croûtons
50g/2oz butter (melted)
200g/7oz Cheddar cheese (grated)

450ml/¾pt milk
6 eggs
1 tablespoon prepared mustard

- Preheat the oven to 170°C/325°F/Gas mark 3.
- Dry-fry the bacon in a frying pan until very crisp, then remove and crumble.
- Place the croûtons in a casserole dish and pour the butter over them. Sprinkle the cheese over.
- Mix the milk, eggs and mustard and pour over the cheese. Finally, sprinkle the bacon over all. Bake in the oven for 45 minutes and allow to stand for 15 minutes before serving.

One-pot potatoes & pepper steak

SERVES 4

INGREDIENTS:

450g/1lb rump steak (thinly sliced)
1 tablespoon garlic salt
2 tablespoons olive oil

1 green pepper (cut into thin strips)
4 potatoes (sliced and boiled)
Salt and pepper

- Toss the steak with the garlic salt. Heat the oil in a large frying pan over a high heat, add the beef and toss for 3 minutes. Remove the steak. Add the green pepper to the pan and toss for a further 3 minutes.
- Add the potatoes and sauté for 5 minutes. Return the steak to the pan, then toss until heated through. Season and serve.

Lamb & vegetable stew

SERVES 4

INGREDIENTS:

2 tablespoons olive oil
400g/14oz lean lamb fillet (cubed)
1 red onion (sliced)
1 garlic clove (crushed)
1 potato (cubed)
400g/14oz canned chopped tomatoes
1 red pepper (chopped)
200g/7oz canned chickpeas

1 aubergine (cut into chunks)
200ml/7fl oz lamb stock
1 tablespoon red wine vinegar
1 teaspoon chopped fresh thyme
1 teaspoon chopped fresh rosemary
1 teaspoon chopped fresh oregano
Salt and pepper
8 pitted black olives (halved)

→

←

- Preheat the oven to 170°C/325°F/Gas mark 3.
- Heat 1 tablespoon oil in a flameproof casserole dish and, over a high heat, brown the lamb. Reduce the heat and add the remaining oil, the onion and garlic, then cook until soft.
- Add the potato, tomatoes, pepper, chickpeas, aubergine, stock, vinegar and herbs to the casserole dish. Season with salt and pepper, stir and bring to the boil.
- Cover and cook in the oven for 1 to 1½ hours, or until tender.
- About 15 minutes before the end of cooking time, add the olives. Serve hot.

One-pot ham dinner

SERVES 6

INGREDIENTS:

1.3kg/3lb ham
300g/11oz fresh green beans
1 medium head of green cabbage
(shredded)

6 medium potatoes (diced)
Salt and pepper

- Put the ham into a large casserole dish and cover with water. Cook over a low heat for 2 hours, adding more water as necessary. Add the beans and cabbage and cook for 25 minutes.
- Add the potatoes and cook until all the vegetables are tender. Season to taste and serve.

Sausage stew

SERVES 4

INGREDIENTS:

450g/1lb pork sausages
2 leeks (sliced)
450g/1lb carrots (thinly sliced)
2 celery sticks (sliced)
400g/14oz canned chopped tomatoes

300ml/½pt vegetable stock
2 tablespoons tomato purée
Salt and pepper
1 bay leaf
450g/1lb potatoes (diced)

- Dry-fry the sausages in a heavy-based saucepan until well browned all over.
- Remove from the pan and drain on kitchen paper.
- Add the remaining ingredients to the pan, except the potatoes. Return the

sausages and bring to the boil. Reduce the heat, cover and simmer gently for 35 minutes. Add the potatoes and continue cooking for a further 30 minutes until the mixture is thick. Remove the bay leaf and serve hot.

Liver hotpot

SERVES 6

INGREDIENTS:

Butter for greasing
500g/1lb 2oz lamb's liver
Salt and pepper
25g/1oz plain flour

2 large onions (thinly sliced)
850g/1¾lb potatoes (thinly sliced)
500ml/18fl oz lamb stock
6 rashers streaky bacon

- Preheat the oven to 180°C/350°F/Gas mark 4. Lightly grease a large casserole dish.
- Remove the skin and tubes from the liver. Season the flour with salt and pepper, then dip each slice of liver in the seasoned flour.
- Arrange layers of liver, onion and potatoes in the prepared casserole dish, ending with a neat layer of potatoes. Heat the stock and pour in just enough to cover the potatoes.
- Cover the casserole dish and bake for about 1 hour, or until the liver is tender.
- Remove the lid and arrange the bacon rashers on top. Continue cooking, uncovered, until the bacon is crisp. Serve hot, straight from the casserole dish.

Ulster Irish stew

SERVES 4

INGREDIENTS:

900g/2lb neck of lamb (cubed)
900g/2lb potatoes (sliced)
450g/1lb onions (thickly sliced)

Salt and pepper
1 sprig thyme

- Layer the meat, potatoes and onion in a casserole dish, seasoning each layer well and finishing with a layer of potatoes. Fill to about two-thirds full with water, add the thyme and cover with a lid.
- Bring to the boil and simmer for 1 to 2 hours, or until the lamb is really tender.
- Serve hot.

Four-hour beef stew

SERVES 6

INGREDIENTS:

700g/1¹/₂lb stewing beef (cubed)
2 onions (quartered)
150ml/¹/₄pt tomato sauce

5 carrots (chopped)
2 tablespoons tapioca
2 potatoes (chopped)

- Preheat the oven to 130°C/250°F/Gas mark ¹/₂.
- Mix all the ingredients except the potatoes and place in a casserole. Cover with a layer of potatoes. Cover and bake for 4 hours.

Spring lamb casserole

SERVES 4

INGREDIENTS:

450g/1lb lamb neck fillet (trimmed and cut into small pieces)
25g/1oz butter
1 garlic clove (crushed)
8 pearl onions
16 baby carrots
4 small turnips (quartered)

25g/1oz plain flour
450ml/³/₄pt lamb stock
2 tablespoons tomato purée
1 sachet bouquet garni
12 baby new potatoes
Salt and pepper

- Preheat the oven to 180°C/350°F/Gas mark 4.
- Brown the lamb in the butter with the garlic in a flameproof casserole dish.
- Remove from the pan with a slotted spoon. Add the onions, carrots and turnips and toss for 3 minutes, until lightly browned. Remove from the pan.
- Stir the flour into the pan, then remove the pan from the heat and gradually blend in the stock and tomato purée. Return to the heat and bring to the boil, stirring. Add the bouquet garni.
- Return the meat and vegetables to the pan. Add the potatoes and season lightly. Cover and transfer to the oven. Cook for 1¹/₄ hours or until the lamb is really tender. Taste and adjust the seasoning if necessary. Remove the bouquet garni and serve hot.

Japanese sukiyaki one-pot

SERVES 4

INGREDIENTS

1 tablespoon vegetable oil
450g/1lb sirloin steak (thinly sliced)
3 spring onions (sliced)
350g/12oz tofu(cut into bite-sized pieces)
275g/10oz spinach (stems removed)
175g/6oz mushrooms (sliced)
1 Chinese cabbage (cut into 5cm/2in pieces)
275g/10oz canned bamboo shoots (drained)

150g/5oz canned water chestnuts (drained)
150g/5oz beansprouts

For the cooking broth:
125ml/4fl oz soy sauce
125ml/4fl oz sake
1 teaspoon granulated sugar

- Mix all the ingredients for the cooking broth together and bring to the boil.
- Heat the oil in a large frying pan. Add the beef and lightly brown over a medium-high heat. Mix in a small of amount of the cooking broth.
- Add the remaining ingredients and cook, adding the cooking broth as it reduces, keeping 5mm/¼in in the pan at all times. Serve immediately.

Hotpot chops

SERVES 4

INGREDIENTS:

4 boneless lamb steaks, about 100g/4oz each
Salt and pepper
1 small onion (thinly sliced)

1 carrot (thinly sliced)
1 medium potato (thinly sliced)
1 teaspoon olive oil

- Preheat the oven to 180°C/350°F/Gas mark 4.
- Trim any excess fat from the steaks, season both sides with salt and pepper and arrange them on a baking tray. Alternate layers of sliced onion, carrot and potato on top of each lamb steak.
- Brush the tops of the potato lightly with oil, season well and bake in the oven for 25 to 30 minutes, until the lamb is tender and cooked through. Drain the lamb on kitchen paper and serve immediately.

Polish stew

SERVES 8

INGREDIENTS:

450g/1lb Polish sausage
3 tablespoons vegetable oil
700g/1½lb stewing beef (cubed)
2 onions (sliced)
175g/6oz mushrooms (sliced)
450g/1lb sauerkraut

225ml/8fl oz white wine
225ml/8fl oz tomato sauce
2 teaspoons soy sauce
1 teaspoon caraway seeds
Salt and pepper

- Preheat the oven to 190°C/375°F/Gas mark 5.
- Sauté the sausages for 15 minutes in a frying pan, then slice into 2.5cm/1in pieces and transfer to a casserole dish.
- Add the oil to the sausage drippings and brown the beef for 15 minutes, then remove to the casserole dish. Sauté the onion until lightly browned and add to the casserole dish.
- Sauté the mushrooms with the sauerkraut and wine. Add the tomato sauce, soy sauce, caraway seeds and seasoning. Add this to the casserole dish and mix well.
- Cover and bake for 2 hours, stirring every 30 minutes.

Beef & lager stew

SERVES 6

INGREDIENTS:

1.5kg/3lb braising steak (cubed)
Salt and pepper
Vegetable oil for frying
1 medium onion (finely chopped)
2 garlic cloves (finely chopped)

2 large cans lager
2 thyme sprigs
2 bay leaves
1 tablespoon tomato purée

- Season the steak with salt and pepper. Heat the oil in a large casserole dish, add the onion and cook until softened, then add the meat. Brown the meat, then add the garlic and sauté for 1 minute.
- Add the remaining ingredients, bring to the boil, cover and simmer for 2½ hours. Serve hot.

Gnocchi casserole

SERVES 6

INGREDIENTS:

300g/11oz gnocchi (cooked)
750g/1lb 11oz minced beef (cooked)
200g/7oz pitted black olives

For the tomato sauce:
2 tablespoons extra-virgin olive oil
100g/4oz onion (diced)

2 garlic cloves
12 tomatoes (diced)
2 teaspoons fresh basil
2 tablespoons chopped fresh parsley
1 teaspoon chopped fresh chives
450ml/³/₄pt red wine

- Preheat the oven to 180°C/350°F/Gas mark 4.
- To make the tomato sauce, heat the oil in a frying pan and sauté the onion and garlic. Add the tomatoes and herbs and simmer for 20 minutes.
- Layer the tomato sauce, gnocchi, beef and olives in a large casserole dish. Bake in the oven for 30 minutes until hot.

Potato, spinach & pork chop bake

SERVES 4

INGREDIENTS:

900g/2lb small potatoes
1 tablespoon vegetable oil
4 pork chops
1 large onion (sliced)
250ml/9fl oz single cream

2 eggs
Salt and pepper
¹/₂ teaspoon freshly grated nutmeg
200g/7oz spinach (trimmed)

- Preheat the oven to 200°C/400°F/Gas mark 6.
- Place the whole, unpeeled potatoes in a large pan of boiling water and cook for about 15 minutes, until just done. Drain, peel and cut into 1cm/¹/₂in slices.
- Heat the oil in a frying pan and brown the pork on both sides over a high heat.
- Remove from the pan. In the same pan, fry the onions for 10 minutes, until soft.
- In a bowl, mix the cream and eggs, season well with salt, pepper and nutmeg and add the onion.

→

←

- Place a layer of potato slices in the base of a casserole dish, then a handful of raw spinach, packing the spinach down with your hand as best you can. Then spoon over half of the onion and cream mixture. Continue to layer the potatoes, spinach and onion mixture, ending with a layer of potatoes.
- Lay the browned pork chops on top, cover with aluminium foil and bake for 35 to 40 minutes or heated through. Leave to stand for 10 minutes before serving.

Lamb stew with wine & rosemary

SERVES 6

INGREDIENTS:

Grated zest and juice of 2 oranges
3 tablespoons olive oil
900g/2lb boneless lamb shoulder
1 onion (thinly sliced)
225ml/8fl oz red wine
125ml/4fl oz chicken stock
2 teaspoons tomato purée
3 garlic cloves (crushed)
1 teaspoon fennel seeds (crushed)
1 bay leaf
2 tablespoons chopped fresh rosemary

225g/8oz shiitake mushrooms (thinly sliced)
225g/8oz button mushrooms (thinly sliced)
12 new potatoes (quartered)
4 carrots (sliced)
2 tablespoons balsamic vinegar
Salt and pepper
15g/½oz butter
2 tablespoon plain flour

- In a casserole dish, heat 1 tablespoon oil over a medium heat. Add half of the lamb and brown on all sides. Remove the lamb from the pan, add the remaining lamb and brown, then remove from pan.
- Add another tablespoon oil to the pan, add the onions and brown. Add the orange juice and red wine and simmer for 5 minutes. Put the lamb back into the pan, adding the orange zest, stock, tomato purée, garlic, fennel seeds, bay leaf and rosemary. Bring to the boil, reduce the heat to medium low, cover and simmer for 1 hour.
- In a large frying pan, heat the remaining olive oil over a medium-high heat.
- When hot add half the mushrooms and sauté until golden, then remove from the pan and add the remaining mushrooms.
- After the stew has cooked for 1 hour, add the potatoes and carrots. Cover and continue cooking for a further 30 minutes. Stir in the mushrooms, vinegar, salt and pepper. Bring to the boil, add the butter and flour, reduce the heat and simmer for 5 minutes, stirring occasionally.

Spicy goatmeat stew

SERVES 6

INGREDIENTS:

900g/2lb goatmeat
Salt and pepper
2 onions (sliced)
1 teaspoon fresh thyme
1 teaspoon curry powder

75ml/3fl oz groundnut oil
225g/8oz red chillies
900g/2Ib tomatoes
200ml/7fl oz tomato purée

- Season the goatmeat with salt, place in a deep frying pan and add the onions, thyme and curry and cook for 30 to 40 minutes until tender.
- In another pot, heat up the rest of the oil and fry the chillies and tomatoes for 20 minutes until fairly dry. Add the tomato purée and stir thoroughly, then add the fried goatmeat pieces. Simmer gently for another 10 minutes, stirring frequently until well blended. Drain off any excessive oil that rises to the top and serve.

TexMex casserole

SERVES 4

INGREDIENTS:

Butter, for greasing
275g/10oz frozen spinach (thawed and chopped)
1 tablespoon vegetable oil
3 medium butternut squash (sliced)
1 red pepper (chopped)
1 onion (chopped)
425g/15oz canned haricot beans (drained)

12 corn tortillas (cut into 2.5cm/1in pieces)
275g/10oz canned condensed mushroom soup
225g/8oz sour cream
200g/7oz salsa
150g/5oz taco seasoning
100g/4oz Cheddar cheese (grated)
200g/7oz minced beef (cooked)

- Preheat the oven to 180°C/350°F/Gas mark 4. Coat a large casserole dish with butter.
- Drain the spinach well. Heat the oil over a medium heat in a large non-stick pan. Cook the squash, pepper and onion for 6 minutes, or until soft. Remove from the heat.
- Stir in the spinach, beans, tortillas, soup, sour cream, salsa, taco seasoning and 75g/3oz cheese. Spoon into the casserole dish and add the beef. Bake in the

$\rightarrow$

←

oven for 30 minutes. Sprinkle evenly with the remaining cheese and bake for a further 5 minutes, until the cheese is melted.

Beef & vegetable stew

SERVES 4

INGREDIENTS:

550g/1lb 4oz lean stewing beef (trimmed and cubed)
2 onions (cut into wedges)
3 carrots (cut into chunks)
1 small swede (cut into chunks)
8 potatoes (chopped)

600ml/1pt beef stock
Salt and pepper
1 bouquet garni
100g/4oz green beans (cut into short lengths)

- Place all the ingredients except the beans in a large saucepan and bring to the boil, skimming the surface. Cover, reduce the heat and simmer gently for 2 hours, removing the lid for the last 30 minutes. Add the beans for the last 15 minutes.
- Discard the bouquet garni, then taste and adjust the seasoning if necessary.

Lamb & okra stew

SERVES 8

INGREDIENTS:

2 large onions (chopped)
2 garlic cloves
50g/2oz butter
900g/2lb lamb (cubed)
900g/2lb okra (chopped)

225g/8oz tomatoes (sliced)
1 tablespoon tomato purée
Salt and pepper
Juice of 1 lemon

- Fry the onions and garlic in the butter until both are golden and the garlic is aromatic. Add the lamb and brown all over. Then add the okra and fry gently for about 10 minutes.
- Add the tomatoes, continue to cook for a few more minutes, and cover with water in which you have diluted the tomato purée. Season with salt and pepper, and stir well. Bring to a boil and simmer over a low heat for 1½ hours or more, until the meat and vegetables are very tender and the sauce is reduced, adding a little more water if necessary. Remove from the heat and add the lemon juice.

Irish stew with dumplings

SERVES 4

INGREDIENTS:

2 tablespoons vegetable oil
2 large onions (sliced)
1 leek (sliced)
1 large carrot (sliced)
2 celery sticks (sliced)
900ml/1½pt lamb stock
700g/1½lb lamb cutlets (trimmed)
50g/2oz pearl barley
2 large potatoes (cut into large chunks)

Salt and pepper

For the dumplings:
100g/4oz self-raising flour
25g/1oz porridge oats
2 tablespoons chopped fresh parsley
Pinch of salt
50g/2oz vegetable suet
Chilled water for mixing

- To make the dumplings, put the flour, oats, parsley and salt into a large mixing bowl. Stir in the suet. Add enough chilled water to make a soft dough. Shape into 8 dumplings, cover with a tea towel and set aside.
- Heat the oil in a large saucepan and gently fry the onions, leek, carrot and celery for 5 minutes, without browning.
- Add the stock, lamb and pearl barley to the saucepan. Bring to the boil and then reduce the heat. Cover and simmer for 20 minutes.
- Add the potatoes and cook for a further 20 minutes. Add the dumplings to the saucepan. Cover and simmer for 15 to 20 minutes, until the dumplings are light and fluffy.
- Season the stew with salt and pepper and serve immediately.

Chilli con carne one-pot

SERVES 6

INGREDIENTS:

700g/1½lb minced beef
1 large onion (chopped)
200g/7oz green pepper (chopped
2 garlic cloves (crushed)
400g/14oz canned chopped tomatoes

400g/14oz canned red kidney beans
(drained)
225ml/8fl oz tomato sauce
2 teaspoons chilli powder

- In a large saucepan, cook the beef, onion, green pepper and garlic until the meat has browned, then drain off any fat.

→

← • Stir in the tomatoes, kidney beans, tomato sauce and chilli powder. Bring the mixture to a boil, and then reduce the heat to a simmer. Cover and allow to simmer for at least 20 minutes.

Beef in beer

SERVES 6

INGREDIENTS:

2 tablespoons sunflower oil
2 onions (thinly sliced)
8 carrots (sliced)
40g/1½oz plain flour
Salt and pepper

1.3kg/3lb stewing steak (cubed)
400ml/14fl oz stout
2 teaspoons muscovado sugar
2 bay leaves
1 tablespoon chopped fresh thyme

- Preheat the oven to 160°C/325°F/Gas mark 3.
- Heat the oil in a flameproof casserole dish. Add the onions and carrots and cook over a low heat, stirring occasionally, for 5 minutes, or until the onions are softened.
- Put the flour in a plastic bag and season. Add the steak to the bag and shake well to coat.
- Remove the vegetables from the casserole dish with a slotted spoon and reserve.
- Add the steak to the casserole dish and cook, stirring frequently, until browned all over. Do this in batches if necessary. Return the steak, onions and carrots to the casserole dish and sprinkle in any remaining flour. Pour in the stout and add the sugar, bay leaves and thyme. Bring to the boil, cover and bake in the oven for 1³/₄ hours.

Beef cabbage casserole

SERVES 4-6

INGREDIENTS:

1 teaspoon vegetable oil
2 teaspoons butter
450g/1lb minced beef
1 head green cabbage (chopped)
1 onion (chopped)

Salt and pepper
175g/6oz Cheddar cheese (grated)
150g/5oz sour cream
3 tablespoons port

- Preheat the oven to 200°C/400°F/Gas mark 6.
- Heat the oil and butter in a frying pan, brown the beef then pour off any excess fat. Add the cabbage, onion, salt and pepper. Cover and cook slowly for about 10 minutes, until the cabbage is translucent.
- Add the cheese, sour cream and port. Mix well and heat through. Transfer the mixture to a casserole dish. Bake in the oven for about 10 to 15 minutes, until the topping is browned.

Beef, Guinness & mushroom stew

SERVES 6

INGREDIENTS:

900g/2lb shin of beef (trimmed, cut into 2.5cm/1in cubes)
Salt and pepper
Plain flour (seasoned), for dusting
50g/2oz butter
2 tablespoons sunflower oil
2 onions (roughly chopped)

100g/4oz button mushrooms
750ml/1¼pt Guinness
2 tablespoons tomato purée
½ tablespoon granulated sugar
1 bay leaf
1 sachet bouquet garni
225g/8oz shiitake mushrooms

- Preheat the oven to 170°C/325°F/Gas mark 3.
- Toss the beef lightly in seasoned flour. Heat a third of the butter and 1 tablespoon oil in a frying pan and brown the meat briskly in batches, then transfer to a casserole dish. Add a little more butter and oil to the pan and fry the onions until lightly browned, then add to the casserole dish. Fry the button mushrooms and add to the casserole dish.
- Pour the Guinness into the pan and bring to the boil. Stir in the tomato purée and sugar, then pour into the casserole dish. Add the bay leaf, bouquet garni and seasoning. Cover the casserole dish and transfer to the oven. Cook for 2 to 3 hours, or until the meat is very tender.
- Remove the stalks from the shiitake mushrooms and discard. Slice the caps thickly. Heat the remaining butter in a frying pan and sauté the mushrooms, then stir into the casserole dish and return to the oven for 5 minutes. Discard the bay leaf and bouquet garni, adjust the seasoning and serve.

Bacon & lentil stew

SERVES 4-6

INGREDIENTS:

450g/1lb rindless smoked back bacon
rashers (diced)
1 onion (chopped)
2 carrots (sliced)
2 celery sticks (chopped)
1 turnip (chopped)

1 large potato (chopped)
75g/3oz Puy lentils
1 bouquet garni
900ml/1½pt chicken stock
Salt and pepper

- Heat a large flameproof casserole dish and add the bacon. Cook over a medium heat, stirring, for 5 minutes or until the fat runs. Add the onion, carrots, celery, turnip and potato and cook, stirring, for 5 minutes.
- Add the lentils, bouquet garni and stock. Bring to the boil, reduce the heat and simmer for 1 hour, or until the lentils are tender.
- Remove and discard the bouquet garni and season to taste. Serve immediately.

Beef macaroni casserole

SERVES 4

INGREDIENTS:

2 tablespoons olive oil
700g/1½lb minced beef
100g/4oz celery (chopped)
150g/5oz onion (chopped)
400g/14oz canned chopped tomatoes
150g/5oz macaroni (cooked and
drained)

200g/7oz Cheddar cheese (grated)
2 teaspoons Worcestershire sauce
¾ teaspoon salt
¼ teaspoon pepper

- Preheat the oven to 180°C/350°F/Gas mark 4.
- In a large frying pan, heat the oil over a medium heat, then add the beef, celery and onions. Fry until the beef is browned and the onions are tender. Remove from the heat and put into a large casserole dish.
- Add the tomatoes, macaroni, cheese, Worcestershire sauce, salt and pepper. Bake in the oven for 30 minutes, until hot and bubbly.

Beef, mushroom & red wine casserole

SERVES 4

INGREDIENTS:

1½ tablespoons vegetable oil
25g/1oz butter
700g/1½lb braising steak (cut into 4cm/1½in cubes)
200g/7oz streaky bacon rashers (cut into strips)
350g/12oz onions (sliced)
3 garlic cloves (crushed)
350g/12oz carrots (chopped)

1 tablespoon tomato purée
1 tablespoon plain flour
225ml/8fl oz red wine
300ml/½pt beef stock
1 bouquet garni
6 juniper berries
Salt and pepper
225g/8oz shiitake mushrooms

- Preheat the oven to 170°C/325°F/Gas mark 3.
- Heat 1 tablespoon oil in a large casserole dish then add the butter. When foaming, add the beef and brown over a high heat on all sides. Remove and reserve.
- Add the bacon and fry until golden, then add the onions, garlic, carrots and tomato purée. Cook over a moderate heat until lightly browned. Sprinkle in the flour and cook for 2 minutes, stirring, then pour in the wine. Mix until smooth, bring to the boil and bubble for 3 minutes. Return the beef to the casserole dish, pour in enough stock to barely cover, add the bouquet garni and juniper berries and season with salt and pepper. Bring to the boil, cover and cook in the oven for 1 hour.
- Heat the remaining oil in a large frying pan, add the mushrooms and stir-fry until just cooked.
- When the beef is tender, remove the bouquet garni and add the mushroom to the casserole. Serve immediately.

Hungarian goulash

SERVES 4

INGREDIENTS:

1 onion (finely chopped)
2 tablespoons shortening
450g/1lb chuck steak (cut into
2.5cm/1in pieces)
1 teaspoon paprika

3 carrots (sliced)
600ml/1pt water
4 potatoes (chopped)
Salt and pepper

- Brown the onion in the shortening, then add the beef and paprika. Allow the beef to simmer in its own juice for 1 hour. Add the carrots and simmer for 30 minutes.
- Add the water and potatoes. Simmer until the potatoes are done, season and serve.

Black bean chilli one-pot

SERVES 12

INGREDIENTS:

450g/1lb sausagemeat
450g/1lb minced beef
2½ teaspoons chilli powder
1 tablespoon olive oil
100g/4oz onion (chopped)
2 tablespoons chopped garlic
3 tablespoons chopped shallots
1 red pepper (chopped)
1 yellow pepper (chopped)
700g/1½lb rump steak (sliced)
225ml/8fl oz vegetable juice

900g/2lb canned black soy beans
(drained)
900g/2lb tomato purée
850g/1¾lb canned chopped tomatoes
2 tablespoons Worcestershire sauce
2 tablespoons red wine
2 tablespoons cayenne pepper
2 tablespoons chopped fresh parsley
1 tablespoon chopped fresh oregano
1 tablespoon chopped fresh basil
2 bay leaves

- Brown the sausagemeat and minced beef with 1 tablespoon of the chilli powder. Drain thoroughly and set aside.
- Sauté the onions, garlic and shallots in a large casserole dish in the olive oil until translucent. Add the peppers and sauté for a further 1 to 2 minutes. Add the steak and sauté until it just begins to brown.
- Add the vegetable juice and simmer for 5 minutes. Add the beans, tomato purée, tomatoes and sausagemeat and minced beef to the casserole dish. Heat to a high

simmer, then turn the heat down to the lowest marked setting.
- Add the Worcestershire sauce, red wine, remaining chilli powder, cayenne pepper and herbs. Simmer on the lowest setting for 6 to 8 hours. Stir every 30 minutes.

Pasta & tomato hotpot

SERVES 4-6

INGREDIENTS:

300g/11oz minced beef
1 teaspoon dried thyme
75g/3oz fresh breadcrumbs
Salt and pepper
2 tablespoons olive oil
1 onion (finely diced)
2 teaspoons minced garlic
3 rashers smoky streaky bacon
(chopped)

For the sauce:
425g/15oz canned condensed tomato
soup
350ml/12fl oz vegetable stock
750g/1lb 11oz pasta

- In a bowl, combine the mince, thyme and breadcrumbs. Season with salt and pepper. With wet hands, shape the mixture into 24 mini meatballs.
- Brown the meatballs in the hot oil in a large saucepan, turning carefully. Reduce the heat, add the onion, garlic and bacon and cook for 1 to 2 minutes.
- Pour in the soup, stock and pasta. Stir well and bring to the boil. Simmer gently for 8 to 10 minutes, until the pasta is cooked.

Mushroom & beef hotpot

SERVES 4

INGREDIENTS:

225g/8oz beef fillet (cut into strips)
10 spring onions (thinly sliced)
6 pine mushrooms (thinly sliced)
2 pyogo mushrooms (sliced)
1 onion (sliced)
1 green cabbage (shredded)
225ml/8fl oz beef stock

For the marinade:
2 tablespoons soy sauce
3 tablespoons finely chopped spring
onions
2 teaspoons minced garlic
1 tablespoon sesame seeds
1 tablespoon sesame oil

→

←
- Mix the marinade ingredients together in a shallow dish and coat the beef in the mixture. Leave to marinate for at least 2 hours.
- Layer the bottom of a thick, shallow casserole with seasoned beef and spring onions.
- Place the mushrooms, onion and cabbage on top of the beef. Add the stock, season and bring to the boil. Heat through until the beef is cooked, about 15 minutes.

Caribbean one-pot stew

SERVES 4

INGREDIENTS:

450g/1lb sweet potatoes
2 tablespoons olive oil
2 tablespoons minced root ginger
3 garlic cloves (minced)
1/4 red chilli (minced)
2 celery sticks (diced)
1 green pepper (diced)
1 small onion (diced)

450g/1lb pork loin (trimmed and cut into 1cm/1/2in pieces)
1 teaspoon ground cumin
Salt and pepper
900g/2lb canned kidney beans (rinsed and drained)
400g/14oz canned chopped tomatoes
400ml/14fl oz vegetable stock

- Prick the sweet potatoes with a fork and microwave on high for 6 to 8 minutes until tender. Set aside. When cool, peel and cut into 1cm/1/2in cubes.
- Heat the oil in a large casserole dish. Add the ginger, garlic and chilli and sauté for about 2 minutes, until soft. Add the celery, green pepper and onion and cook for about 5 minutes, until translucent.
- Season the pork with cumin, salt and pepper. Push the vegetables to one side of stockpot and add the pork, browning on all sides. Add the kidney beans, tomatoes, stock and sweet potato and bring to the boil. Reduce the heat and simmer for 25 to 30 minutes, or until the pork is tender. Adjust seasoning to taste.

Sausage & egg casserole

SERVES 4

INGREDIENTS:

450g/1lb pork sausages
2 tomatoes (halved)
4 eggs

50ml/2fl oz milk
Salt and pepper
150g/5oz Cheddar cheese (grated)

- Preheat the oven to 170°C/325°F/Gas mark 3.
- In a non-stick frying pan, dry-fry the sausages until golden brown and cut into bite-sized pieces. Place the sausages and tomatoes into a casserole dish.
- Beat the eggs with the milk and season to taste. Pour the egg mixture over the sausages and tomatoes. Bake for 45 minutes or until the egg is set. Sprinkle with the cheese and place under a hot grill until golden brown and bubbling.

Persian pumpkin stew

SERVES 4-6

INGREDIENTS:

½ teaspoon coriander seeds
½ teaspoon cardamom seeds
½ teaspoon ground cinnamon
1 teaspoon cumin seeds
1 clove
2 tablespoons vegetable oil
900g/2lb lamb (cubed)
1 onion (minced)
4 garlic cloves (minced)
2 carrots (chopped)

1 celery stick (chopped)
4 tomatoes (peeled and chopped)
1 acorn squash (peeled and chopped)
1.2 litres/2pt vegetable stock
50g/2oz fresh coriander leaves (minced)
50g/2oz fresh parsley leaves (minced)
Salt and pepper
1 pumpkin (chopped)
200g/7oz basmati rice

- Combine the coriander, cardamom, cinnamon, cumin and clove in a spice mill or coffee grinder and grind until smooth. Set aside.
- Heat 1 tablespoon oil in a large, heavy-based saucepan. Add the lamb in one layer and sprinkle with the spice mixture. Sear over a medium heat for about 3 to 5 minutes until lightly browned. Remove the lamb from the pan and set aside.
- Add the onion and garlic to the pan. Sauté, stirring frequently, for about 5 minutes, until translucent.
- Add the carrots, celery, tomatoes, squash and stock. Return the lamb to the pan. Add the coriander, parsley and salt and pepper. Partly cover and gently simmer for 1½ to 2 hours until the lamb is tender.
- Preheat the oven to 180°C/350°F/Gas mark 4.
- Place the pumpkin on a baking tray and brush with the remaining oil. Bake for about 45 to 60 minutes, until tender.
- Cook the rice according to the package directions, set aside.
- Place the pumpkin in a serving dish and top with the stew. Serve with the rice.

Poultry

Perhaps one of the most versatile ingredients ever, poultry –
be it chicken, duck or turkey – can be prepared in many
different ways. Whether it is as Creamy chicken noodle
casserole, Pumpkin turkey stew, Chilli chicken casserole or
French-style stewed duck, the possibilities and pleasures are
endless and guaranteed.

One-pot enchilada casserole

SERVES 4

INGREDIENTS:

2 tablespoons chilli powder
2 tablespoons dried onion (chopped)
2 tablespoons sun-dried tomatoes
(chopped)

750ml/1¼pt water
400g/14oz canned chickpeas
350g/12oz corn chips (crumbled)
175g/6oz Cheddar cheese (grated)

- Combine the chilli powder, dried onion and sun-dried tomatoes in a bowl.
- Bring the water to the boil, then add the chilli mixture and chickpeas. Simmer for about 5 minutes. Add the crumbled corn chips and cheese. Stir until the chips are moistened, then serve.

Spiced chicken casserole

SERVES 4

INGREDIENTS:

4 chicken portions (skinned)
2 tablespoons plain flour
Salt and pepper
1 teaspoon paprika
25g/1oz butter

1 teaspoon curry powder
300g/11oz canned condensed
mushroom soup
2 teaspoons chopped gherkins

- Preheat the oven to 180°C/350°F/Gas mark 4.
- Toss the chicken portions in the flour, season with a little salt and pepper and dust with the paprika.
- Melt the butter in a flameproof casserole dish and brown the chicken on all sides. Remove from the pan and drain off any excess fat.
- Sprinkle the curry powder into the casserole dish and add the soup. Bring to the boil, stirring. Add the chicken and gherkins, cover and cook in the oven for 1½ to 2 hours, until the chicken is cooked. Serve hot.

Broccoli, Spanish rice & chicken

SERVES 4

INGREDIENTS:

50g/2oz butter
4 skinless, boneless chicken breast halves
200g/7oz Spanish rice (cooked)
400ml/14fl oz water

400g/14oz canned chopped tomatoes
275g/10oz frozen broccoli (thawed and chopped)
100g/4oz Parmesan cheese (grated)
Salt and pepper

- Melt the butter over a medium-high heat in a large frying pan. Add the chicken and cook for about 2 minutes on each side or until browned. Remove the chicken from the pan and keep warm.
- Sauté the rice over a medium heat in the frying pan until golden brown, stirring frequently.
- Slowly stir in the water and tomatoes. Place the chicken over the rice mixture. Bring the mixture to a boil.
- Cover and reduce the heat to low. Simmer for 15 minutes.
- Add the broccoli and cover and simmer for a further 5 minutes, or until the liquid is absorbed.
- Sprinkle with the cheese and serve.

Chicken & potato bake

SERVES 4

INGREDIENTS:

2 tablespoons olive oil
4 chicken breasts
1 bunch spring onions (trimmed and chopped)
350g/12oz carrots (sliced)
100g/4oz green beans (trimmed and sliced)

600ml/1pt chicken stock
350g/12oz new potatoes
Salt and pepper
2 tablespoons cornflour
3 tablespoons cold water

→

←

- Preheat the oven to 190°C/375°F/Gas mark 5.
- Heat the oil in a large flameproof casserole dish and add the chicken breasts.
- Gently fry for 5 to 8 minutes until browned on both sides. Lift from the casserole dish with a slotted spoon and set aside.
- Add the spring onions, carrots and green beans and gently fry for 3 to 4 minutes.
- Return the chicken to the casserole dish and pour in the stock. Add the potatoes, season and bring to the boil. Cover the casserole dish, transfer to the oven and bake for 40 to 50 minutes, until the potatoes are tender.
- Blend the cornflour with the cold water. Add to the casserole, stirring until blended and thickened. Cover and cook for a further 5 minutes. Serve immediately.

Turkey one-pot

SERVES 4

INGREDIENTS:

100g/4oz dried kidney beans (soaked overnight and drained)
25g/1oz butter
2 herby pork sausages
450g/1lb turkey casserole meat
3 leeks (sliced)

2 carrots (finely chopped)
400g/14oz canned chopped tomatoes
3 teaspoons tomato purée
1 bouquet garni
400ml/14fl oz chicken stock
Salt and pepper

- Cook the beans in boiling water for 40 minutes, then drain well.
- Meanwhile, heat the butter in a flameproof casserole dish, then cook the sausages until browned and the fat runs. Remove and drain on kitchen paper. Stir the turkey into the casserole dish and cook until lightly browned all over, then transfer to a bowl using a slotted spoon. Stir the leeks and carrots into the casserole dish and brown lightly.
- Add the tomatoes and tomato purée and simmer gently for about 5 minutes.
- Chop the sausages and return to the casserole dish with the beans, turkey, bouquet garni, stock and seasoning. Cover and cook gently for about 1¼ hours, until the beans are tender and there is very little liquid. Serve hot.

Chicken & leek casserole

SERVES 6

INGREDIENTS:

25g/1oz butter
4 skinless, boneless chicken breasts
2 leeks (chopped)
275g/10oz canned condensed vegetable
soup

225ml/8fl oz white wine
1 tablespoon cornflour

- Preheat the oven to 180°C/350°F/Gas mark 4.
- In a frying pan, brown the chicken in the butter over a medium-high heat. Add the leeks and cook until soft. Add the soup and wine and sprinkle the cornflour over the top.
- Mix together. Simmer for about 20 minutes or until the mixture starts to really thicken.
- Pour the mixture into a large casserole dish. Bake in the oven for about 30 minutes.

Chicken pasanda

SERVES 4

INGREDIENTS:

4 cardamom pods
6 black peppercorns
1/2 cinnamon stick
1/2 teaspoon cumin seeds
2 teaspoons garam masala
1 teaspoon chilli powder
1 teaspoon grated fresh root ginger
1 garlic clove (finely chopped)
4 tablespoons natural yogurt

Pinch of salt
700g/1 1/2lb skinless, boneless chicken
breast (diced)
5 tablespoons groundnut oil
2 onions (finely chopped)
3 green chillies (deseeded and chopped)
2 tablespoons chopped fresh coriander
125ml/4fl oz single cream

- Put the cardamom pods in a dish with the peppercorns, cinnamon, cumin, garam masala, chilli powder, ginger, garlic, yogurt and salt. Add the chicken and stir well to coat. Cover and leave to marinate in the refrigerator for 2 hours.
- Heat the oil in a wok. Add the onions and cook over a low heat, stirring occasionally, for 5 minutes, then add the chicken and marinade and cook over a medium heat, stirring, for 15 minutes.

$\rightarrow$

←
- Stir in the chillies and coriander and pour in the cream. Heat through but do not let it boil. Serve immediately.

Duck, tomato & pepper stew

SERVES 4

INGREDIENTS:

4 duck legs (each cut into 2 pieces)
3 tablespoons olive oil
1 small red onion (chopped)
3 garlic cloves (finely chopped)
1 red pepper (cut into strips)
1 green pepper (cut into strips)
700g/1½lb tomatoes (skinned and roughly chopped)

2 thyme sprigs
1 rosemary sprig
Salt and pepper
150ml/¼pt water
15g/½oz plain chocolate (finely chopped)

- Brown the duck legs briskly in the oil over a high heat in a wide, deep frying pan. Set aside. Reduce the heat and cook the onion, garlic and peppers gently in the oil until tender. Add the tomatoes, thyme, rosemary, salt and pepper and water. Bring to the boil, return the duck to the pan and simmer for 40 minutes.
- Stir in the chocolate and cook for a final 5 minutes. Taste, adjust the seasoning and serve.

Chicken broccoli casserole

SERVES 4

INGREDIENTS:

Vegetable oil for greasing
500g/1lb 2oz broccoli florets
500g/1lb 2oz cooked chicken (cubed)
275g/10oz canned condensed chicken soup
125ml/4fl oz mayonnaise

100g/4oz Parmesan cheese (grated)
½ teaspoon curry powder
100g/4oz fresh bread (cubed)
25g/1oz butter (melted)

- Preheat the oven to 180°C/350°F/Gas mark 4. Lightly grease a large baking dish with oil.
- Cook the broccoli in water in a covered saucepan until al dente, then drain.
- Place the broccoli in the prepared baking dish.
- Combine the chicken, soup, mayonnaise, cheese and curry powder, then spoon over the broccoli. Top with the bread and butter. Bake uncovered for 25 to 30 minutes or until heated through.

Jamaican hotpot

SERVES 4

INGREDIENTS:

2 teaspoons sunflower oil
4 chicken drumsticks
4 chicken thighs
1 medium onion (sliced)
750g/1lb 10oz pumpkin (peeled and diced)
1 green pepper (sliced)

2.5cm/1in piece fresh root ginger (finely chopped)
425g/15oz canned chopped tomatoes
300ml/½pt chicken stock
50g/2oz split lentils
Salt and pepper
350g/12oz canned sweetcorn

- Preheat the oven to 190°C/375°F/Gas mark 5.
- Heat the oil in a large flameproof casserole dish and fry the chicken joints, turning frequently, until they are golden all over.
- Drain any excess fat from the pan and add the onion, pumpkin and pepper.
- Gently fry for a few minutes. Add the ginger, tomatoes, stock and lentils. Season with salt and pepper.
- Cover and place in the oven for about 1 hour, until the vegetables are tender and the juices from the chicken run clear.
- Add the drained sweetcorn and cook for a further 5 minutes. Season to taste and serve.

Spanish chicken casserole

SERVES 4

INGREDIENTS:

25g/1oz plain flour
Salt and pepper
1 tablespoon paprika
4 chicken portions
3 tablespoons olive oil
1 large onion (chopped)
2 garlic cloves (crushed)

425g/15oz canned chopped tomatoes
1 green pepper (chopped)
150ml/¹/₄pt Spanish red wine
300ml/¹/₂pt chicken stock
3 medium potatoes (quartered)
12 pitted black olives
1 bay leaf

- Preheat the oven to 190°C/375°F/Gas mark 5.
- Put the flour, salt, pepper and paprika into a large plastic bag. Rinse the chicken portions and pat dry with kitchen paper. Put them into the bag and shake to coat.
- Heat the oil in a large flameproof casserole dish. Add the chicken portions and cook over a medium-high heat for 5 to 8 minutes until well browned on each side. Lift out of the casserole dish with a slotted spoon and set aside.
- Add the onion and garlic to the casserole and cook for a few minutes until browned. Add the tomatoes and pepper and cook for 2 to 3 minutes.
- Return the chicken to the casserole. Add the wine, stock and potatoes and then the olives and bay leaf. Cover and bake in the oven for 1 hour, until the chicken is tender. Adjust seasoning to taste and serve.

Chicken & peach casserole

SERVES 4

INGREDIENTS:

1 tablespoon vegetable oil
1 chicken (skinned and divided into pieces)
1 onion (sliced)
1 green pepper (sliced)
25g/1oz butter

400g/14oz canned chopped peaches
1 tablespoon cornflour
1 tablespoon soy sauce
3 tablespoons white wine vinegar
2 tomatoes (peeled and sliced)

- Preheat the oven to 190°C/375°F/Gas mark 5.
- Heat the oil in a frying pan and brown the chicken. Cover and simmer for 10 minutes, then remove and put into a casserole dish. Sauté the onion and pepper

in the butter. Drain the peaches, reserving the syrup.
- Mix together the cornflour, soy sauce, vinegar and 225ml/8fl oz peach syrup, add to the frying pan and bring to the boil. Add the peaches and tomatoes.
- Pour the contents of the frying pan over the chicken. Cover the casserole dish and bake in the oven for 40 minutes. Serve hot.

Chicken, pepper & bean stew

SERVES 4-6

INGREDIENTS:

1.8kg/4lb chicken (cut into pieces)	450ml/¾pt chicken stock
Salt and pepper	50ml/2fl oz chopped fresh parsley
2 tablespoons olive oil	½ tablespoon Tabasco sauce
25g/1oz butter	1 tablespoon Worcestershire sauce
2 onions (chopped)	400g/14oz canned sweetcorn
½ green pepper (chopped)	100g/4oz broad beans
½ yellow pepper (chopped)	3 tablespoons plain flour
450g/1lb canned chopped tomatoes	Salt and pepper
250ml/9fl oz white wine	

- Rinse the chicken pieces under cold running water and pat dry with kitchen paper. Sprinkle each piece lightly with salt and pepper.
- Heat the oil with the butter in a flameproof casserole dish over a medium-high heat, until the mixture is just starting to change colour.
- Add the chicken pieces and fry until golden on all sides. Remove from the pan with a slotted spoon and set aside.
- Reduce the heat and add the onions and peppers to the casserole dish. Cook for 8 to 10 minutes, until softened. Increase the heat and add the tomatoes and their juice, the wine, stock, parsley and Tabasco and Worcestershire sauces. Stir thoroughly and bring to the boil.
- Add the chicken to the casserole dish, pushing the pieces down into the sauce.
- Cover, reduce the heat, and simmer for 30 minutes, stirring occasionally.
- Remove the lid, add the sweetcorn and beans and mix well. Part-cover the pan and cook for 30 minutes.
- Tilt the pan and skim off as much fat as possible. Mix the flour with a little water in a small bowl to make a paste. Stir about 175ml/6fl oz of the hot sauce from the casserole dish into the flour mixture and then stir into the stew and mix well. Cook for a further 5 to 8 minutes, stirring occasionally. Season to taste.

Cheesy broccoli & carrot casserole

SERVES 6

INGREDIENTS:

275g/10oz frozen broccoli (thawed and chopped)
75g/3oz onion (chopped)
275g/10oz canned chicken soup
200g/7oz sour cream
225g/8oz carrots (grated)

1 tablespoon plain flour
Salt and pepper
225g/8oz Cheddar cheese (grated)
250g/9oz stuffing mix
25g/1oz butter (melted)

- Preheat the oven to 180°C/350°F/Gas mark 4.
- In a saucepan, cook the broccoli and onion in a small amount of boiling water for 5 minutes. Drain and set aside.
- In a large casserole dish, combine the soup and sour cream. Stir in the carrots, flour, salt and pepper. Fold in the broccoli, onion and cheese.
- Combine the stuffing mix and butter and sprinkle over the vegetables. Bake in the oven for 25 to 30 minutes or until heated.

Brown rice & chicken slow-pot

SERVES 4

INGREDIENTS:

1 oven-ready chicken, about 1.2kg/2³/₄lb
225g/8oz brown long-grain rice
8 button onions
2 carrots (cut into chunks)
2 turnips (cut into chunks)

Pinch of grated nutmeg
1 teaspoon chopped fresh sage
Salt and pepper
600ml/1pt hot chicken stock
4 tablespoons single cream

- Preheat the oven to 140°C/275°F/Gas mark 1.
- Wipe the chicken inside and out with kitchen paper and place in a casserole

dish. Wash the rice thoroughly in several changes of water. Drain and surround the chicken.

- Add the vegetables, nutmeg, sage and seasoning and pour the stock over. Cover tightly and cook in the oven for 2 hours. Turn up the heat to 200°C/400°F/Gas mark 6 and cook for a further 30 minutes. Remove the chicken and ease it apart into portions, discarding the skin. Stir the cream into the rice. Taste and add more seasoning if necessary. Serve hot.

Lime fricassée of chicken

SERVES 4

INGREDIENTS:

2 tablespoons vegetable oil
1 large chicken (cut into small portions)
50g/2oz plain flour (seasoned)
500g/1lb 2oz baby onions (sliced)
1 green pepper (sliced)
1 red pepper (sliced)

150ml/¼pt chicken stock
Grated zest and juice of 2 limes
2 red chillies (chopped)
2 tablespoons oyster sauce
1 teaspoon Worcestershire sauce
Salt and pepper

- Preheat the oven to 190°C/375°F/Gas mark 5.
- Heat the oil in a large frying pan. Coat the chicken pieces in the flour and cook for about 4 minutes until browned all over.
- Transfer the chicken to a large casserole dish and sprinkle with the onions.
- Slowly fry the peppers in the juices in the frying pan. Add the chicken stock, lime juice and zest and cook for a further 5 minutes. Add the chillies, oyster sauce and Worcestershire sauce, mixing well. Season to taste with salt and pepper, then pour over the chicken and onions.
- Cover the casserole dish with a lid and cook in the centre of the oven for 1½ hours, until the chicken is very tender, then serve.

Chicken macaroni casserole

SERVES 4

INGREDIENTS:

225g/8oz macaroni
200g/7oz cooked chicken (cubed)
275g/10oz canned condensed
mushroom soup

125ml/4fl oz milk
1 tablespoon chopped frsh parsley
175g/6oz Cheddar cheese (grated)

- Preheat the oven to 200°C/400°F/Gas mark 6.
- Cook the macaroni in boiling salted water according to the package instructions, until it is tender, then rinse and drain.
- Combine the macaroni with the remaining ingredients, reserving enough cheese to sprinkle on top. Put in a casserole dish, cover and bake for about 20 minutes.

Chicken paprika stew

SERVES 6

INGREDIENTS:

2 tablespoons vegetable oil
1.3kg/3lb chicken (chopped into bite-sized pieces)
2 medium onions (sliced)
1 garlic clove (finely chopped)
175g/6oz tomatoes (chopped)

125ml/4fl oz water
2 tablespoons paprika
Salt and pepper
1 green pepper (cut into strips)
175g/6oz sour cream

- Heat the oil in a large frying pan over a medium heat. Cook the chicken in the oil for about 15 minutes or until browned. Remove the chicken from the frying pan.
- Cook the onions and garlic in the same pan, stirring occasionally, until the onions are tender, then drain any fat from the pan.
- Add the tomatoes, water, paprika, salt and pepper to the pan and stir well to loosen the brown particles from the bottom of the pan. Return the chicken and bring to the boil, then reduce the heat. Cover and simmer for 30 minutes.
- Stir in the pepper. Cover and cook for a further 15 minutes, until the juices run clear.
- Remove the chicken to a platter and keep warm. Skim any fat from the liquid in the pan. Stir the sour cream into the liquid in the pan and heat through. Pour the sauce over the chicken and serve.

Chicken casserole with yogurt

SERVES 6

INGREDIENTS:

50g/2oz cornflour
1 teaspoon paprika
1.2kg/3lb chicken fillets (skinned and trimmed)
1 packet chicken noodle soup
250ml/9fl oz warm water
1 garlic clove (crushed)

1 teaspoon Worcestershire sauce
50ml/2fl oz dry sherry
125ml/4fl oz lemon juice
2 tablespoons natural yogurt
1 tablespoon finely chopped fresh parsley

- Preheat the oven to 180°C/350°F/Gas mark 4.
- Mix together the cornflour and paprika and toss the chicken fillets in the mixture. Arrange the fillets in the base of a large shallow casserole dish.
- Combine the remaining ingredients and pour over the chicken. Cook in the oven, uncovered, for approximately 40 minutes until the chicken is tender.

Duck casserole

SERVES 4

INGREDIENTS:

Salt and pepper
25g/1oz plain flour
1 duck (jointed and skinned)
4 shallots (finely chopped)

100g/4oz mushrooms (finely chopped)
400ml/14fl oz beef stock
225g/8oz shelled green peas
1 teaspoon chopped fresh mint

- Preheat the oven to 190°C/375°F/Gas mark 5.
- Season the flour and use to coat the duck. Place the shallots and mushrooms with the duck in a casserole dish.
- Add enough stock to cover, put on a lid and cook in the oven for 45 minutes. Add the peas and mint and continue cooking for a further 30 minutes until the duck is tender.

French-style pot-roast poussin

SERVES 4

INGREDIENTS:

1 tablespoon olive oil
1 onion (sliced)
1 garlic clove (sliced)
50g/2oz smoked back bacon
2 fresh poussins, about 450g/1lb each
25g/1oz butter (melted)
Salt and pepper
2 baby celery hearts (quartered)
8 baby carrots

2 small courgettes (cut into chunks)
8 small new potatoes
600ml/1pt chicken stock
150ml/¼pt dry white wine
1 bay leaf
2 thyme sprigs
2 rosemary sprigs
1 tablespoon butter (softened)
1 tablespoon plain flour

- Preheat the oven to 190°C/375°F/Gas mark 5.
- Heat the olive oil in a large flameproof casserole dish and add the onion, garlic and bacon. Sauté for 5 to 6 minutes, until the onions have softened.
- Brush the poussin with a little of the melted butter and season well. Lay on top of the onion mixture and arrange the prepared vegetables around them. Pour the stock and wine around the poussin and add the herbs.
- Cover, bake for 20 minutes, then remove the lid and brush the pousssins with the remaining melted butter. Cook for a further 25 to 30 minutes until golden.
- Transfer the poussins to a warmed serving platter and cut each in half with poultry shears or scissors. Remove the vegetables with a slotted spoon and arrange them around the birds. Cover with aluminium foil and keep warm.
- Discard the herbs from the pan juices. In a bowl, mix together the softened butter and flour to form a paste. Bring the liquid in the pan to the boil and then whisk in teaspoonfuls of the paste until thickened. Season the sauce and serve with the poussin and vegetables.

One-pot chicken couscous

SERVES 8

INGREDIENTS:

900g/2lb boneless, skinless chicken
breasts (cut into 2.5cm/1in chunks)
50ml/2fl oz olive oil
4 large carrots (peeled and sliced)
2 onions (diced)
3 garlic cloves (crushed)
500g/1lb 2oz canned chicken soup

250g/9oz couscous
2 teaspoons Tabasco sauce
½ teaspoon salt
200g/7oz raisins
200g/7oz slivered almonds (toasted)
50g/2oz fresh parsley (chopped)

- In a large frying pan over a medium-high heat, cook the chicken in the oil until well browned on all sides. With a slotted spoon, remove the chicken to a plate.
- Reduce the heat to medium.
- In the remaining drippings, cook the carrots and onion for 5 minutes. Add the garlic and cook for a further 2 minutes, stirring frequently.
- Add the soup, Tabasco sauce, salt and chicken. Bring to the boil, then reduce the heat to low, cover and simmer for 5 minutes. Stir in the raisins, almonds and parsley. Heat through and serve immediately.

Swiss chicken casserole

SERVES 4

INGREDIENTS:

500g/1lb 5oz cooked chicken (chopped
into bite-sized pieces)
175g/6oz celery (sliced)
200g/7oz herb stuffing (broken up)
225ml/8fl oz salad dressing

125ml/4fl oz milk
50g/2oz onion (chopped)
Salt and pepper
225g/8oz Emmanthal cheese (grated)
50g/2oz toasted slivered almonds

- Preheat the oven to 180°C/350°F/Gas mark 4.
- Combine the chicken, celery, stuffing, salad dressing, milk, onion, salt, pepper and cheese in a large casserole dish and sprinkle with the almonds.
- Cover the casserole with a lid and bake in the oven for 25 minutes. Remove the lid and continue baking for a further 10 minutes.

Brunswick stew

SERVES 6

INGREDIENTS:

1.8kg/4lb boneless, skinless chicken breasts (chopped into bite-sized pieces)
Salt
2 tablespoons paprika
2 tablespoons olive oil
25g/1oz butter
450g/1lb onions (chopped)
2 yellow peppers (deseeded and chopped)
400g/14oz canned chopped tomatoes

225ml/8fl oz dry white wine
450ml/³/₄pt chicken stock
1 tablespoon Worcestershire sauce
½ teaspoon Tabasco sauce
1 tablespoon chopped fresh parsley
350g/12oz canned sweetcorn (drained)
425g/15oz canned butter beans (drained)
2 tablespoons plain flour
4 tablespoons water

- Season the chicken with salt and dust with the paprika. Heat the oil and butter in a casserole dish. Add the chicken and cook over a medium heat, turning, for 10 to 15 minutes, or until golden. Transfer the chicken to a plate, using a slotted spoon.
- Add the onion and peppers to the casserole dish and cook over a low heat, stirring occasionally, for 5 minutes. Add the tomatoes, wine, stock, Worcestershire sauce, Tabasco sauce and parsley and bring to the boil, stirring.
- Return the chicken to the casserole dish, then cover and simmer, stirring occasionally, for 30 minutes.
- Add the sweetcorn and beans to the casserole dish, part-cover and simmer for a further 30 minutes.
- Put the flour and water in a small bowl and mix to make a paste. Stir into the stew. Cook, stirring frequently, for 5 minutes. Serve hot.

Garlic chicken cassoulet

SERVES 4

INGREDIENTS:

4 tablespoons sunflower oil
900g/2lb chicken meat (chopped into 2.5cm/1in cubes)
225g/8oz mushrooms (sliced)
16 shallots
6 garlic cloves (crushed)

1 tablespoon plain flour
225ml/8fl oz white wine
225ml/8fl oz chicken stock
1 bouquet garni
Salt and pepper
400g/14oz canned borlotti beans

- Preheat the oven to 150°C/300°F/Gas mark 2.
- Heat the oil in an ovenproof casserole dish and fry the chicken until browned all over. Remove from the casserole dish with a slotted spoon.
- Add the mushrooms, shallots and garlic to the oil in the casserole dish and cook for 4 minutes. Return the chicken to the casserole dish and sprinkle with the flour, then cook for a further 2 minutes.
- Add the wine and stock, stir until boiling, then add the bouquet garni. Season well with salt and pepper. Stir in the borlotti beans.
- Cover and cook in the centre of the oven for 2 hours, then remove the bouquet garni and serve.

Turkey, pea & ham pot pie

SERVES 6

INGREDIENTS:

50g/2oz plain flour
Salt and pepper
500g/1lb 2oz turkey thighs (diced)
4 tablespoons vegetable oil
1 onion (chopped)
250ml/9fl oz chicken stock
175g/6oz ham (cut into bite-sized chunks)

150g/5oz frozen peas
2 teaspoons chopped fresh tarragon
2 teaspoons chopped fresh chives
2 tablespoons crème fraîche
375g/13oz ready-rolled puff pastry
1 egg (beaten)

- Preheat the oven to 200°C/400°F/Gas mark 6.
- Place the flour in a bowl, season and toss the turkey until coated. Heat half the oil in a large frying pan and brown the turkey on all sides.
- Heat the remaining oil in the same pan and fry the onion for about 10 minutes, until soft. Stir in the remaining flour and cook for 1 minute.
- Pour in the stock, bring to the boil and simmer until thickened. Return the turkey to the pan, add the ham, peas and herbs and simmer for 5 minutes. Stir in the crème fraîche. Transfer the mixture to a medium-sized baking dish and allow to cool.
- Lay out the puff pastry, rolling if necessary, to a size just larger than the top of the baking dish. Brush the edge of the dish with a little egg and lay the pastry on top, pressing gently to seal. Crimp lightly around the edges with your fingers or a fork. Brush the top of the pastry with the egg. Make small slits in the top for steam to escape.
- Bake for 30 to 35 minutes or until the filling is completely heated through and the pastry golden brown.

Chicken & sweet potato casserole

SERVES 4

INGREDIENTS:

175ml/6fl oz coconut milk
2 teaspoons granulated sugar
1 teaspoon salt
1.2 litres/2pt groundnut oil
350g/12oz sweet potatoes (cut into 1cm/½in slices)
450g/1lb chicken pieces (cut into bite-sized pieces)

1 garlic clove (chopped)
4 slices fresh ginger (shredded)

For the sauce:
½ chicken stock cube
1 tablespoon cornflour
350ml/12fl oz water

- Mix the coconut milk with the sugar and salt.
- Heat the oil to boiling point in a wok and fry the sweet potato until golden. Remove and place in a casserole dish. Fry the chicken pieces until brown and remove to the casserole dish.
- Stir-fry the garlic and ginger in 1 tablespoon oil for 2 minutes, then transfer to the casserole dish along with the sauce ingredients. Cover and bring to the boil, reduce the heat and simmer for 30 minutes, until cooked. Add the coconut mixture and heat through but do not boil. Serve hot.

Turkey casserole

SERVES 8

INGREDIENTS:

75g/3oz butter
2 tablespoons plain flour
150ml/¼pt single cream
225ml/8fl oz cold water
Salt and pepper

225g/8oz turkey (cooked and diced)
225g/8oz Cheddar cheese (grated)
450g/1lb potatoes (cooked and mashed)
225g/8oz dry stuffing mix

- Preheat the oven to 180°C/350°F/Gas mark 4.
- Melt half the butter in a saucepan over a low heat, then stir in the flour until thoroughly mixed. Slowly stir in the cream and water and season with salt and

pepper. Stir over a low heat for 5 minutes, then remove from the heat.
- Place the turkey in a lightly greased baking dish. Pour the sauce over the turkey, then sprinkle with the cheese. Spread the mashed potatoes over the cheese.
- Melt the remaining butter and add to the stuffing mix, then sprinkle the stuffing over the potato. Bake, uncovered, for 45 minutes.

One-pot tandoori chicken

SERVES 4

INGREDIENTS:

1.2 litres/2pt water
225g/8oz wholewheat pasta
2 boneless, skinless chicken breasts
(cut into bite-sized pieces)
1 tablespoon vegetable oil
200g/7oz sugar snap peas

200g/7oz red pepper (chopped)
150g/5oz onion (chopped)
1 small courgette (sliced)
250ml/9fl oz plain yogurt
1 teaspoon lemon juice
1 tablespoon tandoori seasoning

- Boil the water in a large, deep frying pan. Add the pasta, cover and continue boiling for about 10 minutes or until the pasta is al dente. Drain the pasta, transfer to a bowl and keep warm.
- Heat a large frying pan, add the chicken and oil, mix and brown on all sides.
- Add the vegetables and cook, stirring constantly, over a medium heat until the chicken is thoroughly cooked.
- Mix the yogurt, lemon juice and tandoori seasoning into the frying pan and stir until well combined and the mixture is well coated. Add reserved pasta and mix to coat.

Wild duck stew

SERVES 4

INGREDIENTS:

100g/4oz mushrooms (sliced)
4 tomatoes (peeled and quartered)
40g/1½oz butter
1 large carrot (diced)
1 green pepper (diced)
1 onion (sliced)
175g/6oz celery (chopped)
1 garlic clove (quartered)
200g/7oz pitted black olives
1 tablespoon tomato purée
50ml/2fl oz olive oil

450ml/³/₄pt red wine
1 tablespoon Worcestershire sauce
⅛ teaspoon cinnamon
⅛ teaspoon ground cloves
⅛ teaspoon allspice
⅛ teaspoon mace
⅛ teaspoon thyme
1 bay leaf (crushed)
Salt and pepper
4 wild ducks (cut into serving pieces)
20 small new potatoes

- Sauté the mushrooms and tomatoes in the butter for 3 minutes.
- Combine with the carrot, green pepper, onion, celery, garlic, olives, tomato purée, olive oil, wine, Worcestershire sauce, cinnamon, cloves, allspice, mace, thyme, bay leaf, salt and pepper to make a marinade. Add the duck pieces and marinate overnight or for at least 10 hours.
- Simmer the duck in the marinade 1½ to 2 hours or until tender.
- Boil the potatoes in salted water for approximately 15 minutes or until tender. Add to stew just before serving.

Chicken & plum casserole

SERVES 4

INGREDIENTS:

2 rashers lean back bacon (rind removed, trimmed and chopped)
1 tablespoon sunflower oil
450g/1lb skinless, boneless chicken thighs (cut into 4 equal strips)
1 garlic cloves (crushed)
175g/6oz shallots (halved)
225g/8oz plums (quartered and stoned)
1 tablespoon muscovado sugar

150ml/¼pt dry sherry
2 tablespoons plum sauce
450ml/³/₄pt chicken stock
2 teaspoons cornflour (mixed with 4 teaspoons cold water to form a paste)
2 tablespoons chopped fresh flat-leaf parsley

- In a large frying pan, dry-fry the bacon for 3 minutes, until the juices run.
- Remove the bacon from the pan with a slotted spoon and set aside.
- In the same frying pan, heat the oil and fry the chicken with the garlic and shallots for 4 to 5 minutes, stirring occasionally, until well browned.
- Return the bacon to the pan and stir in the plums, sugar, sherry, plum sauce and stock. Bring to the boil and simmer for 20 minutes, until the plums are soft and the chicken is cooked through. Add the cornflour paste to the pan and cook, stirring, for a further 3 minutes until thickened. Serve immediately, garnished with the parsley.

Chicken &
crackers casserole

SERVES 6

INGREDIENTS:

2 packets Ritz crackers (crushed)
100g/4oz butter (melted)
6 boneless chicken breasts (cooked and chopped into bite-sized pieces)

400g/14oz canned cream of chicken soup
225g/8oz sour cream
225ml/8fl oz chicken stock

- Preheat the oven to 150°C/300°F/Gas mark 2.
- Place half the crackers in the bottom of a large casserole dish. Drizzle half the butter over the crackers.
- Mix the chicken with the soup, sour cream and stock, then pour over the crackers.
- Sprinkle the remaining crackers over the chicken mixture and drizzle with the remaining butter. Bake in the oven for 30 to 45 minutes.

Chicken & sweetcorn stew

SERVES 4

INGREDIENTS:

4 skinless chicken breasts (chopped into chunks)
Salt and pepper
Plain flour for coating
2 tablespoons olive oil
1 medium onion (sliced)

1 garlic clove (crushed)
150g/5oz canned sweetcorn
2 chicken stock cubes
1 tablespoon clear honey
125ml/4fl oz tomato sauce

- Cut chicken into chunks, season and coat in flour. Fry the chicken in the oil until golden. Remove from pan.
- Fry the onion and garlic in the same pan until soft. Add the chicken, sweetcorn, stock cubes, honey and tomato sauce. Simmer over a medium-high heat for at least 20 minutes, stirring regularly.

Turkey & tomato hotpot

SERVES 4

INGREDIENTS:

25g/1oz white bread (crusts removed)
2 tablespoons skimmed milk
1 garlic clove (crushed)
½ teaspoon caraway seeds
225g/8oz minced turkey
Salt and pepper

1 egg white
350ml/12fl oz chicken stock
400g/14oz canned chopped tomatoes
1 tablespoon tomato purée
100g/4oz long-grain rice

- Cut the bread into small cubes and place in a mixing bowl. Sprinkle the milk over and leave to soak for 5 minutes. Add the garlic, caraway seeds, turkey and seasoning to the bread. Mix together well.
- Whisk the egg white until stiff, then fold, half at a time, into the turkey mixture. Refrigerate for 10 minutes.
- While the turkey mixture is chilling, put the stock, tomatoes and tomato purée into a large saucepan and bring to the boil.
- Add the rice and cook briskly for about 5 minutes. Turn the heat down to a gentle simmer.
- Meanwhile, shape the turkey mixture into 16 small balls. Carefully drop them

into the pan and simmer for a further 8 to 10 minutes, or until both the turkey and rice are cooked. Serve hot.

Chicken & pasta broth

SERVES 4

INGREDIENTS:

2 tablespoons sunflower oil
350g/12oz boneless chicken
breasts (diced)
1 medium onion (diced)
250g/9oz carrots (diced)

250g/9oz cauliflower florets
900ml/1½pt chicken stock
2 teaspoons dried mixed herbs
100g/4oz pasta shapes
Salt and pepper

- Heat the oil in a large saucepan and quickly sauté the chicken, onion, carrots and cauliflower until they are lightly coloured. Stir in the chicken stock and herbs and bring to the boil.
- Add the pasta and return to the boil. Cover the pan and leave the broth to simmer for 10 minutes, stirring occasionally to prevent the pasta shapes from sticking together. Season the broth with salt and pepper and serve.

Winter chicken stew

SERVES 4

INGREDIENTS:

4 chicken portions (skinned and
chopped into bite-sized pieces)
25g/1oz butter
1 onion (sliced)
4 carrots (sliced)
1 swede (sliced)

100g/4oz pearl barley
900ml/1½pt chicken stock
Salt and pepper
3 potatoes (cut into bite-sized chunks)
1 green cabbage (shredded)

- Brown the chicken in the butter in a large saucepan. Remove from the pan with a slotted spoon.
- Add the onion, carrots and swede to the pan and sauté for 2 minutes, stirring.
- Add the barley and stock and return the chicken to the pan. Season to taste. Bring to the boil, then simmer for 45 minutes. Add the potatoes and cabbage, cover and continue cooking for 20 minutes or until all ingredients are tender.

Cheesy turkey casserole

SERVES 4

INGREDIENTS:

100g/4oz medium noodles
275g/10oz frozen broccoli spears
25g/1oz butter
25g/1oz flour
1 teaspoon salt
¼ teaspoon prepared mustard

¼ teaspoon black pepper
450ml/³/₄pt milk
300g/11oz Cheddar cheese (grated)
250g/9oz cooked turkey (diced)
75g/3oz slivered toasted almonds

- Preheat the oven to 180°F/350°F/Gas mark 4.
- Cook the noodles in boiling salted water, following package directions, then drain. Cook the broccoli just until tender.
- In a saucepan over a low heat, melt the butter and blend in the flour, salt, mustard and black pepper. Stir until smooth and bubbly. Gradually add the milk, stirring until thickened. Remove from the heat and stir in the cheese until melted. Dice the broccoli stalks, leaving the florets intact.
- In a 20cm/8in square baking dish, arrange the noodles, broccoli stalks and turkey, then pour the cheese sauce over. Arrange the florets over the top and sprinkle with almonds. Bake for about 15 minutes, or until hot and bubbly.

Pot-roast orange chicken

SERVES 4

INGREDIENTS:

2 tablespoons sunflower oil
1 chicken, about 1.5kg/3lb 5oz
2 large oranges
2 small onions (quartered)
500g/1lb 2oz carrots (cut into 5cm/2in lengths)

Salt and pepper
150ml/¹/₄pt orange juice
2 tablespoons brandy
2 tablespoons sesame seeds
1 tablespoon cornflour
1 tablespoon cold water

- Preheat the oven to 180°C/350°F/Gas mark 4.
- Heat the oil in a large flameproof casserole dish and fry the chicken, turning occasionally until evenly browned.
- Cut 1 orange in half and place half inside the cavity of the chicken. Place the chicken back in the casserole dish and arrange the onions and carrots around it.

Season with salt and pepper and pour the orange juice over. Cut the remaining oranges into wedges and tuck among the vegetables.

- Cover and cook in the oven for 1½ hours, or until the juices run clear. Remove the lid and sprinkle with the brandy and sesame seeds. Return to the oven for 10 minutes.
- To serve, lift the chicken on to a large platter and add the vegetables. Skim any excess fat from the juices. Blend the cornflour with the water to form a paste, then stir into the juices and bring to the boil, stirring all the time. Adjust to taste, then serve the sauce with the chicken.

Chinese chicken hotpot

SERVES 4-6

INGREDIENTS:

175g/6oz dried haricot beans
3 chicken legs
1 tablespoon vegetable oil
350g/12oz lean pork (diced)
1 small carrot (roughly chopped)
1 onion (roughly chopped)
1.7 litres/3pt water
1 garlic clove (crushed)
2 tablespoons tomato purée
1 bay leaf

2 chicken stock cubes
350g/12oz sweet potatoes (cubed)
2 teaspoons chilli sauce
2 tablespoons white wine vinegar
3 tomatoes (skinned, deseeded and chopped)
225g/8oz Chinese leaves (shredded)
Salt and pepper
3 spring onions (shredded)

- Put the haricot beans in a bowl, cover with plenty of cold water and set aside to soak for 8 hours or overnight.
- Separate the chicken drumsticks from the thighs. Chop off the narrow end of each drumstick and discard.
- Heat the vegetable oil in a wok, add the chicken, pork, carrot and onion, then brown evenly.
- Drain the haricot beans and add to the wok with fresh water, the garlic, tomato purée and bay leaf and stir to mix. Bring to the boil, lower the heat and simmer for 2 hours until the beans are almost tender.
- Crumble the chicken stock cubes into the wok, add the sweet potatoes and the chilli sauce, then simmer for 15 to 20 minutes until the potatoes are cooked.
- Add the vinegar, tomatoes and Chinese leaves to the wok, then simmer for 1 to 2 minutes. Season to taste and garnish with the spring onions.

Chicken hotpot

SERVES 4

INGREDIENTS:

450g/1lb chicken joints
25g/1oz lentil flour
1 tablespoon olive oil
100g/4oz onion (chopped)
100g/4oz carrot (chopped)
100g/4oz swede (chopped)
225g/8oz mushrooms

400g/14oz canned chopped tomatoes
2 garlic cloves (crushed)
1 teaspoon dried mixed herbs
25g/1oz lentils
Salt and pepper
300ml/½pt chicken stock

- Preheat the oven to 190°C/375°F/Gas mark 5.
- Remove the skin from the chicken and roll the joints in lentil flour. Fry the joints gently in the oil until browned on both sides and then place in a casserole dish.
- Fry the onion until translucent and then add to the casserole dish, with the carrot, swede, mushrooms, tomatoes, garlic, herbs and lentils.
- Season with salt and pepper and add just enough chicken stock to cover.
- Cook in the oven for 30 minutes, then reduce the oven heat to 150°C/300°F/Gas mark 2 and cook for a further hour. Serve hot.

Stoved chicken one-pot

SERVES 4

INGREDIENTS:

900g/2lb potatoes (cut into 5mm/¼in slices)
2 large onions (thinly sliced)
1 tablespoon chopped fresh thyme
Salt and pepper

25g/1oz butter
1 tablespoon vegetable oil
2 slices streaky bacon (chopped)
4 large chicken joints (halved)
600ml/1pt chicken stock

- Preheat the oven to 150°C/300°F/Gas mark 2.
- Make a thick layer of half the potato slices in the bottom of a large, heavy-based casserole dish, then cover with half the onion. Sprinkle with half the thyme and season.
- Heat the butter and oil in a large frying pan, then brown the bacon and chicken.
- Using a slotted spoon, transfer the chicken and bacon to the casserole.

- Reserve the fat in the pan.
- Sprinkle the remaining thyme and some seasoning over the chicken, then cover with the remaining onion, followed by a neat layer of overlapping potato slices.
- Sprinkle with seasoning.
- Pour the stock into the casserole, brush the potatoes with the reserved fat, then cover tightly and cook in the oven for about 2 hours, until the chicken is tender.
- Preheat the grill. Uncover the casserole dish and place under the grill until the potatoes go brown and crisp. Serve hot.

Creamy chicken noodle casserole

SERVES 4

INGREDIENTS:

1 teaspoon vegetable oil
1 onion (chopped)
2 garlic cloves (crushed)
Salt and pepper
³/₄ teaspoon dried thyme
450g/1lb mushrooms (halved)
450g/1lb boneless, skinless chicken breasts

125ml/4fl oz chicken stock
25g/1oz cornflour
350ml/12fl oz canned evaporated milk
300g/11oz broad egg noodles
200g/7oz frozen peas
1 tablespoon Dijon mustard

- Preheat the oven to 190°C/375°F/Gas mark 5.
- In a large frying pan, heat the oil over medium heat and cook the onion, garlic, salt, pepper and thyme, stirring, for about 5 minutes or until the onion is softened. Add the mushrooms and cook over a high heat, stirring, for about 5 minutes or until browned.
- Meanwhile, cut the chicken into bite-sized pieces and stir into the frying pan.
- Cook, stirring, for about 4 minutes or until no longer pink inside. Scrape the chicken mixture into a bowl and set aside.
- In small bowl, whisk together the stock and cornflour, and pour into the pan along with the evaporated milk. Cook over a medium heat, stirring, for about 5 minutes or until thickened.
- Meanwhile, in large pot of boiling salted water, cook the noodles for about 5 minutes or until almost tender. Drain well and return to the pot.
- Add the reserved chicken mixture, milk sauce, peas and mustard and stir gently to coat the noodles. Pour into a baking dish, cover with aluminium foil and bake for about 30 minutes, or until heated through.

Tortilla chicken casserole

SERVES 6-8

INGREDIENTS:

Vegetable oil for greasing
6 boneless chicken breast halves
(cooked and chopped)
100g/4oz canned chopped green
chillies
225g/8oz Cheddar cheese (grated)

275g/10oz canned condensed
mushroom soup
225ml/8fl oz milk
12 corn tortillas
175g/6oz plain crisps (crushed)

- Preheat the oven to 180°C/350°F/Gas mark 4. Lightly grease a 23cm/9in square baking dish with oil.
- Combine the chicken, green chillies, cheese, soup and milk.
- Place 4 tortillas in the bottom of the prepared baking dish and spread one-third of the chicken mixture over the tortillas. Repeat the layers until all tortillas are used, ending with chicken mixture. Top with the crisps. Bake for 30 minutes, until bubbly.

Duck & pomegranate stew

SERVES 4

INGREDIENTS:

2 small pomegranates
2kg/4lb duck (cut into 8 pieces)
3 tablespoons sunflower oil
1 onion (chopped)
225g/8oz shelled walnuts (coarsely
ground)

450ml/³/₄pt chicken stock
1 cinnamon stick
2 cloves
Juice of ½ lemon
A pinch of granulated sugar
Salt and pepper

- Squeeze the juice from one of the pomegranates using a lemon squeezer. Extract the seeds of the other pomegranate and reserve.
- Brown the duck pieces briskly in half the oil and transfer to a flameproof casserole dish. Fry the onion in the same fat until it is tender and transfer to the casserole dish. Add the walnuts to the pan and fry until they begin to change colour, then scrape into the casserole dish.
- Return the frying pan to the heat and pour in the stock. Bring to the boil, stirring up any pan residue. Pour into the casserole dish and add the cinnamon stick, cloves, pomegranate juice, lemon juice, sugar, salt and pepper. Cover and

simmer for 30 minutes. Uncover and continue simmering for 20 to 30 minutes, or until the meat is very tender and the sauce is thick. Taste and adjust the seasoning and serve.

One-pot chicken broth

SERVES 4

INGREDIENTS:

1.2 litres/2pt chicken stock
1 tablespoon grated fresh ginger
2 red chillies (chopped)
1 stalk lemon grass (bruised)
200g/7oz chicken fillets (cut into bite-sized pieces)
75g/3oz button mushrooms (halved)

2 heads pak choi (shredded)
6 kaffir lime leaves (shredded)
225g/8oz rice noodles
Juice of 1 lime
1 tablespoon fish sauce
2 tablespoons chopped fresh coriander

- Put the stock in a large pan with the ginger, chillies and lemon grass. Bring to the boil, then reduce the heat and simmer for 5 minutes.
- Add the chicken fillets, mushrooms, pak choi and lime leaves and cook for 4 minutes. Remove the lemon grass and add the noodles. Cook for a further 2 minutes. Stir in the lime juice, fish sauce and coriander and serve.

One-pot Cajun chicken gumbo

SERVES 2

INGREDIENTS:

1 tablespoon sunflower oil
4 chicken thighs
1 small onion (diced)
2 celery sticks (diced)
1 green pepper (diced)
100g/4oz long-grain rice

300ml/¹/₂pt chicken stock
1 red chilli (deseeded and thinly sliced)
225g/8oz okra (trimmed)
1 tablespoon tomato purée
Salt and pepper

- Heat the oil in a wide pan and fry the chicken until golden. Remove the chicken

→

from the pan. Stir in the onion, celery and pepper and fry for 1 minute. Pour off any excess oil.

- Add the rice and fry, stirring, for a further minute. Add the stock and heat until boiling. Add the chilli, okra and tomato purée. Season to taste.
- Return the chicken to the pan and stir. Cover tightly and simmer gently for 15 minutes, or until the rice is tender and the chicken is cooked. Serve immediately.

Sherry chicken casserole

SERVES 4

INGREDIENTS:

4 chicken portions (skinned and chopped)
25g/1oz butter
1 large onion (finely chopped)
100g/4oz button mushrooms (quartered)

400g/14oz canned chopped tomatoes
125ml/4fl oz sherry
2 tablespoons tomato purée
1 bouquet garni
Salt and pepper

- Preheat the oven to 180°C/350°F/Gas mark 4.
- Brown the chicken in the butter in a flameproof casserole dish. Remove with a slotted spoon, then add the onion and fry for 2 minutes. Add the mushrooms and cook for 1 minute. Return the chicken to the pan.
- Add the tomatoes. Blend the sherry with the tomato purée and stir in. Add the bouquet garni and seasoning. Bring to the boil, then cover and cook in the oven for 1½ hours, or until the chicken is tender. Skim off any fat and serve.

Duck stew with turnips & onions

SERVES 4

INGREDIENTS:

25g/1oz butter
1 duck (cut in pieces)
1 tablespoon plain flour
1.2 litres/2pt water

2 onions (quartered)
8 turnips (quartered)
Salt and pepper

- Place the butter and pieces of duck in a frying pan and fry quickly until brown.
- Add the flour, stirring all the time.
- Add the water, bring to the boil and boil for 3 minutes. Place the duck and gravy in a casserole dish. Add the onions, turnips and seasoning. Cover and cook slowly for about 45 to 50 minutes. Serve hot.

Rich chicken casserole

SERVES 4

INGREDIENTS:

8 chicken thighs
2 tablespoons olive oil
1 medium red onion (sliced)
2 garlic cloves (crushed)
1 red pepper (thickly sliced)
Thinly pared zest and juice of 1 orange
125ml/4fl oz chicken stock

400g/14oz canned chopped tomatoes
25g/1oz sun-dried tomatoes (thinly sliced)
1 tablespoon chopped fresh thyme
50g/2oz black olives (pitted)
Salt and pepper

- In a heavy-based frying pan, fry the chicken without fat over a high heat, turning occasionally until golden brown. Using a slotted spoon, drain off any excess fat from the chicken and transfer to a flameproof casserole dish.
- Add the olive oil to the pan and fry the onion, garlic and pepper over a moderate heat for 3 to 4 minutes. Transfer the vegetables to the casserole dish. Add the orange zest and juice, chicken stock, canned and sun-dried tomatoes and stir to combine.
- Bring to the boil, then cover the casserole dish with a lid and simmer very gently over a low heat for about 1 hour, stirring occasionally. Add the thyme and olives and adjust the seasoning with salt and pepper to taste. Serve hot.

Almond chicken casserole

SERVES 6

INGREDIENTS:

700g/1½lb chicken (boned, skinned and diced)
200ml/7fl oz mayonnaise
200ml/7fl oz plain yogurt
400g/14oz canned mushroom soup
450ml/¾pt chicken stock
Salt and pepper
2 tablespoons lemon juice

3 tablespoons chopped onion
350g/12oz cooked rice
225g/8oz canned sliced water chestnuts
225g/8oz slivered almonds
175g/6oz celery (chopped)
100g/4oz butter
150g/5oz cornflakes

- Preheat the oven to 180°C/350°F/Gas mark 4.
- Mix the chicken, mayonnaise, yogurt, soup, stock, salt, pepper, lemon juice, onion, rice, water chestnuts, half the almonds and the celery together. Put into a large casserole dish.
- Mix the remaining almonds with the butter and cornflakes and top the casserole with this mixture. Bake in the oven for 35 to 45 minutes.

Chilli chicken casserole

SERVES 4

INGREDIENTS:

Plain flour (seasoned), for dredging
200g/7oz chicken (chopped)
25g/1oz butter
2 tablespoons vegetable oil
2 medium onions (chopped)

1½ teaspoons poultry seasoning
4 tablespoons soy sauce
125ml/4fl oz tomato purée
2 tablespoons chilli powder
175ml/6fl oz medium dry sherry

- Preheat the oven to 180°C/350°F/Gas mark 4.
- Dredge the chicken pieces in the seasoned flour, then brown in a casserole dish with the butter and oil over a medium-high heat.
- Add the remaining ingredients to the casserole dish and mix well. Cover and bake in the oven for 1 hour, or until the chicken is tender.

Pumpkin turkey stew

SERVES 6

INGREDIENTS:

2 tablespoons canola oil
4 onions (finely chopped)
2 teaspoons grated fresh root ginger
700g/1½lb boneless, skinless turkey
thigh meat, cut into 4cm/1½in cubes
400g/14oz canned chopped tomatoes

200g/7oz pumpkin purée
225ml/8fl oz water
½ teaspoon salt
¼ teaspoon pepper
2 tablespoons chopped fresh coriander

- Heat 1 tablespoon oil in a large casserole dish over a medium heat. Cook the onions for 3 minutes, until softened. Add the ginger and cook for a further 2 minutes.
- Transfer to a bowl.
- Heat the remaining oil in the casserole dish. Brown the turkey in batches, 3 to 4 minutes per batch. Return the onions and ginger to the casserole dish. Stir in the tomatoes, pumpkin purée, water, salt and pepper. Bring to the boil.
- Reduce the heat to low and simmer, part-covered, for 40 minutes, until the turkey is tender. Stir occasionally. Add the coriander and cook for a further 2 minutes, then serve.

Chicken macaroni stew

SERVES 2

INGREDIENTS:

225g/8oz canned chopped tomatoes
200g/7oz frozen mixed vegetables
100g/4oz elbow macaroni
50g/2oz onion (chopped)
¼ teaspoon chopped fresh oregano

Salt and pepper
⅛ teaspoon garlic powder
1 bay leaf
225ml/8fl oz chicken stock
200g/7oz chicken (cooked and diced)

- Place all the ingredients except the chicken in a saucepan and bring to the boil. Reduce the heat and boil gently for about 15 minutes, uncovered, until the macaroni is tender. Stir several times to prevent the macaroni from sticking.
- Add the chicken and heat to serving temperature. Remove the bay leaf and serve.

Country cider hotpot

SERVES 4

INGREDIENTS:

2 tablespoons plain flour
Salt and pepper
4 boneless rabbit portions
25g/1oz butter
1 tablespoon vegetable oil
15 baby onions
4 rashers streaky bacon (chopped)

2 teaspoons Dijon mustard
450ml/³/₄pt dry cider
3 carrots (chopped)
2 parsnips (chopped)
12 prunes (stoned)
1 rosemary sprig
1 bay leaf

- Preheat the oven to 160°C/325°F/Gas mark 3.
- Place the flour and seasoning in a plastic bag, add the rabbit portions and shake until coated. Set aside.
- Heat the butter and oil in a flameproof casserole dish and add the onions and bacon. Fry for 4 minutes, until the onions have softened. Remove with a draining spoon and reserve.
- Fry the seasoned rabbit portions in the casserole dish until they are browned all over, then spread a little of the mustard over the top of each portion.
- Return the onions and bacon to the pan. Pour on the cider and add the carrots, parsnips, prunes, rosemary and bay leaf. Season well. Bring to the boil, then cover and transfer to the oven. Cook for about 1¹/₂ hours until tender. Remove the rosemary and bay leaf and serve the rabbit hot.

French-style stewed duck

SERVES 4

INGREDIENTS:

1 oven-ready duck, about 1.8kg/4lb
25g/1oz butter
12 pearl onions
600ml/1pt chicken stock
Salt and pepper
225g/8oz frozen peas

1 tablespoon chopped fresh mint
1 tablespoon chopped fresh oregano
1 tablespoon chopped fresh parsley
1 teaspoon grated nutmeg
25g/1oz plain flour

- Preheat the oven to 200°C/400°F/Gas mark 6.
- Remove the giblets and wipe the duck inside and out with kitchen paper. Prick

all over with a fork.
- Melt the butter in a flameproof casserole dish and brown the duck on all sides.
- Remove the duck and brown the onions. Pour off any fat and return the duck to the pan. Add the stock and a little salt and pepper and bring to the boil. Cover and cook in the oven for 30 minutes.
- Skim the surface of any fat, then add all the remaining ingredients, except the flour. Reduce the oven heat to 180°C/350°F/Gas mark 4 and cook for a further 1½ hours. Remove the duck and keep warm. Skim off any fat.
- Blend the flour with water and stir into the casserole dish, then simmer for 3 minutes, stirring. Taste and adjust the seasoning if necessary.
- Carve the duck, discarding the skin, and transfer to serving plates. Spoon the sauce over to serve.

Chicken & noodle one-pot

SERVES 4

INGREDIENTS:

1 tablespoon sunflower oil
1 onion (sliced)
1 garlic clove (crushed)
2.5cm/1in piece root ginger (peeled and grated)
1 bunch spring onions (sliced)
500g/1lb 2oz chicken breast fillet (skinned and cut into bite-sized pieces)

2 tablespoons mild curry paste
450ml/¾pt coconut milk
300ml/½pt chicken stock
Salt and pepper
250g/9oz Chinese egg noodles
2 teaspoons lime juice

- Heat the oil in a wok or large, heavy-based frying pan. Add the onion, garlic, ginger and spring onions to the wok and stir-fry for 2 minutes, until softened.
- Add the chicken and curry paste and stir-fry for 4 minutes, until the chicken is golden brown. Stir in the coconut milk, stock and seasoning and mix well.
- Bring to the boil and add the noodles to the pan. Cover and simmer for about 6 to 8 minutes until the noodles are just tender, stirring occasionally. Add the lime juice and adjust the seasoning. Serve hot.

Tarragon chicken casserole

SERVES 10

INGREDIENTS:

275g/10oz canned condensed chicken soup
275g/10oz canned condensed mushroom soup
175ml/6fl oz single cream

4 teaspoons dried tarragon
$1/2$ teaspoon ground black pepper
450g/1lb linguine (cooked and drained)
600g/1lb 5oz cooked chicken (cubed)
100g/4oz Parmesan cheese (grated)

- Preheat the oven to 180°C/350°F/Gas mark 4.
- In a large bowl, combine the soup, cream, tarragon and pepper. Stir in the linguine and chicken and transfer to a large baking dish. Sprinkle with the Parmesan.
- Bake, uncovered, for 30 minutes or until heated through.

Butter bean & chicken casserole

SERVES 4

INGREDIENTS:

425g/15oz canned butter beans
50ml/2fl oz tomato ketchup
200g/7oz chicken (cooked and cubed)
1 teaspoon minced onion

75g/3oz green pepper (chopped)
$1/2$ teaspoon Worcestershire sauce
200g/7oz Cheddar cheese (grated)
Salt and pepper

- Preheat the oven to 170°C/325°F/Gas mark 5.
- Put the beans, ketchup, chicken, onion, pepper and Worcestershire sauce in a large casserole dish. Bake, uncovered, in the oven for 20 minutes. Top with cheese and return to the oven until the cheese melts.

Cock-a-leekie

SERVES 6

INGREDIENTS:

1.3kg/3lb chicken
2.4 litres/4pt chicken stock
900g/2lb leeks
1 bouquet garni

Salt and pepper
450g/1lb prunes (stoned and soaked overnight)

- Put the chicken, breast-side down, in a large casserole dish. Pour in the stock and bring to the boil, skimming off any scum from the surface.
- Tie half the leeks together in a bundle with string and thinly slice the remainder.
- Add the bundle of leeks to the casserole dish with the bouquet garni and a pinch of salt. Reduce the heat, then part-cover and simmer for 2 hours.
- Remove and discard the bundle of leeks and the bouquet garni. Drain the prunes, add them to the casserole dish and simmer for 20 minutes. Season to taste, then add the sliced leeks. Simmer for a further 10 minutes, then serve.

Vegetarian

Whether preparing a vegetarian alternative to a meat course, or simply trying something new, this chapter mixes beans, peppers, carrots and potatoes into some truly delicious dishes. Recipes such as Carrot and cabbage casserole, Turnip, potato and onion stew, Chickpea and artichoke stew and Chunky vegetable chilli will make the kids glad to eat their greens.

Sweetcorn &
cheese casserole

SERVES 6

INGREDIENTS:

25g/1oz butter (melted)
1 teaspoon plain flour
¼ teaspoon dry mustard
2 teaspoons dried chives (chopped)
1 teaspoon dried onions (chopped)
1 teaspoon chopped fresh parsley

250g/9oz sweetcorn (drained)
100g/4oz red pepper (chopped)
100g/4oz cottage cheese (whipped)
100g/4oz natural yogurt
Salt and pepper

- Preheat the oven to 170°C/325°F/Gas mark 3.
- Blend the butter with the flour until smooth. Add the mustard, chives, onions, parsley, sweetcorn, red pepper, cottage cheese and yogurt. Mix well and pour into a large casserole dish. Season to taste.
- Bake in the oven for 25 to 30 minutes or until heated through. Serve hot.

One-pot pasta with tomato,
white beans & pesto

SERVES 4

INGREDIENTS:

400g/14oz bow-tie pasta
750ml/1¼pt water
2 chicken stock cubes
200g/7oz pesto

2 medium tomatoes (chopped)
425g/15oz canned cannellini beans
150g/5oz Parmesan cheese (grated)

- Combine the pasta, water and stock cubes in a large saucepan. Bring to the boil.
- Cook, stirring frequently, for about 15 minutes until the pasta is tender and the water has reduced to about 125ml/4fl oz. Reduce the heat and add the pesto.
- Cook, stirring frequently, until sauce has reduced slightly. Stir in the tomatoes and beans. Cook, stirring occasionally, until heated through. Sprinkle with cheese before serving.

Cheese & rice casserole

SERVES 4

INGREDIENTS:

Vegetable oil for greasing
200g/7oz brown rice (cooked)
3 onions (chopped)
200g/7oz cottage cheese

1 teaspoon dried dill
50g/2oz Parmesan cheese (grated)
125ml/4fl oz milk

- Preheat the oven to 180°C/350°F/Gas mark 4. Lightly grease a large casserole dish with oil.
- Combine all the ingredients well in a mixing bowl, then pour into the prepared casserole dish. Bake in the oven for 15 to 20 minutes.

Pasta & bean casserole

SERVES 6

INGREDIENTS:

225g/8oz dried haricot beans (soaked overnight and drained)
225g/8oz penne
75ml/3fl oz olive oil
850ml/1½pt vegetable stock
2 large onions (sliced)
2 garlic cloves (chopped)
2 bay leaves
1 teaspoon dried oregano
1 teaspoon dried thyme

75ml/3fl oz red wine
2 tablespoons tomato purée
2 celery sticks (sliced)
1 fennel bulb (sliced)
100g/4oz mushrooms (sliced)
225g/8oz tomatoes (sliced)
Salt and pepper
1 teaspoon muscovado sugar
4 tablespoons dry white breadcrumbs

- Preheat the oven to 180°C/350°F/Gas mark 4.
- Put the beans in a large pan, cover them with water and bring to the boil. Boil the beans rapidly for 20 minutes, then drain them.
- Cook the pasta for only 3 minutes in a large pan of boiling salted water, adding 1 tablespoon oil. Drain in a colander and set aside.
- Put the beans in a large flameproof casserole dish, pour over the stock and stir in the remaining oil, the onions, garlic, bay leaves, herbs, wine and tomato purée.
- Bring to the boil, cover the casserole dish and cook in the oven for 2 hours.

→

←
- Add the reserved pasta, the celery, fennel, mushrooms and tomatoes and season with salt and pepper. Stir in the sugar and sprinkle on the breadcrumbs. Cover the casserole dish again and cook for a further hour. Serve hot.

Bean & celery stew

SERVES 4

INGREDIENTS:

1 onion (thickly sliced)
4 celery sticks (chopped)
1 tablespoon olive oil
2 garlic cloves (crushed)
400g/14oz canned haricot beans
(drained)

400g/14oz canned chopped tomatoes
1 tablespoon tomato purée
Salt and pepper
1 vegetable stock cube

- Fry the onion and the celery in the olive oil over a medium heat until the onion starts to go translucent. Add the garlic and fry for a few more minutes. Add the beans, tomatoes and the tomato purée and mix well.
- Season, then add the stock cube. Simmer for a further 10 minutes and then serve.

Bulgarian red pepper stew

SERVES 4

INGREDIENTS:

75g/3oz dried lentils
75g/3oz dried haricot beans
2 large onions (chopped)
2 tablespoons vegetable oil
2 tablespoons dry sherry
6 red peppers (chopped)
2 teaspoons dried basil
1 teaspoon dried marjoram
1/4 teaspoon dried thyme

1/4 teaspoon cayenne pepper
1 1/2 teaspoon paprika
1/4 tsp salt
1/8 tsp ground black pepper
700ml/1 1/4pt vegetable stock
50ml/2fl oz red wine
50ml/2fl oz tomato purée
175ml/6fl oz prune juice
Salt and pepper

- Cover the lentils and beans with plenty of water and soak for 4 hours or overnight. Drain.

- In a large saucepan, cook the onions in the oil and sherry for about 5 minutes, until soft. Stir in the peppers and cook for a further 5 minutes. Add the basil, marjoram, thyme, cayenne, paprika and seasoning, and cook for another few minutes.
- Pour in the stock and wine and add the drained lentils and beans. Bring to the boil, then lower the heat and simmer gently for about 1½ hours, or until the beans are soft. Mix in the tomato purée, prune juice and seasoning to taste. Cook for several minutes more. If the stew seems too thick, add water.

Broccoli & cauliflower casserole

SERVES 4

INGREDIENTS:

450g/1lb frozen broccoli (thawed)
450g/1lb frozen cauliflower florets (thawed)
1 large onion (chopped)
50g/2oz butter
2 tablespoons plain flour
1 teaspoon salt
½ teaspoon garlic powder

½ teaspoon dried basil, crushed
¼ teaspoon ground black pepper
300ml/½pt milk
175g/6oz cream cheese with chives (diced)
100g/4oz fresh breadcrumbs
3 tablespoons grated Parmesan cheese

- Preheat the oven to 180°C/350°F/Gas mark 4.
- Cook the broccoli and cauliflower according to package directions, then drain well. Place in a large saucepan and set aside.
- Cook the onion in half the butter until tender but not brown. Stir in the flour, salt, garlic powder, basil and pepper. Add the milk. Cook and stir until thickened and bubbly. Add the cream cheese and stir until the cheese melts. Stir into the vegetable mixture.
- Pour into a large casserole dish. Toss together the breadcrumbs, cheese and remaining butter. Sprinkle over the vegetable mixture. Bake uncovered for 25 to 30 minutes or until heated through.

Potato & leek casserole

SERVES 4

INGREDIENTS:

300g/11oz leeks (cut into 1cm/½in pieces)
150g/5oz carrots (grated)
2 tablespoons olive oil
Salt and pepper

1 teaspoon dried rosemary
900g/2lb potatoes (sliced in thin rounds)
225ml/8fl oz vegetable stock
50g/2oz fresh parsley (chopped)

- Preheat the oven to 190°C/375°F/Gas mark 5. In a deep frying pan, coat the leeks and carrots with oil. Cover and simmer over a low heat until soft. Add the seasoning and rosemary and mix well.
- Layer a casserole dish with one-third of the potatoes, then half the seasoned vegetables. Repeat the layers and finish with the last third of the potatoes. Pour the stock evenly into the casserole dish. Cover and bake for 50 minutes, covered.
- Uncover and bake for a further 20 minutes. Garnish with parsley and serve.

Cabbage casserole

SERVES 10

INGREDIENTS:

1 medium head green cabbage (thinly sliced)
150g/5oz butter
75g/3oz plain flour

Salt and pepper
700ml/1½pt milk
200g/7oz Cheddar cheese (grated)
150g/5oz fresh breadcrumbs

- Preheat the oven to 180°C/350°F/Gas mark 4.
- Boil the cabbage in a large saucepan of salted water for 3 to 4 minutes, add 25g/1oz butter, then drain and set aside.
- In a small saucepan, melt 75g/3oz butter, then stir in the flour, salt and pepper until smooth. Gradually add the milk, stirring constantly. Continue cooking and stirring until thickened and bubbly.
- In a casserole dish, layer half of drained cabbage, half of the cream sauce, then the rest of the cabbage and cream sauce on the top. Sprinkle the top with the cheese.
- Melt the remaining butter and toss with the breadcrumbs, then sprinkle over the cheese layer. Bake uncovered for about 40 to 45 minutes.

Bean stew with herb dumplings

SERVES 4

INGREDIENTS:

425g/15oz canned red kidney beans (drained)
425g/15oz canned haricot beans (drained)
400g/14oz canned chopped tomatoes
1 garlic clove (crushed)
1 tablespoon tomato purée
200g/7oz canned sweetcorn

275g/10oz canned green beans
300ml/¹/₂pt vegetable stock
1 bay leaf
Salt and pepper
100g/4oz self-raising flour
25g/1oz butter
1 teaspoon dried mixed herbs
1 tablespoon chopped fresh parsley

- Put the kidney and haricot beans in a saucepan with the tomatoes, garlic, tomato purée, sweetcorn, green beans, stock and bay leaf. Season lightly. Bring to the boil and simmer gently for 5 minutes.
- Meanwhile, put the flour in a bowl with a little salt and pepper. Rub in the butter and stir in the herbs. Mix with enough cold water to form a soft but not too sticky dough.
- Shape into 8 rough balls and drop into the top of the stew. Cover and simmer gently for 15 to 20 minutes until the dumplings are risen and fluffy. Discard the bay leaf, sprinkle with parsley and serve.

Brown rice stew

SERVES 8

INGREDIENTS:

500ml/16fl oz chicken stock
200g/7oz long-grain brown rice
850g/1³/₄lb canned chopped tomatoes
3 carrots (sliced)
3 onions (chopped)
1 large onion (chopped)
1 celery stick (sliced)

3 garlic cloves (chopped)
1 bay leaf
3 knackwurst sausages (sliced)
1 teaspoon dried oregano
1 teaspoon dried basil
¹/₂ teaspoon dried thyme

→

←
- In a large casserole dish, combine the stock, rice, tomatoes, carrots, onions, celery, garlic and bay leaf. Cover and cook over a high heat for 10 minutes or until boiling, then stir.
- Turn the heat down to medium and simmer, covered, for 45 to 60 minutes or until the rice is tender. Stir in the sausages, oregano, basil and thyme and leave to stand, covered, for 15 minutes. Discard the bay leaf and serve.

One-pot macaroni & cheese

SERVES 2

INGREDIENTS:

450ml/³/₄pt water
¼ teaspoon salt
200g/7oz elbow macaroni
250g/9oz Cheddar cheese (grated)
25g/1oz butter

2 tablespoons double cream
Pinch of paprika
Pinch of white pepper
Pinch of cayenne pepper

- Bring a large saucepan of salted water to a boil. Stir in the macaroni and return the water to the boil. Stirring occasionally, continue boiling for 4 minutes.
- Lower the heat to medium and continue to boil the macaroni with frequent stirring for a further 7 minutes. Drain, then add the remainder of the ingredients, stirring well until the cheese is melted.

Armenian stew

SERVES 4

INGREDIENTS:

200g/7oz dried apricots (soaked in 125ml/4fl oz water for 1 hour)
100g/4oz dried chickpeas (soaked overnight in water)
1.2 litres/2pt water

200g/7oz red lentils (soaked overnight in water)
3 onions (sliced)
Salt and pepper

- In a large pan, bring the apricots and their water to the boil. Add the chickpeas and 150ml/¼pt water. Bring to the boil and simmer for 30 minutes.
- Add the lentils, onions and remaining water to the pan and bring to the boil.
- Lower the heat. Cover and cook for about 2 hours, until the beans are tender.

Baked barley & bean casserole

SERVES 4

INGREDIENTS:

150g/5oz broad beans (cooked)
100g/4oz cooked barley
225ml/8fl oz soy milk
75g/3oz raw wheatgerm
25g/1oz plain flour
1 tablespoon vegetable oil, plus extra
for greasing

50g/2oz onion (minced and sautéed)
3 tablespoons prepared mustard
75ml/3fl oz clear honey
75ml/3fl oz ketchup
½ teaspoon garlic powder
½ teaspoon onion powder
½ teaspoon chilli powder

- Preheat the oven to 180°C/350°F/Gas mark 4.
- Mix all the ingredients together and leave to stand for 30 minutes. Turn into an oiled casserole dish and bake for 40 minutes.

Baked bean & vegetable casserole

SERVES 4

INGREDIENTS:

450g/1lb canned baked beans
100g/4oz celery (finely diced)
100g/4oz carrot (finely grated)
100g/4oz courgette (finely grated)
25g/1oz shallots (finely chopped)

1 tablespoon chopped fresh parsley
50g/2oz red chilli (deseeded and finely chopped)
1 garlic clove (crushed)

- Mix all the ingredients together in a mixing bowl.
- Place into a saucepan and cook, covered, over a medium-high heat for 10 minutes, stirring occasionally. Serve hot.

Japanese tofu hotpot

SERVES 2

INGREDIENTS:

50g/2oz dried fish flakes
300g/11oz tofu (cubed)
2 tablespoons soy sauce
1 tablespoon granulated sugar

1 tablespoon sake
125ml/4fl oz water
1 large egg (beaten)
7 spring onions (roughly chopped)

- Spread the fish flakes evenly in a casserole dish and arrange the tofu on top.
- Add the soy sauce, sugar, sake and water.
- Cover and bring to the boil over a moderate heat and then simmer for 5 minutes.
- Pour in the egg and top with the green onions. Simmer for a final 30 seconds, covered, then serve.

Aromatic green casserole

SERVES 4

INGREDIENTS:

75g/3oz sugar snap peas (cut into bite-sized pieces)
75g/3oz brussel sprouts
75g/3oz broccoli (cut into bite-sized pieces)
50g/2oz walnuts (chopped)
2 tablespoons vegetable oil

½ teaspoon chopped fresh dill
¼ teaspoon sage
½ teaspoon salt
Juice of ½ lemon
1 pinch cayenne pepper
50ml/2fl oz water

- Steam the beans, brussel sprouts and broccoli for 8 minutes. Reserving the sprouts and broccoli, combine the beans with the remaining ingredients.
- Transfer to a blender or food processor and purée until smooth. Pour the sauce over the vegetables. Serve hot or cold.

Corn bean & pumpkin stew

SERVES 4

INGREDIENTS:

200g/7oz haricot beans (soaked overnight and drained)
½ teaspoon salt
1 teaspoon cumin seeds
1 teaspoon dried oregano
2.5cm/1in cinnamon stick (chopped)
1 tablespoon vegetable oil
1 large onion (diced)
2 garlic cloves (finely chopped)

1 tablespoon paprika
500ml/16fl oz vegetable stock
450g/1lb canned chopped tomatoes
175g/6oz pumpkin (peeled and cut into 2.5cm/1in cubes)
200g/7oz canned sweetcorn
2 red chillies (deseeded and finely chopped)

- Cook the beans in water with the salt for 1½ hours or until they are tender.
- Warm a heavy-based frying pan and toast the cumin seeds until their fragrance emerges, then add the oregano, stir for 5 seconds, and quickly transfer to a plate so they do not burn. Combine them with the cinnamon and grind to a powder with a pestle and morter.
- Heat the oil in a large frying pan and sauté the onion briskly over a high heat for 1 minute, then lower the heat to medium. Add the garlic, spice mixture and paprika and stir well to combine. Add half the stock and cook, stirring occasionally, until the onion is soft. Next add the tomatoes and cook for 5 minutes. Then add the pumpkin along with the remaining stock.
- After 20 to 30 minutes, or when the pumpkin is about half-cooked, add the corn, beans and chillies. Cook until the pumpkin is tender.

Hearty bean stew

SERVES 6

INGREDIENTS:

100g/4oz dried chickepeas
100g/4oz dried kidney beans
2 litres/4pt water
1 medium onion (sliced into rings)
1½ chicken gravy granules
2 garlic cloves (minced)
2 medium potatoes (sliced)

2 carrots (sliced)
2 courgettes (thinly sliced)
100g/4oz elbow macaroni
50g/2oz oatmeal
50ml/2fl oz lemon juice
100g/4oz spinach leaves
50g/2oz watercress

→

← In a casserole dish combine the beans and 600ml/1pt water and bring to the boil.

- Boil for 20 minutes and remove from the heat. Cover and stand for 1 hour, then drain.
- In the same casserole dish, combine the beans, the remaining water, the onion, gravy granules and garlic. Bring to a boil, then reduce the heat. Cover and simmer for 1 hour.
- In a small, covered saucepan, cook the potatoes in a small amount of water for about 15 minutes or until very tender. Cool, then transfer the potatoes and water to a blender or food processor and blend until smooth.
- Stir the puréed potatoes, carrots, courgette, macaroni and oatmeal into the bean mixture. Simmer for 15 to 20 minutes or until the vegetables are tender. Stir in the lemon juice and add the spinach and watercress.

Middle Eastern vegetable stew

SERVES 4-6

INGREDIENTS:

50ml/2fl oz vegetable stock
1 green pepper (sliced)
2 courgettes (sliced)
2 carrots (sliced)
2 celery sticks (sliced)
2 medium potatoes (diced)

400g/14oz canned chopped tomatoes
1 teaspoon chilli powder
2 tablespoons chopped fresh mint
1 tablespoon ground cumin
400g/14oz canned chickpeas (drained)
Salt and pepper

- Heat the stock in a large flameproof casserole dish until boiling, then add the pepper, courgettes, carrot and celery. Stir over a high heat for 2 to 3 minutes, until the vegetables are just beginning to soften.
- Add the potatoes, tomatoes, chilli powder, mint and cumin. Add the chickpeas and bring to the boil.
- Reduce the heat, cover the casserole dish and simmer for 30 minutes or until all the vegetables are tender. Season to taste with salt and pepper and serve hot.

Barley mushroom casserole

SERVES 4

INGREDIENTS:

1 tablespoon vegetable oil
200g/7oz onions (sliced)
200g/7oz mushrooms (sliced)

550ml/18fl oz water
Salt and pepper
150g/5oz pearl or pot barley

- In a saucepan over a medium heat, add the oil and fry the onions and mushrooms for about 10 minutes until tender.
- Add the water and seasoning and bring to a boil. Stir in the barley, reduce the heat to low, cover and simmer for 50 minutes until the barley is tender and the liquid is absorbed. Stir occasionally while cooking and add more water if necessary.

Chunky vegetable chilli

SERVES 8-10

INGREDIENTS:

1.2 litres/2pt water
150g/5oz quick-cooking barley
1 medium aubergine (diced)
½ large red pepper (chopped)
½ large green pepper (chopped)
1 medium onion (chopped)
3 garlic cloves (minced)

400g/14oz canned chopped tomatoes
425g/15oz canned black beans
(drained)
½ teaspoon chilli powder
Salt and pepper
150g/5oz fresh spinach (chopped)

- Boil the water in a large, deep frying pan and stir in the barley. Cover and reduce the heat. Simmer for about 10 minutes, or until the barley is tender.
- Add the aubergine, peppers, onion and garlic. Mix thoroughly, cover and cook over a medium heat for about 20 minutes until the aubergine is softened and the other vegetables are tender, removing the cover to stir frequently.
- Add the tomatoes, black beans, chilli powder and seasoning to the frying pan. Stir to combine and cook for a further 5 minutes. Add the spinach, mix and cook for 2 to 3 minutes or until the spinach is wilted.

Cheese casserole

SERVES 46

INGREDIENTS:

25g/1oz butter
1 medium onion (finely chopped)
100g/4oz green chillies (deseeded and chopped)
225g/8oz canned tomato sauce
½ teaspoon salt

2 eggs (beaten)
175g/6oz corn tortilla chips
225g/8oz Cheddar cheese (grated)
200g/7oz sour cream
3 tomatoes (sliced)

- In a non-metallic bowl, melt the butter in the microwave in 30 seconds.
- Add the onion and heat, uncovered, in the microwave for 3 minutes or until tender. Add the chillies, tomato sauce and salt to the onion and heat in the microwave, uncovered, for 6 minutes.
- Gradually add the eggs to the heated sauce mixture, a little at a time, stirring constantly.
- Layer half the corn chips, half the tomato mixture and half the cheese in a casserole dish. Repeat with the remaining corn chips, tomato mixture and the remainder of the cheese.
- Carefully spread the sour cream over the top of the entire casserole and heat, uncovered, in the microwave for 5 minutes or until the mixture begins to set.
- Arrange the tomatoes in a ring around the outside edge of the casserole. Heat, uncovered, in the microwave for 6 minutes or until the tomatoes are cooked.

Carrot & cabbage casserole

SERVES 4

INGREDIENTS:

6 carrots (thinly sliced)
2 tablespoons vegetable oil
2 onions (sliced)
450g/1lb green cabbage (thinly sliced)
Salt and pepper
2 tablespoons nutritional yeast
200g/7oz fresh breadcrumbs
50g/2oz sesame seeds

For the tofu sour cream:
200g/7oz tofu (cubed)
50ml/2fl oz oil
3 tablespoons lemon juice
½ teaspoon salt
1 teaspoon granulated sugar

- Preheat the oven to 180°C/350°F/Gas mark 4.
- To make the tofu sour cream, blend all the ingredients in a blender or food processor until smooth.
- Steam the carrots until al dente. Heat the oil in a large pan and add the onions, cooking until translucent. Then add the cabbage and cook for a further 10 minutes.
- Remove from the heat and stir in the seasoning and carrots. Mix half the tofu sour cream into the vegetables and transfer to a baking dish. Add the nutritional yeast to the remaining tofu and spread this on top of the vegetables. Mix the breadcrumbs and sesame seeds and sprinkle on top of the casserole. Bake for 35 to 40 minutes until the top is lightly browned.

Vegetable cassoulet

SERVES 6

INGREDIENTS:

100g/4oz dried haricot beans (soaked overnight)

1.2 litres/2pt water

2 tablespoons olive oil

2 garlic cloves (chopped)

225g/8oz baby onions (halved)

2 carrots (diced)

2 celery sticks (finely chopped)

1 red pepper (chopped)

175g/6oz mushrooms (sliced)

1 tablespoon chopped fresh rosemary

1 tablespoon chopped fresh thyme

1 tablespoon chopped fresh sage

150ml/¼pt red wine

4 tablespoons tomato purée

1 tablespoon soy sauce

Salt and pepper

50g/2oz fresh breadcrumbs

1 tablespoon chopped fresh parsley

- Preheat the oven to 190°C/375°F/Gas mark 5.
- Drain the beans and place in a saucepan with the water. Bring to the boil and boil rapidly for 10 minutes. Reduce the heat and simmer gently for 45 minutes. Drain the beans, reserving 300ml/½pt of the cooking liquid.
- Heat 1 tablespoon oil in a flameproof casserole dish and add the garlic, onions, carrot, celery and red pepper. Cook gently for 10 to 12 minutes until tender and starting to brown. Add the mushrooms and cook for a further 5 minutes until softened. Add the herbs and stir briefly.
- Stir in the red wine and boil rapidly for about 5 minutes until reduced and syrupy. Stir in the reserved beans and cooking liquid, tomato purée and soy sauce. Season to taste.
- Mix together the breadcrumbs and parsley with the remaining oil. Scatter this mixture evenly over the top of the stew. Cover loosely with aluminium foil, and transfer to the oven and cook for 30 minutes. Remove the foil and cook for a further 15 to 20 minutes until the topping is crisp and golden.

Cauliflower casserole

SERVES 6–8

INGREDIENTS:

1 small head cauliflower
1 courgette (sliced)
100g/4oz onion (chopped)
25g/1oz butter
275g/10oz Cheddar cheese sauce

75ml/3fl oz milk
2 tomatoes (cut into wedges)
½ teaspoon salt
⅛ teaspoon thyme leaves

- Break the cauliflower into florets and cook in boiling salted water for 8 to 10 minutes or until al dente. Drain.
- Sauté the courgette and onion in the butter in a medium frying pan. Combine the cheese sauce and milk until smooth and pour into the frying pan. Add the cauliflower, tomatoes, salt and thyme. Heat through and serve.

Smoked tofu casserole

SERVES 4

INGREDIENTS:

275g/10oz smoked tofu (cubed)
2 tablespoons soy sauce
1 tablespoon dry sherry
1 teaspoon sesame oil
4 dried Chinese mushrooms
250g/9oz egg noodles
Salt and pepper
1 carrot (cut into matchsticks)
1 celery stick (cut into matchsticks)

100g/4oz baby sweetcorn (halved lengthways)
2 tablespoons vegetable oil
1 courgette (sliced)
4 spring onions (chopped)
100g/4oz mangetout (chopped)
2 tablespoons black bean sauce
1 tablespoon cornflour

- Marinate the tofu in the soy sauce, sherry and sesame oil for 30 minutes.
- Place the mushrooms in a small bowl and pour over boiling water to cover. Leave to soak for 20 minutes.
- Place the egg noodles in a large bowl. Pour over enough boiling water to cover by 2.5cm/1in. Add ½ teaspoon salt, cover and cook in the microwave on high power for 4 minutes.
- Place the carrot, celery, sweetcorn and oil in a large bowl. Cover and cook on

high power for 1 minute.

- Drain the mushrooms, reserving 1 tablespoon of the liquid. Squeeze out excess water from the mushrooms and discard the hard cores. Thinly slice the mushrooms.
- Add the mushrooms to the bowl of vegetables with the courgette, spring onions and mangetout. Mix well. Cover and cook on high power for 4 minutes, stirring every 1 minute. Add the black bean sauce to the vegetables, stirring to coat.
- Mix the cornflour with the reserved mushroom water and stir into the vegetables with the tofu and marinade. Cover and cook on high power for 3 minutes.
- Season to taste. Drain the noodles and serve with the vegetables.

Broad bean hotpot

SERVES 4-6

INGREDIENTS:

125ml/4fl oz olive oil
1 onion (chopped)
3 garlic cloves (chopped)
900g/2lb broad beans (topped, tailed and cut into short lengths)
1 sachet bouquet garni
4 tablespoons dry sherry
300ml/½pt water

Salt and pepper
1 teaspoon granulated sugar
2 tablespoons fresh breadcrumbs
1 tablespoon chopped fresh parsley
1 tablespoon finely chopped fresh marjoram
½ teaspoon grated lemon zest

- Heat the oil in a large pan. Add the onion and garlic and fry for a moment without allowing to colour. Add the beans, bouquet garni, sherry and water.
- Bring to the boil, reduce the heat, cover and cook gently for 1 to 1½ hours. Add the salt, pepper and sugar when the beans are tender. Turn up the heat and cook uncovered for 2 minutes.
- Remove the bouquet garni then stir in the breadcrumbs, parsley, marjoram and lemon zest. Serve hot.

Stewed cabbage hotpot

SERVES 4

INGREDIENTS:

300g/11oz Chinese cabbage (shredded)
200g/7oz tofu (cubed and dry-fried)
8 dried Chinese mushrooms (soaked and chopped)

1 carrot (sliced)
2 teaspoons salt
1 tablespoon chopped fresh parsley

- Place all the ingredients in a large casserole dish, except the parsley, and pour over enough water to cover. Bring to the boil, lower the heat and simmer until the vegetables are tender, about 15 minutes.
- Scatter with parsley and serve.

Potato, pancetta & sage one-pot roast

SERVES 4

INGREDIENTS:

25g/1oz butter, plus extra for greasing
750g/1lb 11oz potatoes (sliced)
100g/4oz pancetta (thinly sliced)
12 fresh sage leaves
Salt and pepper

Juice of ½ lemon
300ml/½pt hot vegetable stock
150g/5oz Gruyère cheese (coarsely grated)

- Preheat the oven to 190°C/375°F/Gas mark 5. Lightly butter an ovenproof dish.
- Scatter the potato slices, pancetta and sage leaves into the dish, seasoning with salt and pepper as you go.
- Stir the lemon juice into the stock and pour over the potatoes. Dot the remaining butter over the top and roast for 1 hour, until the top is golden and the potatoes are tender. Top with cheese and serve immediately.

Millet stew

SERVES 6

INGREDIENTS:

225g/8oz millet
700ml/1¼pt water
2 onions (cut into wedges)
2 potatoes (cut into chunks)
2 carrots (cut into chunks)

200g/7oz celery (cut into chunks)
225g/8oz mushrooms (chopped)
2 bay leaves
½ teaspoon dried basil
½ teaspoon dried thyme

- Toast the millet in a dry frying pan for about 5 minutes, stirring constantly to avoid burning. Add all the ingredients to a slow cooker and cook for 4 hours on high or 8 hours on low.
- Alternatively add to a casserole dish and cook over a medium heat for 11/2 to 2 hours, stirring occasionally.

Barley & pine nut casserole

SERVES 6-8

INGREDIENTS:

200g/7oz pearl barley
75g/3oz butter
75g/3oz pine nuts
1 medium onion (chopped)
100g/4oz fresh parsley (minced)

100g/4oz fresh chives (minced)
Salt and pepper
900ml/1¾ pt canned condensed beef soup

- Preheat the oven to 190°C/375°F/Gas mark 4.
- Rinse the barley in cold water and drain well. Set aside.
- Melt 25g/1oz butter in a frying pan over a medium heat, then add the pine nuts and cook until lightly toasted, stirring constantly. Remove the pine nuts with a slotted spoon and set aside.
- Heat the remaining butter in the pan until melted, then add the barley and onion. Cook, stirring constantly, until the barley is lightly toasted and the onion is tender. Remove from the heat and stir in the pine nuts, parsley, chives and seasoning.
- Spoon the barley mixture into a casserole dish.
- Bring the beef soup to the boil in a medium saucepan, pour over the barley mixture in the casserole dish and stir well. Cook in the oven, uncovered, for 1 hour and 10 minutes or until the barley is tender and the liquid is absorbed.

Spicy bean hotpot

SERVES 4

INGREDIENTS:

1 tablespoon sunflower oil
2 onions (sliced)
1 garlic clove (crushed)
1 tablespoon red wine vinegar
400g/14oz canned chopped tomatoes
1 tablespoon tomato purée
1 tablespoon Worcestershire sauce
1 tablespoon wholegrain mustard
1 tablespoon dark brown sugar

250ml/9fl oz vegetable stock
400g/14oz canned red kidney beans
(drained)
400g/14oz canned haricot beans
(drained)
1 bay leaf
75g/3oz raisins
225g/8oz button mushrooms (chopped)
Salt and pepper

- Heat the oil in a large saucepan, add the onions and garlic and cook over a gentle heat for 10 minutes until soft.
- Add all the remaining ingredients except the mushrooms and seasoning. Bring to the boil, lower the heat and simmer for 10 minutes.
- Add the mushrooms and simmer for a further 5 minutes. Stir in seasoning to taste and serve immediately.

Bean burrito casserole

SERVES 6

INGREDIENTS:

12 corn tortillas
300g/11oz canned pinto beans (rinsed)
400g/14oz brown rice (cooked)
200g/7oz onions (chopped)

For the enchilada sauce:
450ml/³/₄pt tomato sauce
600ml/1pt water
¼ teaspoon garlic powder
½ teaspoon onion powder
3 teaspoons chilli powder
50g/2oz cornflour

- Preheat the oven to 180°C/350°F/Gas mark 4.
- To make the enchilada sauce, combine all the ingredients in a saucepan and cook, stirring constantly, for 7 minutes or until the mixture boils and thickens.
- Spread 225ml/8fl oz of the enchilada sauce in the bottom of a casserole dish.
- Take one tortilla at a time and spread some beans, rice and onions down the

centre. Roll up and place seam-side-down in the casserole dish. Repeat until all the ingredients are used. Pour the remaining enchilada sauce over the rolled-up tortillas, cover, and bake for 30 minutes.

Broccoli & cheese casserole

SERVES 6

INGREDIENTS:

225ml/8fl oz water
½ teaspoon salt
225g/8oz instant rice
50g/2oz butter
75g/3oz onion (chopped)
100g/4oz celery (chopped)

275g/10oz canned condensed mushroom soup
275g/10oz canned condensed celery soup
275g/10oz frozen broccoli (thawed)
100g/4oz Cheddar cheese (grated)

- Preheat the oven to 180°C/350°F/Gas mark 4.
- Bring the water and salt to the boil. Add the rice, then cover, remove from the heat and leave to sit for 5 minutes.
- Melt the butter in a frying pan and sauté the onion and celery until tender. In a large mixing bowl, combine the rice, celery and onion with the remaining ingredients.
- Pour into a large casserole dish and bake in the oven for 1 hour.

Cheesy-topped vegetable stew

SERVES 4

INGREDIENTS:

1 onion (sliced)
15g/½oz butter
175g/6oz canned split red lentils (soaked for 2 hours and drained)
2 carrots (chopped)
½ small swede (chopped)
2 turnips (chopped)

4 leeks (chopped)
225g/8oz potatoes (chopped)
450ml/¾pt vegetable stock
1 bouquet garni
Salt and pepper
¼ small green cabbage (shredded)

→

←

- Fry the onion in the butter in a large flameproof casserole dish for 2 minutes.
- Add the lentils and all the remaining vegetables except the cabbage and stir for 1 minute.
- Add the stock, bouquet garni and seasoning. Bring to the boil, reduce the heat, part-cover and simmer gently for 30 minutes. Add the cabbage and cook for a further 20 minutes until all the vegetables are really tender. Discard the bouquet garni and serve.

Sweet potato casserole

SERVES 10

INGREDIENTS:

900g/2lb sweet potatoes (boiled, peeled and mashed)
2 eggs (beaten)
50g/2oz butter (melted)

50g/2oz brown sugar
225ml/8fl oz buttermilk
¼ teaspoon baking powder
½ teaspoon grated nutmeg

- Preheat the oven to 180°C/350°F/Gas mark 4.
- Combine all the ingredients in a large casserole dish and mix together well.
- Bake, covered, in the oven for 1 hour. Serve hot.

Rice verde one-pot

SERVES 3

INGREDIENTS:

50g/2oz butter
1 small onion (finely chopped)
200g/7oz cooked long-grain rice
275g/10oz spinach (chopped)

225ml/8fl oz milk
1 egg (lightly beaten)
½ teaspoon salt
225g/8oz Cheddar cheese (grated)

- Preheat the oven to 180°C/350°F/Gas mark 4.
- Melt the butter in a large casserole dish and sauté the onion until it is transparent. Stir in the rice, spinach, milk, egg, salt and cheese. Mix well with a fork.
- Cover and bake for about 30 minutes, until the mixture is hot and the top is crisp.

Potato & pea stew

SERVES 6

INGREDIENTS:

3 tablespoons ghee
1 tablespoons grated root ginger
2 green chillies (deseeded and finely chopped)
½ tablespoon cumin seeds
1 teaspoon black mustard seeds
¼ teaspoon asafoetida
2 tomatoes (chopped)

700g/1½lb potatoes (cubed)
1 teaspoon ground turmeric
1 tablespoon ground coriander
300ml/½pt water
200g/7oz frozen peas (thawed)
1 teaspoon salt
3 tablespoons chopped fresh coriander

- Heat the ghee in a large casserole dish until hot. Add the ginger, chillies, cumin seeds and mustard seeds. Fry for a few seconds, then add the asafoetida.
- Add the tomatoes and fry for 3 minutes. Add the potatoes, turmeric, coriander and water. Bring to the boil, reduce the heat, cover and simmer for 15 minutes.
- Add the peas, salt and half the fresh coriander. Continue to cook, part-covered, until the potatoes are soft.
- Garnish with the rest of the coriander and serve hot.

Corn & haricot bean stew

SERVES 6

INGREDIENTS:

3 tablespoons vegetable oil
1 large onion (chopped)
1 teaspoon cumin
¼ teaspoon dried thyme
200g/7oz haricot beans
2 garlic cloves (crushed)
3 celery sticks (chopped)

1 green pepper (chopped)
2 tablespoons chopped fresh coriander
1 tablespoon chilli powder
550g/1lb 4oz tomatoes (chopped)
225ml/8fl oz water
Salt and pepper
450g/1lb canned sweetcorn

- Heat the oil in a large pan. Add the onion, cumin and thyme and sauté over a medium-high heat for about 5 minutes, stirring frequently, until the onions begin to colour. Add the beans and continue cooking over a high heat for a further 4 minutes.
- Add the garlic, celery, green pepper, coriander and chilli powder. Cook for 3

→

←

minutes, add the tomatoes and water, then season with salt and pepper.
- Lower the heat, cover the pan and simmer for 15 minutes. When the beans are tender, add the sweetcorn. Heat through and serve.

Turnip, potato & onion stew

SERVES 4

INGREDIENTS:

875g/1lb 15oz turnip (peeled and chopped)
400g/14oz onions (chopped)

8 potatoes (chopped)
Salt and pepper
600ml/1pt vegetable stock

- Mix the turnip and onions and place in the bottom of a saucepan. Cover with the potatoes and season well.
- Add the stock, bring to the boil, cover and simmer for about 15 minutes, until the vegetables are cooked. Serve hot.

Macaroni cheese casserole

SERVES 4

INGREDIENTS:

300g/11oz elbow macaroni
200g/7oz Parmesan cheese (grated)
Salt and pepper

For the mornay sauce:
50g/2oz butter

1 tablespoon plain flour
350ml/12fl oz milk
Salt and pepper
Pinch of grated nutmeg
2 tablespoons grated Parmesan cheese
1 egg yolk

- Preheat the oven to 180°C/350°F/Gas mark 4.
- For the mornay sauce, melt the butter in a small saucepan and add the flour. Stir to form a smooth paste and add the milk. Stir continually and cook over a low flame for 10 minutes. Add salt, pepper and nutmeg. Remove from the heat and stir in the cheese and egg yolk rapidly.
- Cook the macaroni in boiling salted water for about 10 minutes, or until just

tender but still quite firm. Drain. Mix with the sauce, cheese and seasoning. Turn into a casserole dish and bake for 30 minutes.

Vegetable & pasta one-pot

SERVES 4

INGREDIENTS:

2.4 litres/4pt water
1 teaspoon salt
450g/1lb sun-dried tomatoes
225g/8oz spiral pasta
225g/8oz broccoli florets
1 red pepper (sliced)
1 yellow pepper (sliced)
1 bunch spring onions (thinly sliced, white and green parts separated)

½ teaspoon sea salt (dissolved in 1 tablespoon water)
2 tablespoons extra-virgin olive oil
1 tablespoon chopped garlic
50g/2oz fresh parsley (finely chopped)
175g/6oz pitted black olives (halved)
100g/4oz Parmesan cheese (grated)

- Bring the water and salt to the boil in a large casserole dish over a high heat, then transfer 350ml/12fl oz to a small mixing bowl.
- Add the tomatoes and soak for 5 minutes, then drain and slice in thin strips.
- Return the water to a rapid boil over a high heat. Add the pasta gradually, stirring to prevent sticking. Cook the pasta for 3 minutes less than manufacturer's recommended cooking time. Add the broccoli, peppers and white part of the spring onions to the pasta and cook for 3 minutes over a high heat.
- While the vegetables cook, stir the salt-water mixture into the olive oil. When the pasta and vegetables are just done, drain well in a colander, then return the mixture immediately to the casserole dish.
- Stir in the water-oil mixture, tomatoes, garlic, spring onion tops, garlic, parsley and olives and mix well. Serve immediately, topped with Parmesan cheese.

Lentil & rice one-pot supper

SERVES 4

INGREDIENTS:

200g/7oz red lentils
150g/5oz long-grain rice
200g/7oz carrots (sliced)
700ml/1¼pt water

600ml/1pt vegetable stock
1 teaspoon chopped garlic
1 teaspoon dried basil
1 tablespoon olive oila

- Place the lentils in a large saucepan with the rice and carrots. Add the remaining ingredients and bring to the boil.
- Reduce the heat, cover and cook for 30 to 40 minutes until the lentil and rice are both tender. Serve hot.

Peas pilaff one-pot

SERVES 8

INGREDIENTS:

200g/7oz tomatoes (chopped)
150g/5oz green peas
50ml/2fl oz natural yogurt
4 teaspoons minced garlic
4 teaspoons minced root ginger
2 teaspoons ground coriander
1 teaspoon ground cumin
1 teaspoon garam masala
Salt and pepper
¼ teaspoon ground turmeric
2 tablespoons canola oil

200g/7oz onion (finely diced)
2 green chillies (deseeded and chopped)
2 cinnamon sticks
16 black peppercorns
2 teaspoons cumin seeds
700ml/1¼pt water
350g/12oz potatoes (cut into bite-sized pieces)
200g/7oz basmati rice (washed and drained)

- Combine the tomatoes, peas, yogurt, garlic, ginger, coriander, cumin, garam masala, seasoning and turmeric in a large bowl.
- Heat the oil in a large saucepan. Add the onion, chillies, cinnamon, peppercorns and cumin seeds and sauté until the onion starts to turn golden. Add the tomato mixture and stir. Cover and cook over a medium heat for 10 minutes, stirring occasionally.

- Add the water, ³/₄ teaspoon salt and the potatoes and stir well. Cover and bring to the boil. Add the rice, stir gently and cook, covered, until almost all the water has been absorbed, about 10 minutes. Reduce the heat to low and cook for 10 to 15 minutes, or until the rice is tender.

Courgette & aubergine casserole

SERVES 4

INGREDIENTS:

4 tablespoons olive oil
2 small courgettes (trimmed and cubed)
2 small aubergines (trimmed and cubed)
1 garlic clove (finely chopped)
200g/7oz onions (coarsely chopped)
3 tablespoons chives (minced)
4 plum tomatoes (sliced)

1 teaspoon dried thyme
1 bay leaf
1 teaspoon dried rosemary
1 teaspoon dried basil
Salt and pepper
1 tablespoon chopped fresh parsley

- Heat the oil in a large casserole dish. When it is very hot, add the courgettes and aubergines. Cook, stirring, for about 4 minutes. Add the garlic, onions and chives. Cook, stirring, for about 5 minutes.
- Add the tomatoes, thyme, bay leaf, rosemary and basil. Stir well and cook over a medium heat for 10 minutes, stirring regularly. Remove the bay leaf and add the seasoning. Garnish with parsley and serve.

Bean & tomato casserole

SERVES 4

INGREDIENTS:

400g/14oz canned cannellini beans
400g/14oz canned borlotti beans
2 tablespoons olive oil
1 celery stick

2 garlic cloves (chopped)
175g/6oz baby onions (halved)
450g/1lb tomatoes
75g/3oz rocket

→

←

- Drain both cans of beans and reserve 75ml/3fl oz of the liquid.
- Heat the oil in a large pan. Add the celery, garlic and onions and sauté for 5 minutes or until the onions are golden.
- Cut a cross in the base of each tomato and plunge them into a bowl of boiling water for 30 seconds until the skins split. Remove the tomatoes with a slotted spoon and leave until cold enough to handle. Peel off the skin and chop the flesh.
- Add the tomato flesh and reserved bean liquid to the pan and cook for 5 minutes.
- Add the beans to the pan and cook for a further 3 to 4 minutes or until the beans are hot. Stir in the rocket and allow to wilt slightly before serving. Serve hot.

Broccoli casserole

SERVES 6

INGREDIENTS:

900g/2lb frozen chopped broccoli (thawed)
75g/3oz butter
40g/1½oz plain flour

225ml/8fl oz vegetable stock
450ml/¾pt milk
150ml/¼pt water
200g/7oz stuffing mix

- Preheat the oven to 200°C/400°F/Gas mark 6.
- Cook the broccoli according to the package directions, until al dente. Drain well and place in a large casserole dish.
- Melt 25g/1oz butter in a saucepan. Stir in the flour and cook briefly. Add the stock and milk and cook, stirring constantly, until thickened.
- In a separate pan, melt the remaining butter in the water. Mix with the stuffing.
- Pour the stock sauce over the casserole dish, sprinkle with the stuffing mixture and bake in the oven for 20 minutes, or until crisp on top.

One-pot rice & beans

SERVES 4

INGREDIENTS:

200g/7oz tomato salsa
1.2 litres/2pt water
200g/7oz long-grain rice

450g/1lb canned black beans (drained)
425g/15oz canned red kidney beans (drained)

- Over a high heat, heat the salsa and water to boiling point, then stir in the rice.

- Reduce the heat, cover and simmer for 20 minutes or until the rice is tender. Stir in the beans, heat through and serve.

Spinach & peanut butter stew

SERVES 6

INGREDIENTS:

1 tablespoon vegetable oil
2 onions (sliced)
2 tomatoes (peeled and sliced)

900g/2lb spinach (chopped)
40g/1½oz crunchy peanut butter
Salt and pepper

- Heat the oil in a heavy-based pan and fry the onions until they are soft. Add the tomatoes and spinach and cook, covered, over a medium heat for 5 minutes, stirring to prevent sticking.
- Thin the peanut butter with hot water to make a smooth paste and add to the stew. Season with salt and pepper and cook for another 5 to 10 minutes, stirring and adding water if necessary to prevent sticking.

Mexican lentil casserole

SERVES 6

INGREDIENTS:

100g/4oz onions (chopped)
150g/5oz green peppers (chopped)
100g/4oz celery (chopped)
900ml/1½pt water
200g/7oz puy lentils

400g/14oz cooked brown rice
175g/6oz tomato purée
50g/2oz taco seasoning
½ teaspoon chilli powder

- In a medium saucepan, combine the onions, green pepper, celery and water.
- Bring to a boil over medium heat. Stir in the lentils, cover the pot, reduce the heat to low and simmer for 40 minutes.
- Preheat the oven to 190°C/375°F/Gas mark 5.
- Remove the saucepan from the heat and stir in the remaining ingredients, mixing well. Spoon into a casserole dish and bake, uncovered, for 25 minutes.

Yellow split pea casserole

SERVES 4

INGREDIENTS:

2 tablespoons ghee
1 teaspoon black mustard seeds
1 onion (finely chopped)
2 garlic cloves (crushed)
1 carrot (grated).
2.5cm/1in piece root ginger (grated)
1 green chilli (deseeded and finely chopped)
1 tablespoon tomato purée
250g/9oz yellow split peas (soaked in water for 2 hours)

400g/14oz canned chopped tomatoes
500ml/16fl oz vegetable stock
Salt and pepper
225g/8oz pumpkin (cubed)
225g/8oz cauliflower (cut into florets)
2 tablespoons vegetable oil
1 large aubergine (cubed)
1 tablespoon chopped fresh coriander
1 teaspoon garam masala

- Melt the ghee over a medium heat in a large pan. Add the mustard seeds, and when they start to splutter, add the onion, garlic, carrot and ginger.
- Cook until soft, about 5 minutes. Add the chilli and stir in the tomato purée. Stir in the split peas. Add the tomatoes and stock and bring to the boil. Season well.
- Simmer for 40 minutes, stirring occasionally.
- Add the pumpkin and cauliflower and simmer for a further 30 minutes, covered, until the split peas are soft.
- Meanwhile, heat the oil in a frying pan over a high heat. Add the aubergine and stir until sealed on all sides, then remove and drain on kitchen paper.
- Stir the aubergine into the split pea mixture with the coriander and garam masala. Serve immediately.

Courgette casserole

SERVES 6

INGREDIENTS:

Butter for greasing
225ml/8fl oz water
150g/5oz onion (diced)
200g/7oz courgette (sliced)
200g/7oz Cheddar cheese (grated)

2 eggs (beaten)
Salt and pepper
100g/4oz green chillies (diced)
400g/14oz canned chopped tomatoes

- Preheat the oven to 190°C/375°F/Gas mark 5. Grease a casserole dish with butter.
- Bring the water to a boil and cook the onion and courgette until the courgette is al dente, 12 to 15 minutes. Remove from the heat and drain.
- Combine the courgette, onion, cheese, beaten eggs, salt, pepper, chillies and tomatoes in a mixing bowl, then pour into the casserole dish and bake for 40 minutes.

Kidney bean stew with cornmeal dumplings

SERVES 4

INGREDIENTS:

300g/11oz kidney beans
700ml/1½pt water
250g/9oz onions (chopped)
150g/5oz celery (chopped)
175g/6oz carrots (sliced)
3 bay leaves
225ml/8fl oz tomato purée
1 tablespoon balsamic vinegar
2 tablespoons tamari

For the dumplings:
100g/4oz cornmeal
¼ teaspoon sea salt
⅛ teaspoon baking powder
150g/5oz tofu (cubed)

- Combine the beans, water, onions, celery, carrots, bay leaves and tomato purée in a large casserole dish. Bring to the boil, reduce the heat and simmer for about 45 minutes until the beans and vegetables are tender. Stir in the vinegar and tamari.
- While the stew is cooking, prepare the dumplings. In a medium-size mixing bowl, combine the cornmeal, salt and baking powder. Blend the tofu in a blender or food processor until smooth and creamy. Add the tofu to the cornmeal mixture and mix well.
- Bring the stew to a slow boil over medium heat and drop tablespoonfuls of dumpling batter on to the surface. Cover and cook for 10 minutes.
- Remove the dumplings with a slotted spoon to a serving bowl. Stir the stew to mix well. Ladle the stew into individual serving bowls and top with the dumplings.
- Serve immediately.

Asparagus & egg casserole

SERVES 6

INGREDIENTS:

100g/4oz celery (chopped)
50g/2oz butter
50g/2oz flour
Salt and pepper
½ teaspoon dry mustard
450ml/³/₄pt milk

1 teaspoon chicken gravy granules
100g/4oz mushrooms (chopped)
450g/1lb frozen asparagus (chopped)
2 eggs (hard-boiled and sliced)
12 Ritz crackers (crushed)

- Preheat the oven to 190°C/375°F/Gas mark 4.
- In a saucepan, cook the celery in the butter, then blend in the flour, seasoning and mustard. Add the milk and gravy granules. Cook and stir until thickened.
- Stir in the mushrooms and set the mixture aside.
- Cook the asparagus according to the packet directions and drain thoroughly.
- Reserve 50g/2oz asparagus for garnish. Arrange the remaining asparagus and egg in a large baking dish. Pour the sauce over. Bake, covered, for 15 minutes. Arrange the reserved asparagus on top and sprinkle with the crackers.
- Bake, uncovered, for a further 10 minutes, then serve.

Red bean & dumpling stew

SERVES 4

INGREDIENTS:

1 tablespoon vegetable oil
1 red onion (sliced)
2 celery sticks (chopped)
850ml/1½pt vegetable stock
225g/8oz carrots (diced)
225g/8oz potatoes (diced)
225g/8oz courgettes (diced)
4 tomatoes (peeled and chopped)
100g/4oz red lentils
400g/14oz canned kidney beans
(drained)

1 teaspoon paprika
Salt and pepper

For the dumplings:
100g/4oz plain flour
½ teaspoon salt
2 teaspoons baking powder
1 teaspoon paprika
1 teaspoon dried mixed herbs
25g/1oz vegetable suet
125ml/4fl oz water

- Heat the oil in a flameproof casserole dish and gently fry the onion and celery for 3 to 4 minutes until just softened. Pour in the stock and stir in the carrots and potatoes. Bring to the boil, cover and cook for 5 minutes.

- Stir in the courgettes, tomatoes, lentils, kidney beans, paprika and seasoning.
- Bring to the boil, cover and cook for 5 minutes.
- To make the dumplings, sift the flour, salt, baking powder and paprika into a bowl. Stir in the herbs and suet. Bind together with the water to form a soft dough. Divide into 8 and roll into balls.
- Add the dumplings to the stew, pushing them slightly into it. Cover and simmer for 15 minutes until the dumplings have risen and are cooked through.

Brown rice & lentil stew

SERVES 4

INGREDIENTS:

300g/11oz brown rice
200g/7oz dried puy lentils
175g/6oz onions (chopped)
150g/5oz celery (sliced)
175g/6oz carrots (sliced)
50g/2oz fresh parsley (chopped)

1 teaspoon Italian seasoning
1 garlic clove (crushed)
1 bay leaf
450ml/³⁄₄pt vegetable stock
400g/14oz canned chopped tomatoes
1 tablespoon cider vinegar

- Combine all the ingredients in a large saucepan and bring to the boil. Reduce the heat and simmer, uncovered, stirring occasionally, for 40 minutes or until the rice is tender. Remove and discard the bay leaf before serving.

Vegetable & egg casserole

SERVES 10

INGREDIENTS:

200g/7oz brown rice
1 vegetable stock cube
500ml/18fl oz warm water
2 eggs (lightly beaten)
25g/1oz butter
100g/4oz onion (diced)
100g/4oz red pepper (diced)

100g/4oz broccoli (chopped)
100g/4oz cauliflower (chopped)
425g/15oz canned chopped tomatoes
3 eggs (hard-boiled and chopped)
1 tablespoon chopped fresh parsley
¹⁄₂ teaspoon dried mixed herbs
50g/2oz Cheddar cheese (grated)

→

←
- Preheat the oven to 180°C/350°F/Gas mark 4.
- Place the rice, stock cube and water in a large saucepan. Cook for about 40 minutes or until the rice is tender, then strain, discarding any liquid.
- Combine the rice and beaten egg and spread in the base of a 2.4 litre/4pt casserole dish.
- Melt half the butter in a large frying pan. Add the onion and sauté. Add the red pepper, broccoli and cauliflower.
- Drain and discard any liquid from the tomatoes. Add the tomatoes to the pan. Cover and simmer for 5 minutes. Add the hard-boiled eggs, parsley, herbs and cheese and spoon over the rice in the casserole dish. Bake in the oven for 15 minutes, or until heated through.

Chilli bean casserole

SERVES 4

INGREDIENTS:

200g/7oz long-grain rice
225ml/8fl oz plain yogurt
2 teaspoons chopped fresh coriander
75g/3oz green taco sauce
1 onion (sliced)
3 garlic cloves (minced)
75ml/3fl oz white wine

200g/7oz canned sweetcorn (drained)
100g/4oz sliced black olives
1 medium courgette (sliced)
400g/14oz canned chilli beans
1 tomato (chopped)
Salt and pepper

- Preheat the oven to 180°C/350°F/Gas mark 4.
- Cook the rice in boiling water. Mix the yogurt with the coriander and taco sauce. Set aside.
- Cook the onion and garlic in the wine until soft. Layer the sweetcorn, cooked rice, olives, courgette, onion and garlic in a casserole dish. Pour the beans over all.
- Cover and cook in the oven for 30 minutes or until heated thoroughly. Sprinkle the tomato over the top and drizzle with the yogurt mixture. Season to taste and serve.

Baked leek casserole

SERVES 4

INGREDIENTS:

75g/3oz butter
8 large leeks (chopped)
1 small onion (finely chopped)
600ml/1pt tomato juice

½ teaspoon Worcestershire sauce
½ teaspoon lemon juice
Pinch of granulated sugar
Salt and pepper

- Preheat the oven to 190°C/375°F/Gas mark 5.
- Melt 50g/2oz butter and fry the leeks and onion until the leeks are just golden-brown and the onion is transparent. Transfer to a large casserole dish. Pour in the tomato juice.
- Stir in the Worcestershire sauce, lemon juice and sugar. Season well. Dot with the remaining butter.
- Cover the casserole securely and bake in the oven for 1 hour. Serve with the cooking liquor.

Leek & mushroom hotpot

SERVES 3

INGREDIENTS:

2 tablespoons vegetable oil
2 large leeks (white part only, chopped)
6 large mushrooms (quartered)
175g/6oz canned chopped tomatoes
200g/7oz cooked haricot beans

¼ teaspoon dried marjoram
Salt and pepper
300ml/½pt vegetable stock
5 large potatoes (thinly sliced)
100g/4oz Gruyère cheese (grated)

- Preheat the oven to 200°C/400°F/Gas mark 6.
- Put the oil into a large casserole dish over a medium heat. Add the leeks and cook until softened. Add mushrooms to the leeks and stir together.
- Add the tomatoes, beans, marjoram, salt and pepper. Stir well. Add enough stock to reach the top of the casserole contents and stir well. Bring to the boil, turn the heat down to simmer, cover tightly and allow to simmer for 10 minutes.
- In a saucepan, boil the potatoes until they are nearly cooked. Drain well.
- Put half the potatoes in a layer on top of the casserole, completely covering the contents. Sprinkle on a layer of half the cheese. Add another layer of potatoes

→

←

and finish with the remaining cheese.
- Replace the lid and bake in the oven for 25 minutes.
- Remove the lid and cook for a further 5 to 10 minutes until the cheese is brown and bubbly.

Autumn barley stew

SERVES 10

INGREDIENTS:

200g/7oz barley
1.8 litres/3pt vegetable stock
2 onions (chopped)
3 potatoes (cut into chunks)
1 large sweet potato (cut into chunks)
450g/1lb Brussels sprouts

2 tablespoons tamari
1 teaspoon chopped fresh parsley
2 teaspoons oregano
1 teaspoon dill weed
3 tomatoes (chopped)

- Place the barley and stock in large casserole dish and bring to the boil. Add the remaining ingredients, except the tomatoes.
- Reduce the heat, cover and simmer for about 50 minutes. Add the tomatoes and cook for a further 10 minutes. Serve hot.

Greek vegetable casserole

SERVES 6

INGREDIENTS:

1 aubergine (chopped)
900g/2lb courgettes (chopped)
4 medium potatoes (chopped)
2 green peppers (sliced)
1 red pepper (sliced)

225ml/8fl oz olive oil
4 medium tomatoes (diced)
2 garlic cloves (crushed)
1 teaspoon granulated sugar
Salt and pepper

- Preheat the oven to 180°C/350°F/Gas mark 4.
- Sauté the aubergine, courgettes, potatoes and peppers in the oil in batches. Sauté each batch for 2 to 3 minutes, then remove from the pan.
- Place the vegetables in a baking dish and toss them briefly so they are well mixed.
- Add the tomatoes to the frying pan and sauté for 2 minutes. Add the garlic, sugar and salt and pepper to taste and simmer for a further 1 minute.

- Pour the tomato mixture on top of the vegetables and bake in the oven for 25 minutes, or until the vegetables are tender.

Root hotpot with herby dumplings

SERVES 4

INGREDIENTS:

1 teaspoon coriander seeds
1 teaspoon cumin seeds
1 garlic clove (finely chopped)
1 onion (finely chopped)
3 tablespoons olive oil
1.2 litres/2pt vegetable stock
2 teaspoons clear honey
300g/11oz carrots (chopped)
400g/14oz parsnips (chopped)
300g/11oz Jerusalem artichokes (chopped)
½ small swede (chopped)
300g/11oz potatoes (chopped)

½ head of green cabbage (shredded)

For the dumplings:
3 shallots
15g/½oz butter
25g/1oz vegetable suet
200g/7oz self-raising flour
Salt and pepper
2 tablespoons chopped fresh herbs, such as parsley, sage or thyme
3 tablespoons Parmesan cheese (freshly grated)
Pinch of ground nutmeg

- Fry the coriander and cumin seeds, garlic and onion in the oil until soft. Add the stock, the honey and the root vegetables and simmer until tender.
- For the dumplings, fry the shallots in butter until soft. Mix the suet, flour, seasoning, herbs, Parmesan and nutmeg. Add the shallots, then add enough water to make a dough. Shape into small dumplings and poach in a pan of boiling water for about 10 minutes.
- Stir the cabbage into the hotpot and simmer for 3 minutes. Serve with the dumplings.

Aubergine, mozzarella & Cheddar hotpot

SERVES 4

INGREDIENTS:

4 large white potatoes (peeled and thinly sliced)
2 tablespoons olive oil
1 medium aubergine (sliced)
1 large onion (sliced)
275g/10oz canned chopped tomatoes
425g/15oz canned chickpeas
25g/1oz green lentils

2 garlic cloves (crushed)
2 tablespoons chopped fresh parsley
Salt and pepper
25g/1oz Mozzarella cheese (finely grated)
25g/1oz Cheddar cheese (finely grated)
1 tablespoon boiling water

- Place the potatoes in a saucepan of cold, salted water. Bring to the boil and cook until beginning to soften. Drain and set aside.
- Heat the oil in a frying pan and gently sauté the aubergine until it begins to brown. Turn and repeat on the other side. As each piece is done, remove to kitchen paper.
- When the aubergine is cooked, stir the onion in the frying pan until softened, but not browned. Stir in the tomatoes, chickpeas, lentils, garlic, parsley and seasoning. Cook over a medium heat for 40 to 45 minutes, or until the lentils are tender.
- Preheat the oven to 200°C/400°F/Gas mark 6.
- Mix the cheeses together. Add the boiling water to make a paste.
- When the tomato mixture is ready, spoon the remaining mixture over the bottom of a large casserole dish. Cover with half the aubergine and add another third of the tomato mixture. Layer on the remaining aubergine.
- Spread a third of the cheese mixture on to the aubergine. Add half the potatoes, another third of the cheese and then the remaining potatoes. Finish with the final third of cheese.
- Cover and bake in the middle of oven for 30 minutes. Remove the lid and bake for a further 10 minutes to brown.

Greek-style chickpea casserole

SERVES 4

INGREDIENTS:

450g/1lb spinach
25g/1oz butter
1 garlic clove (crushed)
400g/14oz canned chickpeas (drained)
100g/4oz feta cheese (cubed)

Salt and pepper
Pinch of ground cinnamon
4 tomatoes (skinned and chopped)
125ml/4fl oz crème fraîche

- Wash the spinach thoroughly under running water and remove any tough stems. Cut into shreds.
- Heat the butter in a saucepan and fry the spinach and garlic, stirring, for 4 minutes. Add the chickpeas, cheese, seasoning and cinnamon. Toss over a gentle heat for 2 minutes.
- Add the tomatoes and crème fraîche and heat through, tossing and stirring. Serve hot.

Tofu & courgette stew

SERVES 4

INGREDIENTS:

300g/11oz tofu (chopped)
1 large onion (chopped)
1 tablespoon vegetable oil
600g/1lb 5oz courgettes (chopped)
1 medium dessert apple (cored and chopped)
350g/12oz long-grain rice

1 tablespoon ground cumin
Salt and pepper

For the marinade:
1 tablespoon Dijon mustard
1 tablespoon lemon juice
50ml/2fl oz soy sauce

- Combine the marinade ingredients in a large bowl and leave the tofu to marinate in the mixture in the refrigerator overnight.
- Place the onion in a frying pan with the oil and fry until soft. Add the tofu and stir until lightly browned. Add the apple and courgette and heat through, stirring, for about 10 minutes.

→

←

- Place the rice and cumin in a large pan of water. Bring to the boil, reduce the heat and cook until soft. Serve the stew with the rice, seasoned to taste.

Mexican bean stew

SERVES 6

INGREDIENTS:

275g/10oz canned kidney beans (drained)
2 carrots (cut into chunks)
200g/7oz courgette (cut into chunks)
400ml/14fl oz tomato sauce

1 teaspoon ground cumin
1 teaspoon chilli powder
2 teaspoons minced onions
1 tablespoon minced garlic
Salt and pepper

- In a large casserole dish, combine the beans, carrots, courgette, tomato sauce, cumin, chilli powder, onions and garlic. Add enough water to achieve the desired consistency, remembering that the stew will reduce.
- Simmer, covered, for 50 to 60 minutes. Season and serve hot.

Chinese vegetable casserole

SERVES 4

INGREDIENTS:

4 tablespoons vegetable oil
2 medium carrots (sliced)
1 courgette (sliced)
4 baby sweetcorn (halved lengthways)
100g/4oz cauliflower florets
1 leek (sliced)
100g/4oz water chestnuts (halved)
225g/8oz tofu (diced)

300ml/¹/₂pt vegetable stock
1 teaspoon salt
2 teaspoons dark brown sugar
2 teaspoons soy sauce
2 tablespoons dry sherry
1 tablespoon cornflour
2 tablespoons water
1 tablespoon chopped fresh coriander

- Heat the oil in a preheated wok until it is almost smoking. Lower the heat slightly, add the carrots, courgette, sweetcorn, cauliflower and leek to the wok and stir-fry for 2 to 3 minutes.
- Stir in the water chestnuts, tofu, stock, salt, sugar, soy sauce and sherry and bring to the boil. Reduce the heat, cover and simmer for 20 minutes.
- Blend the cornflour with the water to form a smooth paste. Stir into the wok,

bring the sauce to the boil and cook, stirring constantly until it thickens. Scatter the coriander over and serve immediately.

Vegetable hotpot

SERVES 4

INGREDIENTS:

2 potatoes (thinly sliced)
2 tablespoons vegetable oil
2 garlic cloves (finely chopped)
1 onion (chopped)
1 leek (chopped)
200g/7oz carrots (chopped)
150g/5oz cauliflower florets
150g/5oz broccoli florets

100g/4oz turnip (chopped)
1 teaspoon chilli powder
1/2 teaspoon ground cumin
1 tablespoon cornflour
700ml/1 1/4pt vegetable stock
1/2 teaspoon chopped fresh sage
200g/7oz Cheddar cheese (grated)

- Preheat the oven to 180°C/375°F/Gas mark 4.
- Cook the potato in boiling water for 5 minutes and drain.
- Heat the oil in a frying pan, add the garlic, onion and leek and fry until translucent. Mix in the rest of the vegetables, the chilli and the cumin and cook, covered, for 3 minutes.
- Mix the cornflour with the stock and add to the vegetables. Add the sage and bring to the boil.
- Transfer to a casserole dish. Layer with potato rounds on top. Sprinkle with cheese and bake for 8 minutes until the potatoes are brown and the cheese is melted. Serve immediately.

Baked squash casserole

SERVES 10

INGREDIENTS:

1.8kg/4lb butternut squash (topped, tailed and chopped)
1 egg
200g/7oz breadcrumbs

75g/3oz brown sugar
Salt and pepper
1/2 tablespoon chopped onion
100g/4oz green pepper (diced)

- Preheat the oven to 180°C/350°F/Gas mark 4.

→

←

- Drop the squash into a large saucepan with enough boiling water to cover.
- Return to the boil, reduce the heat and cook until tender, then mash, reserving the liquid.
- Combine the squash and liquid, egg, two-thirds of the breadcrumbs, the sugar, salt, onion and green pepper. Turn into a large casserole dish and cover with the remaining breadcrumbs. Bake for about 30 minutes, or until lightly browned.

Spinach & artichoke casserole

SERVES 4

INGREDIENTS:

275g/10oz frozen spinach (thawed)
450g/1lb mushrooms (sliced)
1 tablespoon vegetable oil
1 medium onion (chopped)
175g/6oz marinated artichoke hearts
(with liquid)

5 eggs (beaten)
1 garlic clove (crushed)
75g/3oz Parmesan cheese (grated)
75g/3oz Cheddar cheese (grated)

- Preheat the oven to 180°C/350°F/Gas mark 4.
- In a frying pan sauté the mushrooms and onion in the oil.
- Combine all the ingredients in a large casserole dish and mix well.
- Heat, covered, in the oven for 30 to 40 minutes.

Chickpea & artichoke stew

SERVES 4

INGREDIENTS:

1.2 litres/2pt vegetable stock
2 medium onions (chopped)
2 garlic cloves (minced)
1 tablespoon olive oil
1 teaspoon ground turmeric
1 teaspoon paprika
4 potatoes (cubed)

5 fresh sage leaves (crushed)
200g/7oz cooked sweet potato (puréed)
900g/2lb cooked chickpeas
400g/14oz canned artichoke hearts
(quartered)
Salt and pepper

- In a large saucepan, bring the stock to a simmer. Meanwhile, in a large frying pan, sauté the onions and garlic in the oil for about 8 minutes or until soft. Stir in the turmeric and paprika and sauté for 1 minute.
- Add the potatoes, sage and the stock. Cook for about 12 minutes, until the potatoes are tender. Stir in the sweet potato and add the chickpeas and artichoke hearts. Add salt and pepper to taste, then return to a simmer. Heat through and serve.

Baked lentil & vegetable stew

SERVES 4

INGREDIENTS:

450g/1lb Brussel sprouts
200g/7oz green lentils
700ml/1½pt water
200g/7oz onions (chopped)
150g/5oz celery (chopped)

200g/7oz carrots (sliced)
400g/14oz rutabaga (chopped)
4 bay leaves
1 tablespoon fresh root ginger (grated)
2 tablespoons tamari

- Preheat the oven to 180°C/350°F/Gas mark 4.
- Cut across in the bottom of each sprout. Combine the sprouts and remaining ingredients except the tamari in a large baking dish. Bake, stirring occasionally, for about 1 hour, until the lentils and vegetables are tender.
- Add more water to the stew while baking if necessary. Stir in the tamari and serve warm.

Courgette & corn casserole

SERVES 8

INGREDIENTS:

Butter for greasing
600g/1lb 5oz courgettes (grated)
425g/15oz canned creamed sweetcorn
200g/7oz red pepper (finely diced)
50g/2oz Cheddar cheese (finely grated)
50g/2oz potato flour

75g/3oz rice flour
1 teaspoon baking powder
2 tablespoons olive oil
2 eggs (lightly beaten)
100g/4oz onion (finely diced)

→

- Preheat the oven to 200°C/400°F/Gas mark 6. Grease a casserole dish with butter.
- Place all the ingredients into a medium-sized mixing bowl and mix well. Pour into the prepared casserole dish and bake for 30 minutes, or until set in the centre.

Potato & spinach casserole

SERVES 4

INGREDIENTS:

Vegetable oil for greasing
2 tablespoons breadcrumbs
50g/1lb potatoes (boiled and mashed)
3 tablespoons grated Cheddar cheese
75g/3oz butter
Salt and pepper
1 medium egg yolk (beaten)
2 teaspoons sunflower oil

1 small onion (finely chopped)
450g/1lb fresh spinach (chopped)
1 tablespoon tomato purée
1 green chilli (finely chopped)
1 chicken stock cube
1 medium egg white (whisked until stiff)
Pinch of grated nutmeg

- Preheat the oven to 180°C/350°F/Gas mark 4. Grease an ovenproof casserole dish and coat the inside surface with the breadcrumbs.
- Mix the mashed potato with the cheese, butter, salt, pepper and egg yolk and place in the casserole dish, over the breadcrumbs.
- Heat the sunflower oil in a frying pan and fry the onion until soft but not browned. Add the spinach, tomato purée, chilli and stock cube and simmer gently for 5 minutes. Allow to cool until just warm, then fold in the egg white and nutmeg.
- Pour the mixture over the potato and bake in the oven for 25 minutes.

Carrot casserole

SERVES 6

INGREDIENTS:

Butter for greasing
350ml/12fl oz water
225g/8oz carrot (chopped)
175g/6oz potato (chopped)
200g/7oz sweet potato (chopped)
25g/1oz onions (chopped)

300g/11oz brown rice (cooked)
75ml/3fl oz milk
75g/3oz Parmesan cheese (grated)
Salt and pepper
1 tablespoon soy sauce

- Preheat the oven to 180°C/350°F/Gas mark 4. Lightly grease a large casserole dish with butter.
- In a large saucepan, bring 225ml/8fl oz water to the boil then add the carrot, potato and sweet potato. Cover and cook for 5 minutes.
- Add the remaining water to the cooked vegetables, then add the remaining ingredients and mix well. Pour into the casserole dish and bake in the oven for 25 to 30 minutes.

Pasta & potato stew

SERVES 8

INGREDIENTS:

1 large onion (coarsely chopped)
75g/3oz celery (chopped)
1 teaspoon olive oil
50ml/2fl oz red wine
2 garlic cloves (crushed)
200g/7oz tomatoes (chopped)
75g/3oz fresh parsley (chopped)
100g/4oz carrots (chopped)

150g/5oz cooked red potatoes (diced)
150g/5oz macaroni (cooked)
300g/11oz cooked kidney beans
1.8 litres/3pt vegetable stock
1 tablespoon dried basil
½ teaspoon dried oregano
1 teaspoon dried chives

- In a large casserole dish over a medium-high heat, sauté the onion and celery in the oil and red wine until the onion is limp but not brown. Add the garlic, tomatoes, parsley and carrots and cook for 5 minutes, stirring frequently.
- Add the remaining ingredients and bring to the boil. Reduce the heat to medium and cook for about 15 minutes, uncovered, until the vegetables are soft. Before serving, purée 200ml/7fl oz of the stew in a blender or food processor, and add back.
- Adjust seasonings as needed.

Apple cranberry casserole

SERVES 2

INGREDIENTS:

250g/9oz Granny Smith apples (peeled and diced)
200g/7oz cranberries
175g/6oz granulated sugar

100g/4oz oatmeal
75g/3oz brown sugar
100g/4oz chopped pecan nuts
50g/2oz butter

→

←
- Preheat the oven to 170°C/325°F/Gas mark 3.
- Spread the apples and cranberries in the bottom of a large casserole dish. Spread the rest of the ingredients except the butter over the apples and cranberries.
- Dot with butter and bake for 1 hour.

Armenian pumpkin stew

SERVES 6-8

INGREDIENTS:

½ teaspoon coriander seeds
½ teaspoon cardamom seeds
½ teaspoon ground cinnamon
1 teaspoon cumin seeds
1 clove
2 tablespoons vegetable oil
900g/2lb lamb (cubed)
1 large onion (minced)
4 garlic cloves (crushed)
2 carrots (sliced)

1 celery stick (sliced)
4 tomatoes (peeled and sliced)
1 acorn squash (peeled and chopped)
1.2 litres/2pt vegetable stock
Salt and pepper
1 pumpkin (flesh chopped, keep shell whole)
200g/7oz basmati rice
50g/2oz fresh coriander (minced)

- Combine the coriander, cardamom, cinnamon, cumin and cloves in a spice mill or coffee grinder. Grind until smooth. Set aside.
- Heat 1 tablespoon oil in a large saucepan. Add the lamb in one layer and sprinkle with the spice mixture. Sear over a medium heat for about 3 to 5 minutes until lightly browned. Remove the lamb from the pan and set aside.
- Add the onion and garlic to the pan. Sauté, stirring frequently, for about 5 minutes until translucent. Add the carrots, celery, tomatoes and squash. Add the stock and return the lamb to the pan. Partly cover and gently simmer for 1½ to 2 hours, until the lamb is tender. Season with salt and pepper.
- Preheat the oven to 180°C/350°F/Gas mark 4.
- Place the chopped pumpkin flesh on a baking sheet and drizzle with the remaining oil. Bake until tender, about 45 to 60 minutes.
- Meanwhile, cook the rice according to package directions and set aside.
- Place the cooked pumpkin flesh back into its shell and fill with the lamb stew. Divide the rice among 4 warmed bowls. Ladle the stew from the pumpkin over the rice. Garnish with coriander and serve immediately.

Lentil hotpot

SERVES 4

INGREDIENTS:

1 tablespoon olive oil
1 onion (chopped)
1 garlic clove (crushed)
2 medium potatoes (diced)
2 carrots (finely chopped)
2 celery sticks (chopped)
225g/8oz red lentils

425g/15oz canned chopped tomatoes
2 tablespoons tomato purée
1 bay leaf
½ teaspoon dried oregano
1 vegetable stock cube
450ml/¾pt water
Salt and pepper

- Heat the oil in a large pan and fry the onion and garlic until the onion is softened. Add the potatoes, carrots, celery and lentils and fry for a further 2 minutes.
- Add the tomatoes, tomato purée, bay leaf and oregano and season to taste.
- Crumble in the stock cube and stir in the water. Bring to the boil, then simmer for 25 to 30 minutes. Ladle into warm bowls and serve.

Spicy bean & vegetable stew

SERVES 6

INGREDIENTS:

3 tablespoons olive oil
2 small onions (sliced)
2 garlic cloves (crushed)
1 tablespoon paprika
1 small dried red chilli (deseeded and finely chopped)
700g/1½lb sweet potatoes (peeled and cubed)

700g/1½lb pumpkin (peeled and cut into chunks)
100g/4oz okra (trimmed)
500g/1lb 2oz passata
900ml/1½pt water
Salt and pepper
400g/14oz canned haricot beans (drained)

- Heat the oil in a large heavy-based pan, add the onions and garlic and cook over a very gentle heat to 5 minutes.
- Stir in the paprika and chilli and cook for 2 minutes, then add the sweet potatoes,

→

←

pumpkin, okra, passata and water. Season well. Cover, bring to the boil and simmer for 20 minutes until the vegetables are tender. Add the beans and cook for 3 minutes to heat through.

Sweetcorn casserole

SERVES 8

INGREDIENTS:

50g/2oz butter, plus extra for greasing
2 tablespoons vegetable shortening
75g/3oz plain flour
3 tablespoons cold water
250g/9oz frozen sweetcorn (partially thawed)

25g/1oz cornflour
50g/2oz granulated sugar
2 tablespoons evaporated milk
¼ teaspoon baking powder
¼ teaspoon salt
1 teaspoon chilli powder

- Preheat the oven to 180°C/350°F/Gas mark 4. Lightly grease a 23cm/9in baking dish.
- Place the butter, shortening and flour in a blender or food processor and process until creamy. Add the water and sweetcorn and process.
- Combine the cornflour, sugar, evaporated milk, baking powder and salt in a medium bowl. Stir in the sweetcorn mixture until combined. Spread into the prepared baking dish. Sprinkle with chilli powder.
- Bake in the oven for 40 to 50 minutes or until firm and lightly browned around the edge. Cool on a wire rack for 15 minutes before serving.

Polish noodle casserole

SERVES 6

INGREDIENTS:

225g/8oz cooked noodles
100g/4oz sour cream
100g/4oz cottage cheese
2 tablespoons minced onion

2 teaspoons salt
½ teaspoon powdered mustard
¼ teaspoon ground white pepper

- Preheat the oven to 180°C/350°F/Gas mark 4.
- Place the noodles in a large casserole dish. Add the sour cream, cottage cheese, onion, salt, powdered mustard and white pepper and mix well with the noodles. Bake in the oven for 25 minutes.

Tofu casserole

SERVES 4

INGREDIENTS:

2 tablespoons groundnut oil
8 spring onions (cut into batons)
2 celery sticks (sliced)
100g/4oz broccoli florets
100g/4oz courgettes (sliced)
2 garlic cloves (thinly sliced)
450g/1lb baby spinach
450g/1lb tofu (cut into 2.5cm/1in cubes)

For the sauce:
400ml/14fl oz vegetable stock
2 tablespoons soy sauce
3 tablespoons hoisin sauce
½ teaspoon chilli powder
1 tablespoon sesame oil

- Heat the oil in a preheated wok. Add the spring onions, celery, broccoli, courgettes, garlic, spinach and tofu to the wok and stir-fry for 3 to 4 minutes.
- To make the sauce, mix together the stock, soy sauce, hoisin sauce, chilli powder and sesame oil in a flameproof casserole dish and bring to the boil.
- Add the vegetables and tofu to the dish, reduce the heat, cover and simmer for 10 minutes. Serve immediately.

Carrot & cumin stew

SERVES 8

INGREDIENTS:

1 tablespoon cumin seeds
½ tablespoon caraway seeds
½ tablespoon mustard seeds
200ml/7fl oz carrot juice
25g/1oz butter (melted)

900g/2lb baby carrots (peeled)
2 tablespoons olive oil
Salt and pepper
Juice of 1 lime
1 tablespoon dried mixed herbs

- Lightly toast the cumin, caraway and mustard seeds and add to the carrot juice in a heavy-based saucepan. Cook over a high heat until reduced by three-quarters.
- Pour into a blender or food processor. On a medium speed, add the butter in a slow, steady stream. Strain out any solids.
- Cut the baby carrots on a bias and sweat in the oil. When tender, add the carrot juice mixture and season with salt, pepper, lime and herbs. Heat through and serve.

Game

A casserole or stew is the ideal way to experiment with game
– for example, pigeon, venison, pheasant, rabbit or quail. This
versatile ingredient has many interesting tastes and textures,
so, if you are tempted to try something different, look no
further than this selection, which includes Pot-roast of
venison and Grouse casserole.

Woodpigeon casserole

SERVES 4

INGREDIENTS:

2 pig's trotters
25g/1oz butter
1 tablespoon vegetable oil
4 woodpigeon
12 pickling onions
1 carrot (diced)
1 celery stick (diced)
100g/4oz streaky back bacon (cut into strips)

1 cinnamon stick
1 bay leaf
2 sprigs thyme
1½ tablespoons plain flour
16 pitted prunes
2 sprigs parsley
300ml/½pt red wine
Salt and pepper

- Place the trotters in a pan and cover with water. Bring to the boil, cover and simmer for 1 hour, skimming any scum from the cooking liquid. Reserve the liquid and trotters.
- Melt the butter and oil in a flameproof casserole dish. Quickly brown the pigeons then remove and reserve. Add the onions, carrot, celery and bacon to the pan with the cinnamon, bay leaf and thyme. Stir to coat with the fat, then lower the heat, cover and sweat gently for 10 minutes. Sprinkle with flour and stir.
- Return the pigeons to the pan, together with the trotters, prunes, parsley, wine and 600ml/1pt of the trotters' cooking liquid. Season lightly with salt and pepper. Bring to the boil, cover and simmer gently, turning the pigeons occasionally, for 45 to 60 minutes, until they are tender.

Grouse casserole

SERVES 5

INGREDIENTS:

2 grouse (trussed)
Salt and pepper
75g/3oz butter
100g/4oz mushrooms (chopped)
2 carrots (diced)

1 celery stick (diced)
1 onion (chopped)
2 tablespoons whisky
300ml/½pt chicken stock
1 tablespoon redcurrant jelly

- Preheat the oven to 180°C/350°F/Gas mark 4.
- Season the grouse well with salt and pepper. Heat the butter in a flameproof

casserole dish and brown the grouse on all sides. Remove the grouse and reserve.
- Add the vegetables to the casserole dish and cook over a low heat until tender but not browned.
- Return the grouse, add the whisky, light it and allow the flames to die down.
- Add the stock and cook, covered, for 1¼ hours.
- When cooked remove and use poultry shears to cut the grouse in half, place on a serving dish and keep warm.
- Strain the sauce into a small saucepan, boil until it thickens and add the redcurrant jelly. Spoon the sauce over the grouse before serving.

Irish venison stew

SERVES 8

INGREDIENTS:

1.3kg/3lb shoulder of venison (trimmed and cubed)
Plain flour (seasoned), for coating
2 tablespoons olive oil
225g/8oz streaky back bacon (diced)
2 large onions (chopped)
1 large carrot (diced)
1 garlic clove (crushed)
450ml/³/₄pt beef stock

1 sachet bouquet garni
Salt and pepper

For the marinade:
300ml/¹/₂pt red wine
1 medium onion (sliced)
3 tablespoons brandy
3 tablespoons olive oil
Salt and pepper

- Mix together the ingredients for the marinade. Add the venison and marinate for 24 hours. Drain well, pat dry on kitchen paper and toss in the seasoned flour.
- Heat the oil in a frying pan and add the bacon. Cook it slowly so the fat runs, then raise the heat so it crisps on the outside. Transfer to a casserole dish.
- Brown the venison in the bacon fat and add to the bacon. Toss the onions, carrot and garlic in the remaining bacon fat and add to the casserole dish. Add any surplus fat from the pan and strain the marinade into the casserole dish. Stir to dissolve the caramelized juices, bring to the boil and pour over the venison. Add the stock and bouquet garni and bring to the boil. Cover and simmer gently over a medium heat for 2¹/₂ hours.
- Adjust the seasoning to taste and serve hot.

Venison & wild rice casserole

SERVES 5

INGREDIENTS:

500ml/18fl oz water
375ml/13fl oz cream of
mushroom soup
75g/3oz button mushrooms
250g/9oz wild rice

6 lean venison chops
Salt and pepper
1 medium onion (thinly sliced)
3 rashers lean back bacon

- Preheat the oven to 180°C/350°F/Gas mark 4.
- Put the water, soup and mushrooms into a large casserole dish.
- Rinse the rice in cold water a few times, drain and add to the casserole dish. Spread the venison chops out in the sauce, season to taste, and arrange the onions on top, followed by the bacon.
- Cover and bake in the oven for about 1 to 1½ hours, or until the meat and rice are soft and cooked. Serve hot.

Grouse stew

SERVES 4

INGREDIENTS:

1 grouse (cut into bite-sized pieces)
Plain flour for dusting
Salt and pepper
25g/1oz butter
1.8 litres/3pt boiling water
1 teaspoon thyme

200g/7oz sweetcorn
2 potatoes (cubed)
¼ teaspoon cayenne pepper
3 medium onions (sliced)
400g/14oz canned chopped tomatoes

- Roll the grouse pieces in the flour, salt and pepper. Melt the butter in a large frying pan and brown the grouse on all sides.
- Place the grouse and all the other ingredients except the tomatoes in a large casserole dish. Add the boiling water, then cover and simmer for 1½ to 2 hours. Add the tomatoes and continue to simmer for a further 1 hour.

Rabbit casserole with white wine & mushrooms

SERVES 4

INGREDIENTS:

1 rabbit (cut into 10 pieces)
Plain flour (seasoned), for dusting
2 tablespoons vegetable oil
25g/1oz butter
225g/8oz button mushrooms
(quartered)
16 pickling onions (topped and tailed)
125ml/4fl oz dry white wine

600ml/1pt chicken stock
1 bay leaf
2 tablespoons chopped fresh parsley
Salt and pepper
50g/2oz beurre manié
150ml/¼pt crème fraîche
Squeeze of lemon juice

- Toss the rabbit in the seasoned flour.
- Heat half the oil with half the butter in a wide frying pan and brown the rabbit in batches. Transfer with a slotted spoon to a large casserole dish.
- Add a little more oil and butter to the pan and sauté the mushrooms over a high heat until browned, then transfer to the casserole dish.
- Add the remaining oil and butter and brown the onions, then add to the casserole dish.
- Pour the wine into the frying pan and bring to the boil, scraping in the residues from frying. Boil until reduced by half. Pour over the rabbit in the casserole dish, then add the stock, bay leaf, half the parsley and salt and pepper. Bring to the boil, part-cover and simmer for 45 minutes, or until the rabbit is tender. Remove the rabbit, mushrooms and onions with a slotted spoon and place in a serving dish.
- Pour the juices into a wide frying pan and boil rapidly until reduced by half. Reduce the heat to a simmer and add the beurre manié. Cook for a further 3 to 4 minutes without boiling. Stir in the crème fraîche and lemon juice. Taste and adjust the seasoning. Pour over the rabbit and serve, scattered with the remaining parsley.

Rabbit casserole

SERVES 4

INGREDIENTS:

25g/1oz butter
900g/2lb rabbit pieces
200g/7oz tomatoes
1 tablespoon cornflour
100g/4oz carrot (coarsely grated)
1 tablespoon finely grated orange zest

1 teaspoon dried oregano
50ml/2fl oz brandy
25ml/1fl oz white wine vinegar
375ml/13fl oz warm water
2 bay leaves

- Preheat the oven to 180°C/350°F/Gas mark 4.
- Melt the butter in a large frying pan and brown the rabbit pieces well, turning frequently, then transfer the pieces to a large casserole dish.
- Place the tomatoes in boiling water and leave for 2 minutes. Remove the skins and chop into small cubes, then add to the casserole dish.
- Combine the cornflour, carrot, orange zest and oregano in a small bowl. Pour in the brandy, vinegar and water and stir well. Pour over the contents of the casserole dish and add the bay leaves.
- Cover and bake for 1½ hours or until the rabbit is tender. Serve hot.

Pheasant & wild rice casserole

SERVES 6

INGREDIENTS:

400g/14oz pheasant (diced)
250g/9oz wild rice
225g/8oz mushrooms (sliced)
75g/3oz butter
1 onion (chopped)
50g/2oz plain flour

300ml/½pt chicken stock
300ml/½pt milk
2 tablespoons chopped fresh parsley
Salt and pepper
50g/2oz slivered almonds (toasted)

- Preheat the oven to 180°C/350°F/Gas mark 4.
- Poach the pheasant in simmering water for 1 hour or until tender.
- Prepare the rice according to the packet directions.

- Sauté the mushrooms in half the butter, then remove from the pan and reserve. Sauté the onion in the remaining butter until tender. Remove from the heat, stir in the flour until smooth. Gradually stir the stock into the flour mixture, add the milk and cook stirring constantly until thick.
- Add the rice, mushrooms, pheasant, parsley and salt and pepper. Place in large casserole dish and sprinkle with the almonds.

Venison, chestnut & fruit stew

SERVES 6

INGREDIENTS:

100g/4oz dried apricots
100g/4oz pitted prunes
50ml/2fl oz brandy
225g/8oz fresh chestnuts
½ tablespoon coriander seeds
1 tablespoon plain flour
1 onion (sliced)

1.3kg/3lb venison (cut into 5cm/2in squares)
2 tablespoons sunflower oil
1 cinnamon stick
2 strips dried orange zest
900ml/1½pt water
Salt and pepper

- Put the apricots and prunes to soak in the brandy and leave for 1 hour, turning occasionally.
- Preheat the oven to 150°C/300°F/Gas mark 2.
- Score a cross in the curved side of each chestnut then place in a pan, cover with water and bring to the boil. Simmer for 1 minute and turn off the heat. Strip each chestnut of the tough outer skin and papery inner skin and set aside.
- Dry-fry the coriander seeds in a heavy-based frying pan over a high heat, until they start to pop. Tip into a bowl and when cool, crush with a pestle. Mix with the flour.
- Cook the onion in a frying pan, in the oil, until lightly browned and then scoop into a flameproof casserole dish. Raise the heat and brown the venison in batches, then transfer to the casserole dish. Sprinkle the flour mixture over the meat, then add the cinnamon stick, apricots, prunes, orange zest and salt.
- Tip the excess fat from the frying pan and pour in the water. Bring to the boil, scraping in the residues from frying. Pour over the contents of the casserole dish, cover and immediately transfer to the oven. Cook for 2 hours, then stir in the chestnuts. Cook for a further hour, until the meat is tender and the sauce is reduced and thickened. Adjust the seasoning to taste and serve.

Guinea fowl stew

SERVES 4

INGREDIENTS:

50ml/2fl oz groundnut oil
900g/2lb guinea fowl (cut into bite-sized pieces)
1 teaspoon dried thyme
1 teaspoon curry powder
2 large onions (sliced)

225g/8oz red chillies (deseeded and chopped)
900g/2lb tomatoes
225g/8oz tomato purée
2 garlic clove
2 onions (sliced)

- In a large frying pan, heat half the oil and brown the guinea fowl pieces, in batches if necessary, with the thyme and the curry powder. Remove to a plate and keep warm.
- Add the remaining oil to the pan and fry the onions, chillies and tomatoes for 20 minutes, until fairly dry. Add the tomato purée, stir thoroughly and add the guinea fowl pieces.
- Cook and simmer gently for another 10 minutes, stirring frequently.

Shooting stew with dumplings

SERVES 10

INGREDIENTS:

2 oven-ready pheasants
2 litres/3½pt chicken stock
450g/1lb smoked fat bacon (cut into lardons)
4 tablespoons sunflower oil
2.7kg/6lb shin of beef (cut into 225g/8oz portions)
Plain flour for dusting
1.3kg/3lb onions (sliced)
450g/1lb carrots (sliced)
4 celery sticks (sliced)
4 garlic cloves (chopped)

2 tablespoons plain flour
2 bay leaves
4 tablespoons Worcestershire sauce
600ml/1pt red wine
Salt and pepper

For the dumplings:
450g/1lb self-raising flour
175g/6oz butter (diced)
2 eggs
25g/1oz flat-leaf parsley

- Place the pheasants and chicken stock in a large saucepan and simmer for 45 minutes. Allow the pheasant to cool in the stock and then strip off the meat and reserve, returning the carcass to the stock and continue to simmer for 1 hour. Strain and reserve the stock.
- Fry the bacon gently until the fat runs and it starts to brown. Transfer with a slotted spoon into a large casserole dish.
- Add half the oil to the pan and turn up the heat. Dust the beef in the flour and sear in batches, then add to the casserole dish.
- Add the remaining oil to the pan and sweat the onions until soft but not brown, then scatter over the meat. Fry the carrot slowly until caramelized. Add the celery, garlic and the flour. Stir and fry for 1 to 2 minutes, then add to the casserole dish with the bay leaves and Worcestershire sauce.
- Pour over the red wine and top up with the reserved stock to cover. Bring to the boil, skim the surface, lower the heat and season. Simmer, uncovered, for 2 hours.
- To make the dumplings, put the flour in a blender or food processor with the butter and a pinch of salt and pepper. Process quickly so the mixture resembles breadcrumbs. Add the eggs and parsley and process again, adding a little water until the mixture starts to hold as a coherent mass. Remove and transfer to a lightly floured surface.
- Divide into 24 and roll into small balls. Poach in simmering salted water for 20 minutes. Add to the stew and heat through. Serve immediately.

Pheasant casserole

SERVES 4

INGREDIENTS:

2 tablespoons beef dripping
2 pheasants (jointed, breast and
legs only)
1 onion (chopped)

1 carrot (chopped)
1 celery stalk (chopped)
Salt and pepper
350ml/12fl oz red wine

- Preheat the oven to 180°C/350°F/Gas mark 4.
- Heat the dripping in a frying pan and brown the pheasant joints. Remove from the pan and place in a casserole dish. Place the vegetables in the frying pan and cook for 2 minutes, then add the red wine and bring to the boil.
- Pour the mixture over the pheasant joints, season and cover the casserole dish.
- Cook in the oven for 1 to 1½ hours until tender.

Rabbit hotpot

SERVES 4

INGREDIENTS:

900g/2lb rabbit (jointed)
2 medium onions (sliced)
2 tablespoons wholegrain mustard
12 pitted prunes
4 bay leaves
450ml/³/₄pt dry cider
450ml/³/₄pt chicken stock

4 tablespoons plain flour (seasoned),
plus extra for dusting
2 tablespoons vegetable oil
15g/¹/₂oz butter
450g/1lb parsnips (cut into chunks)
400g/14oz canned kidney beans
(drained)

- Place the rabbit joints, onions, mustard, prunes and bay leaves into a bowl, cover with the cider and stock. Mix, cover tightly, and place in the refrigerator overnight.
- Preheat the oven to 180°C/350°F/Gas mark 4.
- Remove the rabbit joints and prunes from the marinade and reserve. Pat the rabbit dry with kitchen paper and coat in seasoned flour.
- Heat the oil and butter in a large flameproof casserole dish, add the joints and fry until browned. Sprinkle with any remaining flour. Add the marinade and parsnips and bring to the boil.
- Cover and transfer to the oven. Bake for 40 minutes. Add the prunes and kidney beans and bake for 20 to 30 minutes or until tender.

Spring rabbit casserole with bacon

SERVES 4

INGREDIENTS:

1 tablespoon sunflower oil
450g/1lb boneless rabbit
4 rashers rindless streaky back bacon
(chopped)
2 leeks (sliced)
4 spring onions (sliced)
3 celery sticks (chopped)

4 small carrots (sliced)
300ml/¹/₂pt vegetable stock
2 teaspoons Dijon mustard
1 teaspoon grated lemon zest
50ml/2fl oz crème fraîche
Salt and pepper

- Preheat the oven to 190°C/375°F/Gas mark 5.
- Heat the oil in a large casserole dish and fry the rabbit pieces until browned all over. Add the bacon and vegetables and toss over the heat for 1 minute. Add the stock, mustard, lemon zest and crème fraîche and seasoning to taste, then bring to the boil.
- Cover and cook for 35 to 40 minutes, or until the rabbit is tender. Serve hot.

Spanish partridge & chocolate stew

SERVES 4

INGREDIENTS:

2 partridges (halved)
2 tablespoons olive oil
1 large onion (chopped)
8 garlic cloves
2 cloves

1 bay leaf
300ml/½pt dry white wine
1 tablespoon sherry vinegar
Salt and pepper
25g/1oz plain chocolate (grated)

- Brown the partridges in the oil in a frying pan over a high heat and transfer to a casserole dish. Fry the onion in the same oil, then transfer to the casserole dish.
- Add all the remaining ingredients to the casserole dish except the chocolate and bring to a gentle simmer, cover tightly and continue simmering for 45 to 50 minutes, until the partridges are tender. Transfer the meat to a serving dish.
- Stir the chocolate into the remaining liquid in the pan and simmer for a further 3 minutes. Stir and adjust the seasoning. Pour over the partridges and serve immediately.

Beef & pigeon stew

SERVES 4

INGREDIENTS:

450g/1lb steak and kidney (cut into 2.5cm/1in cubes)
Plain flour for dusting
Salt and pepper
2 pigeons (prepared, drawn and halved)
4 rashers lean back bacon

100g/4oz onion (finely sliced)
15g/¹/₂oz butter
300ml/¹/₂pt stout
2 tablespoons cider vinegar
1 bay leaf
1 tablespoon chopped fresh parsley
1 tablespoon chopped fresh thyme

- Preheat the oven to 160°C/325°F/Gas mark 3.
- Toss the steak and kidney in seasoned flour until each cube is coated. Wrap each pigeon half in a bacon rasher.
- Fry the onions lightly in the butter, add the meat and let it brown, stirring. Stir in the stout and vinegar and simmer for 15 minutes.
- Arrange half of the meat and onion mixture in a large casserole dish, lay the pigeon halves on top and cover with the rest of the meat and onion, pour the juices over. Add the herbs and a sprinkling of salt and pepper.
- Cover well and cook in the oven for about 3 hours.

Rabbit stew

SERVES 4

INGREDIENTS:

1.8kg/4lb rabbit (jointed)
2 tablespoons plain flour (seasoned)
50g/2oz butter
300ml/¹/₂pt chicken stock
150ml/¹/₄pt white wine
2 teaspoon tomato purée

1 sachet bouquet garni
1 garlic clove (crushed)
Salt and pepper
2 tablespoons double cream
2 teaspoons cornflour
1 tablespoon chopped fresh parsley

- Coat the rabbit joints in the seasoned flour and fry in the butter in a flameproof casserole dish, browning on all sides.
- Add the stock, wine and tomato purée, then bring to the boil. Add the bouquet garni, garlic and season to taste. Reduce the heat and cook gently for 1¹/₂ to 2 hours or until the rabbit is tender. Transfer the rabbit to a serving dish, keep

warm. Transfer the sauce to a saucepan, removing the bouquet garni.
- Mix the cream and cornflour together, and stir into the sauce until thickened.
- Pour sauce over rabbit and garnish with parsley.

Hare stew

SERVES 6

INGREDIENTS:

225g/8oz smoked back bacon (cut into strips)
125ml/4fl oz olive oil
225g/8oz onions (sliced)
2 garlic cloves (chopped)
Salt and pepper
Plain flour, for dusting
1.8kg/4lb hare (cut into 12 pieces)

600ml/1pt red wine
600ml/1pt chicken stock
1 sachet bouquet garni
24 pickling onions
25g/1oz butter
225g/8oz button mushrooms
2 tablespoons chopped fresh parsley

- Fry the bacon slowly in 2 tablespoons oil until almost crisp, then transfer to a casserole dish with a slotted spoon. Fry the onions in this fat until soft and translucent. Add the garlic and cook for a further 2 minutes, then add the onions and garlic to the casserole dish.
- Season and flour the hare. Add 2 tablespoons oil to the pan, increase the heat to medium and brown the hare pieces on all sides. Transfer to the casserole dish.
- Raise the heat under the frying pan, add the wine and deglaze, scraping up any bits clinging to the pan. Pour the wine mixture over the hare and add the stock, bouquet garni and salt and pepper. Bring to the boil, skim the surface, then lower the heat, cover and simmer for about 1 hour.
- About 15 minutes before the end of the cooking time, fry the pickling onions in the butter and remaining oil. Season lightly with salt and pepper and sauté for 5 to 10 minutes until golden brown. Transfer to a dish and keep warm while you fry the button mushrooms. Add these to the onions, and stir both into the casserole dish.
- Scatter the parsley over and serve hot.

Partridge stew

SERVES 4

INGREDIENTS:

225g/8oz streaky back bacon (cut into 2.5cm/1in squares)
1 tablespoon vegetable oil
4 partridges
4 onions (quartered)
12 black peppercorns
3 bay leaves

2 tablespoons white wine vinegar
300ml/½pt chicken stock
150ml/¼pt port
Salt and pepper
15g/½oz butter
2 teaspoons plain flour

- Preheat the oven to 170°C/325°F/Gas mark 3.
- Place the bacon in a large casserole dish with the oil and heat gently for a few minutes.
- Increase the heat, add the partridges and brown them on all sides. Remove them from them with a slotted spoon.
- Add the onions and allow to soften, but do not colour. Then add the peppercorns, bay leaves, vinegar, stock and port.
- Season the partridges and return to the dish. Bake, covered, for 1½ hours.
- Remove the partridges and onions. Skim the fat from the liquid, then strain.
- Mix the butter with the flour into a paste. Bring the liquid to the boil. Reduce to a simmer and gradually add in the flour paste a little at a time, stirring constantly. Simmer for 3 to 4 minutes until the sauce has thickened. Pour over the partridges and onions to serve.

Pot roast of venison

SERVES 4

INGREDIENTS:

1.8kg/4lb boned joint of venison
75ml/3fl oz vegetable oil
4 cloves
8 black peppercorns (lightly crushed)
250ml/9fl oz red wine
100g/4oz streaky back bacon (chopped)
2 onions (finely chopped)

2 carrots (chopped)
150g/5oz mushrooms (sliced)
1 tablespoon plain flour
250ml/9fl oz chicken stock
2 tablespoons redcurrant jelly
Salt and pepper

- Put the venison in a bowl, add half the oil, the spices and wine, cover and leave in a cool place for 24 hours, turning the meat occasionally.
- Preheat the oven to 160°C/325°F/Gas mark 3. Remove the venison from the bowl and pat dry. Reserve the marinade. Heat the remaining oil in a shallow pan, then brown the venison evenly. Transfer to a plate.
- Stir the bacon, onions, carrot and mushrooms into the pan and cook for about 5 minutes.
- Stir in the flour and cook for 2 minutes, then remove from the heat and   stir in the marinade, stock, redcurrant jelly and seasoning. Return to the heat, bring to t the boil, stirring, then simmer for 2 to 3 minutes.
- Transfer the venison and sauce to a casserole dish, cover and cook in the oven, turning the joint occasionally, for about 3 hours, until tender.

Czech hare & plum stew

SERVES 4-6

INGREDIENTS:

1 medium onion (grated)
3 rashers streaky back bacon (diced)
50g/2oz butter
1 hare (cut into 12 pieces)
5 black peppercorns (crushed)
3 allspice berries (crushed)
1 bay leaf

2 strips lemon zest
Salt and pepper
300ml/½pt water
450g/1lb damson plums (pitted and quartered)
2 tablespoons redcurrant jelly
1 tablespoon tomato purée

- Cook the onion and bacon gently in the butter in a flameproof casserole dish without browning. Add the hare, spices, bay leaf, lemon zest, salt and water. Cover and simmer very gently for about 1½ hours, until the hare is tender, turning occasionally.
- Meanwhile, place the plums in a pan with just enough water to prevent them from burning. Simmer gently until the fruit is soft, then pass through a sieve.
- Add this purée to the hare, together with the redcurrant jelly and tomato purée.
- Stir well, then simmer for a final 15 minutes. Lift the meat out of the pot and keep hot. Strain the sauce, taste and adjust the seasoning to taste, then pour over the hare and serve.

Guinea fowl & red wine casserole

SERVES 4

INGREDIENTS:

50g/2oz butter
1 guinea fowl (cut into 6 pieces)
100g/4oz streaky back bacon (chopped)
2 onions (chopped)
50g/2oz plain flour
600ml/1pt red wine

300ml/½pt chicken stock
1 teaspoon dried tarragon
100g/4oz button mushrooms (sliced)
250g/9oz pumpkin (cubed)
Salt and pepper

- Heat the butter in a large saucepan. Add the guinea fowl pieces and bacon and fry over a high heat to brown. Add the onions and cook for a further 1 minute.
- Add the flour and cook, stirring, for 1 minute. Stir in the wine and stock gradually. Add the tarragon, cover and allow to simmer for 30 minutes.
- Add the mushrooms, pumpkin and seasoning, cover and cook for a further 30 minutes, until the guinea fowl is tender.

Hare casserole

SERVES 6

INGREDIENTS:

1 hare (jointed)
1 onion (sliced)
2 carrots (sliced)
2 tablespoons olive oil
25g/1oz butter
4 tablespoons plain flour, plus extra
for dusting
1 sprig rosemary
1 sprig thyme
1 bay leaf
6 juniper berries (crushed)
450ml/¾pt chicken stock

Salt and pepper
2 tablespoons tomato ketchup
1 tablespoon redcurrant jelly

For the marinade:
300ml/½pt red wine
1 carrot (sliced)
1 onion (sliced)
2 bay leaves
1 sprig thyme
4 juniper berries (lightly crushed)

- Mix together the marinade ingredients and pour over the hare. Leave to marinate for at least 12 hours, turning occasionally. Remove from the marinade and dry thoroughly. Strain the marinade and reserve.
- Preheat the oven to 150°C/300°F/Gas mark 2.
- Fry the onion and carrots in half the oil and butter until brown and tender. Transfer to a casserole dish.
- Dust the hare in a little flour and fry briskly until brown. Add to the casserole dish with the herbs and juniper berries. Sprinkle over the flour.
- Pour the excess fat from the pan and add the marinade. Bring to the boil, scraping in all the frying residues, then pour over the hare. Bring the stock to the boil in the frying pan and add that too, then season and stir in the ketchup. Cover and transfer to the oven and cook gently for 3 to 4 hours, until the meat is very tender. Stir in the redcurrant jelly, then taste and adjust the seasoning before serving.

Quail stew

SERVES 4

INGREDIENTS:

8 medium quails
1 tablespoon ground cumin
1 tablespoon vegetable oil
15g/½oz butter
2 large onions (finely chopped)

1 tablespoon crushed garlic
1 teaspoon tomato purée
Salt and pepper
1 teaspoon allspice
4 cardamom pods

- Wash the quails inside out thoroughly, removing all fat from the tops and bottoms of quails. Cut each quail in two, with bottoms and chests separated. Season with cumin.
- In a large cooking pan, heat the oil and butter. Add the onions and garlic and stir until the onions begin to brown. Add the quails, turning to brown all over. Then, add the tomato purée, cover the pan and lower the heat. Add the salt and pepper, allspice, cardamom and enough boiling water just to keep a thick sauce. Leave to cook for 30 minutes until well done.
- Remove the cardamom and serve.

Fish & seafood

Although a less obvious choice for stews and casseroles, fish and seafood do, however, offer a delicious alternative to meat or poultry. Influences for the dishes in this section are from around the world, and all types of seafood can be found, including monkfish, prawns, clams and oysters to name but a few. Sea bass stew, Potato, onion & salt cod casserole and Alaska halibut chowder are just a few examples to inspire you.

Squid stew

SERVES 4

INGREDIENTS:

700g/1½lb prepared squid (sliced into rings)
1 tablespoon olive oil
1 onion (chopped)
3 garlic cloves (finely chopped)
1 teaspoon fresh thyme leaves

400g/14oz canned chopped tomatoes
150ml/¼pt red wine
300ml/½pt water
1 tablespoon chopped fresh parsley
Salt and pepper

- Wash the squid well under running water and drain on kitchen paper.
- Heat the oil in a large casserole dish over a medium heat. Add the squid and cook, stirring occasionally, until lightly browned.
- Reduce the heat and add the onion, garlic and thyme. Cook for a further 5 minutes until softened.
- Stir in the tomatoes, red wine and water. Bring to the boil and simmer gently for 2 hours. Stir in the parsley and season to taste. Serve immediately.

Prawn casserole

SERVES 4

INGREDIENTS:

Vegetable oil for greasing
700ml/1pt 4fl oz water
200g/7oz long-grain rice
Salt and pepper
1 egg white
50g/2oz fresh parsley (chopped)
25g/1oz butter
1 garlic clove (minced)
250g/9oz mushrooms (sliced)

100g/4oz celery (sliced)
150g/5oz onion (chopped)
½ teaspoon dried dill weed
450g/1lb raw unpeeled prawns
25g/1oz plain flour
300ml/½pt milk
200g/7oz Cheddar cheese (grated)
2 teaspoons grated lemon zest
150g/5oz fresh breadcrumbs

- Preheat the oven to 160°C/325°F/Gas mark 3. Lightly oil a 20cm/8in baking tin.
- In a saucepan, bring 300ml/½pt water to the boil. Stir in the rice and a pinch of salt, cover and simmer over a low heat for 15 to 20 minutes or until tender. Remove from the heat and stir in the egg white and 1 tablespoon parsley. Press the mixture into the bottom of the prepared baking tin and set aside.

- In a frying pan, melt 15g/½oz butter over a medium-high heat and cook the garlic, mushrooms and celery, stirring, for about 5 minutes. Stir in the onions, dill and seasoning, then cook over a high heat for 2 minutes. Transfer the vegetables to large bowl.
- Pour the remaining water into the frying pan and bring to a simmer. Cook the prawns for about 1 minute or just until pink. Reserving 225ml/8fl oz of the cooking liquid, drain and rinse the prawns under cold running water. Shell and devein the prawns, then arrange over the rice.
- In a heavy saucepan, melt the remaining butter over a medium heat and stir in the flour. Cook, stirring, for about 2 minutes, without browning, then gradually whisk in the reserved liquid and milk. Cook, stirring, for about 20 minutes or until thickened.
- Remove from the heat and stir in half the cheese and the lemon zest and cook until the cheese is melted. Stir into the vegetable mixture along with the remaining parsley, then pour over the prawns in the baking tin.
- In a small bowl, stir together the remaining cheese and breadcrumbs, then sprinkle evenly over the casserole.
- Bake in the oven for 40 to 50 minutes or until heated through. Leave to stand for 15 minutes before serving.

Mussel stew

SERVES 4

INGREDIENTS:

350ml/12fl oz dry white wine
2 bay leaves
1 tablespoon chopped fresh thyme
Pinch of powdered saffron
Pinch of cayenne pepper
900g/2lb mussels (scrubbed and debearded)
25g/1oz butter
200g/7oz shallots (chopped)

1 tablespoon chopped garlic
2 tablespoons plain flour
75ml/3fl oz whipping cream
50g/2oz fresh parsley (chopped)
3 tablespoons white grape juice
1½ teaspoon brandy
Salt and pepper

- Combine the wine, bay leaves, thyme, saffron and cayenne pepper in a large casserole dish over a high heat. Boil for 3 minutes, then add the mussels. Cover and cook for about 4 minutes until the mussels open.
- Remove from the heat and, using a slotted spoon, transfer the mussels to a serving bowl, discarding any that do not open. Cover and keep warm. Reserve the cooking liquid.
- Melt the butter in a frying pan over a medium heat. Add the shallots and garlic

→

← and sauté for 3 minutes. Add the flour and stir for 1 minute. Whisk in the reserved cooking liquid. Boil until reduced to 175ml/6fl oz, about 7 minutes.

- Whisk in the cream and parsley, then reduce the heat to medium and simmer for about 3 minutes until the liquid is reduced to 225ml/8fl oz. Mix in the grape juice and brandy and season with salt and pepper. Pour the sauce over the mussels and serve.

Salmon & potato casserole

SERVES 4-6

INGREDIENTS:

Vegetable oil for greasing
250g/9oz smoked salmon (flaked)
900g/2lb medium white potatoes
(thinly sliced)
1 medium onion (chopped)

25g/1oz butter
2 tablespoons chopped fresh parsley
¼ teaspoon pepper
75ml/3fl oz water

- Preheat the oven to 180°C/350°F/Gas mark 4. Grease a large casserole with oil.
- Layer half the salmon, potato, onion, butter, parsley and pepper in the casserole dish. Repeat the layers.
- Pour the water over the layers in the casserole dish, then cover. Bake for about 1¼ hours until the potatoes are tender. Serve hot.

Potato, onion & salt cod casserole

SERVES 4-6

INGREDIENTS:

450g/1lb dried salt cod
1.8 litres/3pt boiling water
900g/2lb new potatoes
3 tablespoons olive oil

1 large onion (thinly sliced)
3 garlic cloves (finely chopped)
50g/2oz fresh parsley (chopped)
Salt and pepper

- Soak the cod in water overnight in the refrigerator. Drain and rinse well. Place the cod in a large saucepan and add the boiling water. Simmer over a moderate heat for 10 to 15 minutes, until the cod flakes easily. Drain and rinse well, then flake into small pieces, removing any bones.

- Preheat the oven to 180°C/350°F/Gas mark 4.
- Boil the potatoes until tender but firm, then drain and allow to cool. Peel and slice the potatoes.
- Heat 2 tablespoons olive oil in a large, heavy frying pan over a moderate heat.
- Add the onion and garlic and cook for 5 minutes, stirring frequently, until tender but not brown. Remove the onions and garlic from the pan and set aside.
- Add the potatoes to the pan, along with the remaining oil, and cook for 5 minutes, stirring frequently, until golden brown.
- Layer half the potatoes in a large casserole dish. Sprinkle with parsley, salt and pepper, add a third of the onion mixture and half the cod. Repeat, ending with a layer of the onion mixture. Bake the oven for 30 to 40 minutes, until hot and lightly browned.

Corn & scallop casserole

SERVES 4

INGREDIENTS:

4 rashers smoked streaky bacon (chopped)
2 large potatoes (peeled and diced)
1 medium red onion (diced)
¼ teaspoon dried thyme
Salt and pepper

1 red pepper (diced)
275g/10oz frozen sweetcorn (thawed)
450g/1lb scallops
50ml/2fl oz chicken stock
2 tablespoons double cream

- Place the bacon in a microwave-safe dish. Microwave on high for 3 to 4 minutes or until crisp. Using a slotted spoon, transfer the bacon to drain on kitchen paper and set aside.
- Add the potatoes, onion, thyme, salt and pepper to the bacon fat in the dish and stir to coat. Cover the dish with clingfilm, leaving one corner open to vent.
- Microwave on high for 8 to 9 minutes, until the potatoes are tender, stirring twice during cooking.
- Stir the pepper, sweetcorn, scallops, stock and cream into the potato mixture.
- Microwave, covered and vented, until the scallops are just cooked through, 2 to 3 minutes.
- Sprinkle the bacon over the casserole and serve hot.

Hotpot with crab wontons

SERVES 6

INGREDIENTS:

For the hotpot:
2 Dungeness crabs, about 700g/1½lb each
1 tablespoon groundnut oil
5cm/2in piece fresh root ginger (peeled and flattened)
2 shallots (halved)
1 red chilli (split)
2 tablespoons miso
1.2 litres/2pt water
275g/10oz shiitake mushrooms
Juice of 1 lime

For the crab wontons:
1 tablespoon groundnut oil
5cm/in piece fresh root ginger (peeled and grated)
2 shallots (finely chopped)
½ carrot (finely chopped)
450g/1lb Dungeness crabmeat
1 spring onion (finely chopped)
2 tablespoons chopped coriander
2 tablespoons mayonnaise
Juice of ½ lemon
Salt and pepper
350g/12oz square wonton wrappers
1 egg white
Cornflour for dusting

- To make the hotpot, remove the claws from the crabs and quarter the bodies. In a large casserole dish, add the oil, ginger, shallots and chilli and stir for 2 minutes over a medium heat until fragrant. Then add the crabs and miso. Add the water and simmer for 30 minutes.
- To make the wontons, heat a skillet over a medium heat and coat with the peanut oil. Add the ginger, shallot and carrot and sauté for 2 minutes to soften.
- Put the crabmeat in a mixing bowl and scrape in the ginger mixture. Fold in the spring onion, coriander, mayonnaise and lemon juice and season with salt and pepper.
- Lay a wonton wrapper on a flat surface and brush with the egg white. Drop 1 tablespoon of the crab filling onto the centre of the wrapper. Fold the wonton in half, corner to corner, to form a triangle, then press the seam together to seal.
- Brush the 2 side points with beaten egg white. Lay your index finger in the centre so you have something to press up against, then fold the 2 sides into the centre and press the dough against your finger with your thumb to form a tight seal.
- Lightly dust the filled wontons with cornflour to keep them from sticking together and place them on a baking tray.
- When the wontons are all filled and folded, strain the hotpot broth to remove the solids and return it to the casserole dish. Bring the hotpot to a simmer. Toss in the mushrooms and wontons and simmer for 15 minutes until the wontons are cooked. Add the lime juice and serve.

Spanish fish stew

SERVES 6

INGREDIENTS:

75ml/3fl oz olive oil
2 large onions (finely chopped)
2 tomatoes (peeled and diced)
2 slices white bread (crusts removed)
4 almonds (toasted)
2 garlic cloves (roughly chopped)
350g/12oz cooked lobster
200g/7oz monkfish fillet
200g/7oz cod fillet (skinned)
Salt and pepper

1 tablespoon plain flour
200g/7oz prepared squid (cut into rings)
6 large raw prawns
18 mussels (scrubbed, beards removed)
8 large live clams (scrubbed)
1 tablespoon chopped fresh parsley
125ml/4fl oz brandy
Salt and pepper
Lemon wedges, to garnish

- Heat 3 tablespoons oil in a frying pan over a low heat. Add the onions and cook for 10 to 15 minutes until lightly golden. Add the tomatoes and cook until they are melted down.
- Heat 1 tablespoon oil in a separate frying pan over a medium heat. Add the bread slices and fry until crisp. Break into rough pieces and put in a blender or food processor with the almonds and garlic cloves, then process to a fine paste.
- Split the lobster lengthways. Remove and discard the intestinal vein, stomach sac and gills. Crack the claws and remove the meat. Remove the flesh from the tail and chop into chunks.
- Season the monkfish, cod and lobster with salt and pepper and dust with a little flour.
- Heat the remaining oil in a frying pan and add the monkfish, cod, lobster, squid and prawns and fry until browned, then arrange in a large casserole dish.
- Add the mussels, clams and parsley to the casserole dish. Place over a low heat, then add the brandy and ignite. When the flames have died down, add the tomato mixture and just enough water to cover. Bring to the boil and simmer for 3 to 4 minutes until the mussels and clams have opened. Discard any that remain closed. Stir in the bread paste and season to taste. Simmer for a further 5 minutes until all the fish is tender. Serve hot, garnished with lemon wedges.

Crab & seafood one-pot

SERVES 4

INGREDIENTS:

225g/8oz crabmeat (shredded)
225g/8oz cooked prawns (chopped)
125ml/4fl oz sour cream
150g/5oz green chillies (sliced)
1 teaspoon chilli powder
½ teaspoon ground cumin

¼ teaspoon salt
225g/8oz tortilla chips (crushed)
225ml/8fl oz salsa
200g/7oz Cheddar cheese (grated)
100g/4oz pitted black olives (halved)
2 spring onions (sliced)

- Preheat the oven to 180°C/350°F/Gas mark 4.
- In large bowl, mix together the crabmeat, prawns, sour cream, chillies, chilli powder, cumin and salt.
- Line the bottom of a large baking dish with tortilla chips. Spoon the crab mixture over the chips and top with salsa, cheese, olives and spring onions. Bake in the oven for 16 minutes or until heated through and the cheese is melted.

Apple tuna pasta casserole

SERVES 8

INGREDIENTS:

300g/11oz macaroni
100g/4oz butter (melted)
50g/2oz plain flour
700ml/1¼pt milk

200g/7oz Cheddar cheese
225g/8oz canned tuna (drained)
200g/7oz tart apples (cored and diced)
150g/5oz fresh breadcrumbs

- Preheat the oven to 180°C/350°F/Gas mark 4.
- Cook the macaroni according to package directions, then drain.
- In a saucepan, mix together 75g/3oz butter with the flour. Add the milk and cook quickly, stirring constantly, until the mixture thickens and bubbles.
- Add the cheese and stir until it is melted. Stir in the tuna, apples and macaroni, then transfer to a casserole dish.
- Combine the remaining butter and breadcrumbs. Sprinkle on top of the casserole.
- Bake in the oven for 30 minutes, or until the apples are tender.

Prawn stew

SERVES 4

INGREDIENTS:

2 tablespoons olive oil
1 large onion (finely chopped)
2 rashers lean bacon (finely chopped)
2 garlic cloves (chopped)
1 red pepper (finely chopped)
850ml/1½pt vegetable stock
1 bay leaf
Pinch of ground allspice
50g/2oz long-grain rice

1 tablespoon white wine vinegar
Salt and pepper
150g/5oz okra (trimmed and thinly sliced)
100g/4oz peeled prawns
1 tablespoon anchovy essence
2 teaspoons tomato purée
2 tablespoons chopped fresh parsley

- Heat the oil in a large saucepan and gently fry the onion, bacon and garlic for 5 minutes, until soft. Add the pepper to the pan and continue to fry gently for a further 2 minutes.
- Add the stock, bay leaf, allspice, rice, vinegar and seasoning and bring to the boil. Cover and simmer gently for about 20 minutes, stirring occasionally, until the rice is just tender.
- Add the okra, prawns, anchovy essence and tomato purée. Cover and simmer gently for about 15 minutes until the okra is tender and the mixture slightly thickened.
- Discard the bay leaf from the stew and adjust the seasoning. Stir in the parsley and serve immediately.

Oyster & cauliflower stew

SERVES 4

INGREDIENTS:

25g/1oz butter
600ml/1pt canned shucked oysters with liquid
100g/4oz cauliflower florets (half-cooked)

1 tablespoon cornflour
400ml/14fl oz milk
¼ teaspoon salt
¼ teaspoon black pepper
¼ teaspoon onion powder

- In a large microwave-safe baking dish place place the butter and heat in the microwave, covered with kitchen paper, on high for 45 seconds or until melted.

→

←

- Drain the oysters, reserving the liquid. Add the oysters to the butter and cook on high for 1 minute. With a slotted spoon, remove the oysters to a container or pot with the cauliflower.
- Gradually add the cornflour to the oyster liquid and stir until blended. Add the milk and transfer the liquid to the baking dish. Add salt, pepper and onion powder. Cook on high for 4 to 5 minutes or until slightly thickened, stirring twice. Add the oysters and cauliflower to the dish and cook on high for 2 minutes. Serve hot.

Vietnamese whole fish hotpot

SERVES 4

INGREDIENTS:

1.2 litres/2pt fish stock
50ml/2fl oz tamarind water
25g/1oz granulated sugar
3 red chillies (deseeded and bruised)
3 tablespoons fish sauce
1 tomato (cut into wedges)
175g/6oz canned pineapple cubes

50g/2oz fresh root ginger (peeled and chopped)
900g/2lb sea bass fillets (cut into chunks)
1 packet rice noodles (boiled for 1 to 2 minutes, then rinsed), to serve

- Place the stock, tamarind, sugar and chillies in a shallow and wide pot and bring to a simmer. Add the fish sauce, tomato, pineapple and ginger and simmer for 2 to 3 minutes.
- Taste and adjust the seasonings – there should be a nice balance of sweet, sour and spicy. Add the fish and simmer until cooked, about 15 minutes.
- Serve hot with the noodles.

Fried oyster hotpot

SERVES 6

INGREDIENTS:

450g/1lb fresh oysters
2 tablespoons olive oil
50g/2oz plain flour
2 eggs (beaten)
1 onion (finely chopped)
1 medium carrot (finely chopped)
225g/8oz beef rib-eye steak (thinly sliced)

4 tablespoons soy sauce
2 teaspoons sesame oil
2 teaspoons minced garlic
Salt and pepper
400g/14oz vegetable stock
100g/4oz watercress
2 spring onions (sliced)

- Clean the oysters in salted water and drain.
- Heat the oil in a frying pan. Dredge the oysters in the flour and then in the eggs, then place in the pan and fry until cooked.
- Blanch the onion and carrot separately in boiling salted water. Season the beef with 2 tablespoons soy sauce, 1 teaspoon sesame oil, 1 teaspoon garlic, salt and pepper and place in a large frying pan. Layer the vegetables on the beef.
- Combine the stock with the remaining soy sauce, sesame oil, garlic and seasoning, and pour over the vegetables and beef. Cover and bring to a boil.
- Top with the oysters, watercress and onions and heat through.

Alaska halibut chowder

SERVES 6-8

INGREDIENTS:

225g/8oz onions (finely chopped)
175g/6oz green peppers (finely chopped)
150g/5oz celery (finely chopped)
225g/8oz carrots (finely chopped)
75g/3oz butter
900g/2lb halibut (skinned, boned and cut into bite-sized pieces)

450ml/³⁄₄pt chicken stock
³⁄₄ teaspoon salt
¹⁄₂ teaspoon freshly ground white pepper
450ml/³⁄₄pt milk
25g/1oz plain flour
200g/7oz Cheddar cheese (grated)
1 tablespoon chopped fresh parsley

- In a large frying pan, sauté the onions, peppers, celery and carrots in half the butter. Add the halibut, stock, salt and pepper. Simmer, covered, for 5 minutes.
- Add the milk and heat gently. Combine the remaining butter with the flour and

→

←

add to the chowder. Cook and stir until slightly thickened.
- Add the cheese and cook, stirring, over a low heat until the cheese melts. Sprinkle with parsley and serve.

Baked tuna chow mein casserole

SERVE 4

INGREDIENTS:

40g/1¹/₂oz butter
175g/6oz celery (chopped)
75g/3oz onion (chopped)
1 green pepper (chopped)
200g/7oz canned tuna

275g/10oz canned condensed mushroom soup
200g/7oz chow mein noodles (cooked)
Salt and pepper

- In a deep, non-metallic casserole, melt 25g/1oz butter in the microwave for 30 seconds. Add the celery, onion and green pepper to the butter and heat, uncovered, in the microwave for 3 minutes or until the vegetables are tender.
- Combine the remaining ingredients with the vegetables and blend well. Heat in the microwave, uncovered, for 10 minutes or until the sauce bubbles.

Sardine casserole

SERVES 6

INGREDIENTS:

50g/2oz butter
150g/5oz onion (chopped)
175g/6oz green pepper (chopped)
25g/1oz plain flour
Salt and pepper
400ml/14fl oz milk
200g/7oz Cheddar cheese (grated)

275g/10oz canned sardines (drained and chopped into bite-sized pieces)
1 tablespoon chopped fresh parsley
¹/₂ teaspoon dried oregano
200g/7oz canned chopped tomatoes

- Preheat the oven to 180°C/350°F/Gas mark 4.
- Melt the butter in a large frying pan, add the onion and green pepper and cook

until tender. Blend in the flour, ½ teaspoon salt and pepper. Add the milk gradually and cook, stirring constantly, until thick and smooth. Add the cheese and stir until it melts.

- Remove from the heat and stir in the sardines. Sprinkle with parsley, oregano and salt. Transfer the mixture to a large casserole dish and top with the tomatoes. Bake in the oven for 30 to 35 minutes.

Hearty fish stew

SERVES 4

INGREDIENTS:

1 large onion (thinly sliced)
2 carrots (thinly sliced)
1 large potato (diced)
1 parsnip (diced)
1 turnip (diced)
¼ small green cabbage (shredded)
25g/1oz butter

400g/14oz canned chopped tomatoes
300ml/½pt water
1 fish stock cube
350g/12oz cod fillet (skinned and cubed)
Salt and pepper
½ teaspoon dried mixed herbs

- Put all the vegetables in a large saucepan with the butter. Cook, stirring, for 5 minutes. Add the tomatoes, water and crumbled stock cube. Bring to the boil, reduce the heat, part-cover and simmer for 15 minutes or until the vegetables are nearly tender.
- Add the fish, a little salt and pepper and the herbs and cook for a further 5 minutes. Taste and adjust the seasoning if necessary. Serve hot.

Clam stew

SERVES 6

INGREDIENTS:

18 clams
2 tablespoons olive oil
175g/6oz onion (chopped)
1 teaspoon chopped garlic
850g/1¾lb canned chopped tomatoes
175ml/6fl oz tomato purée

50g/2oz fresh basil (chopped)
2 teaspoons paprika
¼ teaspoon black pepper
225ml/8fl oz dry white wine
700g/1½lb swordfish (cut into 2.5cm/1in pieces)

→

←

- Wash the clams under cold running water and set aside.
- Heat the oil in a large saucepan over a medium heat. Add the onion and garlic and cook until tender. Add the tomatoes, tomato purée, basil, paprika and pepper.
- Cover and bring to a boil, then reduce the heat and simmer for 10 minutes, stirring occasionally.
- Add the wine, clams and fish. Cover and simmer over a medium heat until the clams open. Remove the clam meat from the shells and return to the stew, discarding the shells. Heat through, mix thoroughly and serve.

Jambalaya one-pot

SERVES 4

INGREDIENTS:

2 tablespoons olive oil
2 garlic cloves (minced)
200g/7oz onion (onion)
1 celery stick (sliced)
1 medium green pepper (cut into strips)
200g/7oz long-grain white rice
450g/1lb canned chopped tomatoes

225ml/8fl oz water
⅛ teaspoon hot pepper sauce
150g/5oz chopped cooked ham
8 thin slices chorizo
1 teaspoon dried thyme
Salt and pepper
450g/1lb medium prawns (shelled and deveined)

- In a large frying pan, heat the oil over a medium heat. Add the garlic, onion, celery and green pepper and sauté for about 3 minutes, until just softened.
- Add the rice, tomatoes and their juice, the water, pepper sauce, ham, chorizo, thyme, salt and pepper. Bring to the boil, cover, reduce the heat and simmer for 15 minutes.
- Quickly add the prawns, then cover and cook for a further 5 minutes, or until the rice is tender and the prawns have turned pink.

Oyster stew

SERVES 6

INGREDIENTS:

50g/2oz butter
700g/1½lb leeks (chopped)
700g/1½lb potatoes (sliced)
2.4 litres/4pt water
50ml/2fl oz vegetable oil
100g/4oz fresh breadcrumbs

225ml/8fl oz double cream
Salt and pepper
⅛ teaspoon ground nutmeg
450g/1lb oysters
50g/2oz fresh parsley (chopped)

- Heat 25g/1oz butter in a large saucepan and add the leeks. Cook, stirring often, for about 5 minutes. Add the potatoes and water and bring to the boil. Simmer for 20 minutes. Drain in a colander, reserving the liquid.
- Heat the oil and remaining butter in a heavy skillet and add the breadcrumbs to make croûtons. Cook, stirring, until golden brown. Drain in a sieve.
- In a blender or food processor, blend the leek and potato thoroughly while adding small amounts of the reserved cooking liquid. Add only enough liquid to make a fine purée. Combine the purée with the remaining liquid in a saucepan and bring to a simmer. Add the cream and salt and pepper to taste. Add the nutmeg and heat thoroughly. Add the oysters and cook briefly, until the oysters just curl.
- Serve sprinkled with parsley and the croûtons.

Halibut stew

SERVES 3

INGREDIENTS:

25g/1oz butter
1 large onion (finely chopped)
2 garlic cloves (finely minced)
1 small green pepper (diced)
1 tomato (skinned and chopped)
250g/9oz potatoes (peeled and finely chopped)

125ml/4fl oz water
Salt and pepper
1 teaspoon dried marjoram
5 halibut fillets

- Melt the butter in a microwave-safe baking dish for 1 minute on high then mix in the onion, garlic and green pepper and mix well. Microwave on high for 2 minutes.

→

←

- Stir well, then mix in the tomato, potatoes, water, salt, pepper and marjoram.
- Stir well. Microwave for 5 minutes on a medium-high setting.
- Cut the fish fillets into individual servings and arrange over the hot vegetable mixture. Lightly season, cover and microwave for 5 minutes on high. Leave to stande for 3 minutes before serving.

Prawn & snapper stew

SERVES 6

INGREDIENTS:

850g/1³/₄lb canned chopped tomatoes
400ml/14fl oz fish stock
350ml/12fl oz canned beer
200g/7oz carrots (very thinly sliced)
1 medium onion (chopped)
250g/9oz long-grain rice
1 tablespoon chilli powder
1 teaspoon ground cumin

½ teaspoon dried oregano
2 garlic cloves (minced)
225g/8oz red snapper fillets (cut into 2.5cm/1in pieces)
225g/8oz large prawns (peeled and deveined)
1 large green pepper (chopped)

- In a large casserole dish, combine the tomatoes, stock and beer. Bring to the boil and add the carrots, onion, rice, chilli powder, cumin, oregano and garlic. Return to the boil, then reduce the heat. Cover and simmer for about 20 minutes or until the rice and carrots are nearly tender.
- Add the red snapper, prawns and green pepper. Return to the boil, then reduce the heat, cover and simmer gently for 3 to 5 minutes or until the snapper flakes easily with a fork and prawns turn pink. Serve hot.

Celery & salt cod casserole

SERVES 4

INGREDIENTS:

250g/9oz salt cod (soaked overnight)
1 tablespoon vegetable oil
4 shallots (finely chopped)
2 garlic cloves (chopped)
3 celery sticks (chopped)

400g/14oz canned chopped tomatoes
150ml/¹/₄pt fish stock
50g/2oz pine nuts
2 tablespoons chopped fresh tarragon
2 tablespoons capers

- Drain the cod, rinse under running water and drain again thoroughly. Remove and discard any skin and bones. Pat the fish dry with kitchen paper and cut it into chunks.
- Heat the oil in a large frying pan. Add the shallots and garlic and cook for 3 minutes. Add the celery and cook for a further 2 minutes, then add the tomatoes and stock.
- Bring the mixture to the boil, reduce the heat and leave to simmer for about 5 minutes. Add the fish and cook for 10 minutes or until tender.
- Meanwhile, place the pine nuts on a baking tray. Place under a preheated grill and toast for 3 minutes or until golden.
- Stir the tarragon, capers and pine nuts into the fish casserole and heat gently to warm through. Serve immediately.

Trout stew

SERVES 4

INGREDIENTS:

50ml/2fl oz water
1 teaspoon salt
1 onion (thinly sliced)
225ml/8fl oz tomato juice
2 garlic cloves (crushed)
4 small potatoes (peeled and diced)

1 green pepper (chopped)
1 medium tomato (skinned and chopped)
1.2kg/2½lb trout fillets
275g/10oz frozen green beans

- Combine all the ingredients except the trout and green beans in a large, microwave-safe casserole dish. Cover and microwave for 10 minutes on high, or until the potatoes are tender.
- Add the fish and green beans to the stew, cover, and microwave for a further 5 minutes on high.

Cajun crayfish casserole

SERVES 4

INGREDIENTS:

200g/7oz crayfish tails (coarsely chopped)
4 eggs (hard-boiled and coarsely chopped)
150g/5oz celery (finely chopped)
200g/7oz red pepper (chopped)
150g/5oz breadcrumbs (toasted)
50g/2oz butter (melted)

200g/7oz butternut squash (chopped, boiled and drained)
4 tablespoons chopped shallots
1 tablespoon finely chopped garlic
Salt and pepper
250g/9oz crackers (crumbled coarsely)
50g/2oz fresh parsley (finely chopped)

- Preheat the oven to 200°C/400°F/Gas mark 6.
- Combine all the ingredients in a large bowl, except the crackers and parsley, and mix well. Spoon the mixture in a large casserole dish and sprinkle the crackers over the top and garnish with the parsley.
- Bake the dish for about 20 to 25 minutes in the oven. Serve hot.

Cod with chickpeas & courgette stew

SERVES 4

INGREDIENTS:

75ml/3fl oz extra-virgin olive oil
1 teaspoon chopped fresh rosemary
1 bay leaf
1 large onion (finely diced)
1 celery stick (trimmed and chopped)
1 medium carrot (chopped)
1 red chilli (deseeded and chopped)
900g/2lb courgettes (trimmed and chopped)
4 sun-dried tomatoes (finely diced)

850g/1¾lb canned chickpeas (drained)
150ml/¼pt fish stock
2 tablespoons chopped fresh parsley
Juice of ½ lemon
Salt and pepper
25g/1oz plain flour
2 garlic cloves
4 cod fillets (boned), about 175g/6oz each

- Heat a third of the oil in a deep frying pan until hot. Add the rosemary and bay leaf and cook for 1 minute. Stir in the onion, celery, carrot and chilli and cook for 7 to 8 minutes until soft.

- Add the courgette and tomatoes and cook for a further 3 to 5 minutes until the courgettes are al dente. Add the chickpeas and stock and simmer for 10 minutes. Add the parsley, lemon juice and seasoning and simmer for a further 5 minutes.
- Spread the flour on a flat plate and season with salt and pepper. Heat the remaining oil in a frying pan, add the garlic cloves and fry for 3 minutes, then remove and discard them. Coat the fish in the seasoned flour and place in the pan, skin side down. Cook for 5 minutes until golden brown, then flip the fish over and cook for a further 3 minutes. The fish should just flake. Serve the stew immediately with the fish placed on top.

Creole fish stew

SERVES 4

INGREDIENTS:

4 fillets red snapper
Salt and pepper
1 tablespoon Worcestershire sauce
2 teaspoons garlic powder
1 teaspoon English mustard powder
4 tablespoons vegetable oil

225g/8oz tomatoes (skinned and chopped)
1 sprig thyme
100g/4oz coconut cream
2 large onions (finely chopped)
3 garlic cloves (crushed)

- Wash the fish well, then dry on kitchen paper and season with salt, pepper,
- Worcestershire sauce, garlic powder and mustard powder. Rub well into the fish and leave to marinate overnight.
- Heat the oil in a heavy-based frying pan, fry the fish and drain kitchen paper.
- Place the tomatoes, thyme and coconut cream in a saucepan and bring to the boil. Lower the heat and simmer for 10 minutes. Sauté the onions and garlic in the pan used to fry the fish, then add to the sauce. Add the fish to the sauce and leave to simmer for 4 minutes. Serve immediately.

Prawn & scallop casserole

SERVES 2

INGREDIENTS:

125ml/4fl oz dry white wine
100g/4oz onion (chopped)
50g/2oz fresh parsley (chopped)
50g/2oz butter
1 teaspoon salt
225g/8oz fresh prawns (peeled and deveined)
450g/1lb scallops

25g/1oz plain flour
225ml/8fl oz milk
150ml/¼pt fish stock
100g/4oz Emmenthal cheese
1 tablespoon lemon juice
100g/4oz fresh breadcrumbs
50g/2oz Parmesan cheese (grated)
50g/2oz sliced almonds

- Preheat the oven to 180°C/350°F/Gas mark 4.
- Combine the wine, onion, parsley, 15g/1/2oz butter and salt in a large saucepan and bring to the boil. Add the prawns and scallops and cook for about 3 minutes or until the prawns turn pink. Drain the prawns and scallops and set aside, reserving 150ml/¼pt of the cooking liquid.
- Melt the remaining butter in a large casserole dish over a low heat. Add the flour, stirring until smooth. Cook, stirring constantly, for 1 minute. Gradually add the milk and reserved cooking liquid, stirring until thickened. Add the cheese and lemon juice and stir until smooth. Stir in the prawns and scallops. Bake, covered, for about 30 minutes.
- Combine the breadcrumbs, Parmesan and almonds and mix well. Uncover the casserole and add the breadcrumb topping. Bake for a further 10 minutes and serve immediately.

One-pot tuna pasta

SERVES 4

INGREDIENTS:

600ml/1pt water
2 chicken stock cubes
⅛ teaspoon pepper
1 teaspoon fresh basil
225g/8oz elbow macaroni
100g/4oz red pepper (diced)

250g/9oz frozen green beans (chopped)
225ml/8fl oz milk
100g/4oz Cheddar cheese (grated)
400g/14oz canned tuna (drained)
50g/2oz fresh parsley (chopped)

- Bring the water, stock cubes, pepper and basil to the boil in large casserole dish.
- Gradually add the pasta, keeping the water at boiling point. Cover and simmer for 7 minutes, stirring occasionally.
- Stir the red pepper, green beans and milk into the casserole dish, then cover and simmer for 6 to 8 minutes or until the pasta and beans are tender. Stir in the cheese, tuna and parsley until the cheese is melted. Serve immediately.

Chinese seafood hotpot

SERVES 6

INGREDIENTS:

2.4 litres/4pt fish stock
1 tablespoon chopped root ginger
1 tablespoon chopped garlic
6 spring onions (finely chopped)
100g/4oz dried bean thread noodles
(soaked and cut into bite-sized pieces)
8 scallops (sliced)
4 small squid (cut into rings)

12 prawns (peeled, deveined and butterflied)
8 shucked oysters
450g/1lb spinach (chopped into bite-sized pieces)
450g/1lb tofu (cut into 2.5cm/1in cubes)
Soy sauce or black bean sauce, to serve

- Place the stock, ginger, garlic and spring onions in a large pot and bring to the boil. Reduce the heat, cover and simmer for 30 minutes.
- Arrange the noodles, seafood, spinach and tofu on a large platter. Cover and chill until ready to cook. Reheat the stock to simmering. Set a Mongolian hotpot or electric wok in the centre of the table. Pour the stock into the pot and adjust the heat to a gentle simmer. The guests use chopsticks to cook the seafood, vegetables and tofu slices in the stock and then dip into a traditional Chinese sauces such as soy sauce or black bean sauce.

Prawn & spinach stew

SERVES 4

INGREDIENTS:

175g/6oz mushrooms (sliced)
1 medium onion (chopped)
1 garlic clove (minced)
25g/1oz butter
25g/1oz plain flour
1 bay leaf
⅛ teaspoon ground nutmeg

⅛ teaspoon pepper
400ml/14fl oz vegetable stock
225ml/8fl oz milk
225g/8oz peeled prawns (deveined)
200g/7oz fresh spinach (torn)
75g/3oz Gruyère cheese (grated)

- In a medium saucepan, cook the mushrooms, onion and garlic in the butter until tender. Stir in the flour, bay leaf, nutmeg and pepper. Add the stock and milk.
- Cook and stir until the mixture is thickened.
- Add the prawns and cook for a further 2 minutes. Add the spinach and cheese.
- Cook and stir until the spinach wilts and cheese melts. Remove and discard the bay leaf before serving.

Seafood, fennel & potato stew

SERVES 6

INGREDIENTS:

20 black mussels
6 baby octopus
2 tablespoons olive oil
1 large fennel bulb (thinly sliced)
2 leeks (thinly sliced)
2 garlic cloves (crushed)
½ teaspoon paprika
Salt and pepper
2 tablespoons Pernod

175ml/6fl oz dry white wine
¼ teaspoon saffron threads
¼ teaspoon fresh thyme leaves
16 raw medium prawns (peeled and deveined)
500g/1lb 2oz monkfish cutlets (cut into large chunks)
400g/14oz baby new potatoes

- Scrub the mussels and remove the hairy beards. Discard any mussels that do not close when tapped on the the work surface. Rinse well.

- Use a small sharp knife to cut off the octopus heads. Grasp the bodies and push the beaks out, then remove and discard. Slit the heads and remove the gut, then wash well. Then slice.
- Heat the oil in a large pan over a medium heat. Add the fennel, leek and garlic.
- Stir in the paprika, season lightly with salt and pepper and cook for 8 minutes, or until softened. Add the Pernod and wine and boil for 1 minute, or until reduced by a third.
- Add the mussels to the pan, cover and cook, shaking the pan occasionally, for 4 to 5 minutes, or until opened, discarding any unopened mussels. Remove from the pan and allow to cool. Remove the meat from the shells and set aside.
- Add the saffron and thyme to the pan and cook, stirring, over a medium heat, for 1 to 2 minutes. Season if necessary, then transfer to a large casserole dish.
- Stir the octopus, prawns, monkfish and potatoes into the stew. Cover and cook gently for 10 minutes, or until the potatoes and seafood are tender. Add the mussel meat, cover and heat through. Serve hot.

Monkfish & prawn casserole

SERVES 4

INGREDIENTS:

25g/1oz butter
6 celery sticks (chopped)
1 large onion (chopped)
450g/1lb button mushrooms
1 tablespoon tomato purée
2 tablespoons plain flour

300ml/½pt white wine
700g/1½lb monkfish (cubed)
450g/1lb tomatoes (quartered)
350g/12oz peeled prawns (deveined)
Salt and pepper
1 tablespoon chopped fresh parsley

- Preheat the oven to 180°C/350°F/Gas mark 4.
- Melt the butter in a large casserole dish, then add the celery and onion and cook slowly until just beginning to brown. Add the mushrooms and cook for 2 to 3 minutes.
- Add the tomato purée and flour, stir well and cook for 1 minute before adding the wine. Boil for a further 1 minute and add the monkfish.
- Cover and bake in the oven for 10 minutes. Add the tomatoes with the prawns and salt and pepper to taste. Return the dish to the oven for a further 15 minutes. Sprinkle with the parsley before serving.

Sea bass stew

SERVES 10

INGREDIENTS:

450g/1lb back bacon rashers
1.3kg/3lb sea bass fillet (cubed)
1.5 litres/2½pt water
3 medium onions (sliced)
8 celery sticks (sliced)
450g/1lb carrots (sliced)

600ml/1pt fish stock
4 bay leaves
850g/1¾lb canned chopped tomatoes
Salt and pepper
4 large potatoes (cubed)

- Dry-fry the bacon slowly in a large frying pan and reserve the grease.
- Steam the sea bass over half the water for 15 minutes.
- In a large casserole dish, sauté the onions in the bacon grease until light golden brown. Add the celery, carrots and fish and stir lightly to coat.
- Add the stock, the remaining water, bay leaves, tomatoes, salt and pepper. Bring to the boil, add the potatoes, lower the heat and simmer for 40 minutes, stirring occasionally.

Red snapper casserole

SERVES 6

INGREDIENTS:

700g/1½lb red snapper fillets
Plain flour (seasoned), for dusting
50g/2oz butter

175g/6oz green chilli sauce
350g/12oz Cheddar cheese (grated)
2 tablespoons chopped fresh parsley

- Preheat the oven to 180°C/350°F/Gas mark 4.
- Coat the snapper fillets with the seasoned flour. Heat the butter in a frying pan and lightly sauté the fillets on both sides, in batches if necessary.
- Transfer the fillets to a large casserole dish. Divide the chilli sauce and cheese among them. Bake for about 12 minutes. Sprinkle with parsley before serving.

Calamari stew

SERVES 4

INGREDIENTS:

3 garlic cloves (minced)
2 tablespoons white wine vinegar
1 tablespoon soy sauce

1 tablespoon water
Salt and pepper
900g/2lb fresh squid (cleaned)

- Put the garlic, vinegar, soy sauce, water and salt and pepper to taste in a frying pan over a medium heat and bring to the boil.
- Add the squid while the mixture is still boiling and cook for another 3 to 4 minutes, stirring occasionally. Serve immediately.

Cod stew

SERVES 4-6

INGREDIENTS:

50g/2oz butter
4 carrots (chopped)
2 medium onions (chopped)
900g/2lb potatoes (sliced)
4 tomatoes (sliced)

Salt and pepper
1½ tablespoons plain flour
125ml/4fl oz milk
3 cod fillets

- Melt the butter in a saucepan, then add the carrots and onions and cook until soft.
- Add the potatoes and tomatoes and season with salt and pepper
- Add enough water to come to just below the top layer of tomatoes and boil slowly for 20 minutes. Mix the flour and milk and add to the stew. Lay the cod on top of the stew and cook for 10 to 20 minutes.

Red snapper stew

SERVES 6

INGREDIENTS:

700g/1½lb red snapper fillets (cut into 5cm/2in pieces)
2 tablespoons olive oil
1 garlic clove (minced)
1 large onion (sliced)
1 green pepper (cut into 2.5cm/1in pieces)

1 courgette (sliced)
425g/15oz tomatoes (chopped)
½ teaspoon basil
½ teaspoon oregano
Salt and pepper
50ml/2fl oz dry white wine
100g/4oz mushrooms (sliced)

- Combine all the ingredients in a large casserole dish and stir well.
- Cover and cook over a high heat for 4 hours, adding water if the stew becomes to dry.

Potato, ham & scallop casserole

SERVES 4

INGREDIENTS:

250g/9oz cooked ham (cubed)
250g/9oz cooked scallops
8 medium potatoes (thinly sliced)
75g/3oz onion (finely chopped)
100g/4oz plain flour

Salt and pepper
350ml/12fl oz milk
3 tablespoons fine dry breadcrumbs
1 tablespoon butter (melted)
2 tablespoons chopped fresh parsley

- Preheat the oven to 180°C/350°F/Gas mark 4
- Place half the ham in a large casserole dish. Cover with half the scallops, half the potatoes and half the onion. Sift half the flour over, then season with salt and pepper. Repeat the layers of ham, scallops, potato and onion and seasoning, then sift the remaining flour over the top. Pour the milk over all.
- Bake, covered, in the oven for 1 to 1¼ hours, until the potatoes are tender.
- Uncover. Combine the breadcrumbs and butter and sprinkle over the top of the casserole. Top with parsley. Bake, uncovered, for a further 15 minutes.

Crab & vegetable one-pot

SERVES 4

INGREDIENTS :

900g/2lb crab
4 clams
1.8 litres/3pt cold water
Salt and pepper
4 tablespoons chilli powder
6 garlic cloves (chopped)

½ red pepper (chopped)
½ green pepper (chopped)
1 leek (white part only, sliced)
2 spring onions (sliced)
2 tablespoons chopped fresh coriander

- To prepare the crabs, remove their backs, then wash the flesh and discard any spongy matter. Cut each crab into 4 pieces, cracking the claws with a cleaver, and set aside.
- Simmer the clams in hot water until they just begin to open.
- Put the cold water, salt and chilli powder in a saucepan and bring to the boil, then cover, lower the heat and simmer for 10 minutes. Add the crabs and clams and simmer, uncovered, for approximately 5 minutes.
- Add the garlic, peppers, leek and spring onions. Simmer until the crabs are cooked. Sprinkle with coriander and serve.

Dover sole stew

SERVES 4

INGREDIENTS:

400ml/14fl oz chicken stock
275g/10oz canned condensed French onion soup
200g/7oz potatoes (cubed)
175g/6oz celery (sliced)
450g/1lb Dover sole (cut into 2.5cm/1in pieces)

150g/5oz baby carrots
150g/5oz courgette (thinly sliced)
400g/14oz canned chopped tomatoes
½ teaspoon dried thyme
½ teaspoon dried rosemary

- Combine the stock, soup, potatoes and celery in a large casserole dish and bring to the boil. Reduce the heat to medium, cover and cook for 5 minutes.
- Add the remaining ingredients and cook, covered, for a further 10 minutes or until the fish is cooked and the vegetables are tender.

Thai jasmine rice & prawn casserole

SERVES 3

INGREDIENTS:

500g/1lb 2oz jasmine rice (cooked)
30 cooked tiger prawns (shelled and chopped)

400g/14oz canned sweetcorn (drained)
200g/7oz carrots (thinly sliced)
600g/1lb 5oz mild ginger stir-fry sauce

- Add the cooked rice to a large frying pan. Add the prawns, sweetcorn and carrots and cook over a high heat for 5 minutes, until the carrots are tender.
- Add the sauce and simmer for a further 5 minutes.

Squid & macaroni stew

SERVES 6

INGREDIENTS:

225g/8oz pasta shapes
125ml/4fl oz olive oil
2 onions (sliced)
350g/12oz prepared squid (cut into 4cm/1¹/₂in strips)
225ml/8fl oz fish stock
150ml/¹/₄pt red wine

350g/12oz tomatoes (skinned and thinly sliced)
2 tablespoons tomato purée
1 teaspoon dried oregano
2 bay leaves
Salt and pepper
2 tablespoons chopped fresh parsley

- Bring a large saucepan of lightly salted water to the boil. Add the pasta and 1 tablespoon olive oil and cook for 3 minutes. Drain, return to the pan, cover and keep warm.
- Heat the remaining oil in a pan over a medium heat. Add the onions and fry until they are translucent. Add the squid and stock and simmer for 5 minutes.
- Pour in the wine and add the tomatoes, tomato purée, oregano and bay leaves.
- Bring the sauce to the boil, season to taste and cook for 5 minutes.
- Stir the pasta into the pan, cover and simmer for about 10 minutes, or until the squid and macaroni are tender and the sauce has thickened.
- Remove and discard the bay leaves. Stir the parsley into the pan and serve.

Cheese &
crabmeat casserole

SERVES 4

INGREDIENTS:

450g/1lb Cheddar cheese (cubed)
8 slices bread (crusts removed, cubed)
275g/10oz frozen crabmeat

5 eggs
600ml/1pt milk
75g/3oz butter (melted)

- Preheat the oven to 180°C/350°F/Gas mark 4.
- Alternate layers of cheese, bread and crabmeat in a casserole dish. Beat the eggs, milk and butter and pour over the layered mixture. Bake in a pan of water for 1 to 1½ hours.

Basque tuna stew

SERVES 4

INGREDIENTS:

2 tablespoons olive oil
1 onion (chopped)
2 garlic cloves (chopped)
200g/7oz canned chopped tomatoes
700g/1½lb potatoes (cut into 5cm/2in chunks)

3 green peppers (roughly chopped)
300ml/½pt cold water
900g/2lb fresh tuna (cut into chunks)
Salt and pepper

- Heat the olive oil in a saucepan over a low heat. Add the onion and cook for 8 to 10 minutes until softened and browned. Add the garlic and cook for a further 1 minute. Add the tomatoes, cover and simmer for about 30 minutes until thickened.
- Meanwhile, mix the potatoes and peppers together in a large, clean saucepan. Add the water, which should just cover the vegetables. Bring to the boil over a medium heat and simmer for 15 minutes, until the vegetables are almost tender.
- Add the tuna chunks and the tomato mixture to the potatoes and peppers and season to taste with salt and pepper. Cover and simmer for 6 to 8 minutes until the tuna is tender. Transfer to 4 large warmed serving bowls and serve.

Halibut casserole

SERVES 8

INGREDIENTS:

450g/1lb halibut
2 bay leaves
½ onion (sliced)
25g/1oz butter

4 tablespoons plain flour
400ml/14fl oz milk
Salt and pepper
225g/8oz Cheddar cheese (grated)

- Preheat the oven to 180°C/350°F/Gas mark 4.
- Steam the halibut, bay leaves and onion for 30 minutes.
- Prepare a white sauce by combining the butter, flour, milk, salt and pepper.
- Break the halibut into bite-sized pieces and layer in a large casserole dish with the cheese and white sauce. Cover and bake in the oven for 35 minutes.

Pickled herring casserole

SERVES 6

INGREDIENTS:

15g/½oz butter
100g/4oz dried breadcrumbs
1 tablespoon chopped fresh parsley
2 ounces grated Parmesan cheese
Salt and pepper
450g/1lb potatoes (sliced 1cm/½in thick)

200g/7oz onions (thinly sliced)
25g/1oz plain flour
6 pickled herrings
300ml/½pt milk

- Preheat the oven to 200°C/400°F/Gas mark 6.
- Grease a baking dish with the butter. In a small mixing bowl, combine the breadcrumbs, parsley and cheese. Season with salt and pepper and mix well. Set aside. Season the potatoes and onions with salt and pepper. Place a layer of potatoes on the bottom of the prepared baking dish. Place a layer of onions over the potatoes. Sprinkle half the flour over the onions and top with half the herring. Repeat the layering process with the remaining potatoes, onions, flour and herring.
- Pour the milk over the entire casserole and sprinkle the top with the breadcrumb mixture. Bake, covered, for 30 minutes, or until cooked through.

Lobster casserole

SERVES 4

INGREDIENTS:

40g/1½oz butter
100g/4oz fresh breadcrumbs
2 tablespoons finely chopped onion
½ garlic clove (crushed)
150ml/¼pt condensed Cheddar cheese
soup

100g/4oz mushrooms (sliced)
50ml/2fl oz milk
2 tablespoons dry sherry
1 tablespoon chopped fresh parsley
175g/6oz cooked peas (drained)
250g/9oz cooked lobster (cubed)

- In a small, heat-resistant, non-metallic bowl, melt 25g/1oz butter in the microwave for 15 seconds. Place the breadcrumbs in the butter and turn to coat. Set aside.
- Place the remaining butter in a deep, non-metallic casserole dish. Heat for 15 seconds in the microwave. Add the onion and garlic and heat, uncovered, in the microwave for 2 minutes or until the onion is tender.
- Stir the soup and mushrooms into the onions and garlic. Gradually blend in the milk, sherry and parsley. Add the peas, lobster and breadcrumbs to the soup mixture. Stir to combine all the ingredients. Heat, uncovered, in the microwave for 5 minutes or until the sauce bubbles.

Spicy scallop & cauliflower stew

SERVES 4

INGREDIENTS:

2 tablespoons olive oil
1 onion (chopped)
1 large carrot (sliced)
1 garlic clove (crushed)
¼ tablespoon ground cumin
¼ teaspoon crushed red chilli flakes
850g/1¾lb canned chopped tomatoes

225ml/8fl oz clam juice
50ml/2fl oz dry white wine
½ tablespoon dried thyme
½ medium cauliflower head (cut into florets)
350g/12oz scallops
Salt and pepper

- Heat the oil in a large casserole dish over a medium heat. Add the onion and

→

← cook for about 8 minutes, stirring. Add the carrot, garlic, cumin, chilli flakes and cook for 1 minute.

- Purée the tomatoes and their juices in a blender or food processor and add to the casserole dish. Mix in the clam juice, wine and thyme. Stir well and simmer for 10 minutes.
- Add the cauliflower and simmer for a further 10 minutes. Add the scallops and cook for about 2 minutes, until done. Season with salt and pepper and serve.

Mediterranean fish stew

SERVES 4

INGREDIENTS:

2 teaspoons olive oil
2 red onions (sliced)
2 garlic cloves (crushed)
2 tablespoons red wine vinegar
2 teaspoons caster sugar
300ml/½pt fish stock
300ml/½pt red wine
800g/1 lb 14oz canned chopped tomatoes
225g/8oz baby aubergines (quartered)

225g/8oz courgettes (sliced)
1 green pepper (sliced)
1 tablespoon chopped fresh rosemary
500g/1lb 2oz halibut fillet (skinned and cut into 2.5cm/1in chunks)
750g/1lb 11oz fresh prepared mussels
225g/8oz fresh tiger prawns (peeled and deveined)
Salt and pepper

- Heat the oil in a large saucepan and fry the onions and garlic gently for 3 minutes. Stir in the vinegar and sugar and cook for a further 2 minutes.
- Stir in the stock, wine, tomatoes, aubergines, courgettes, pepper and rosemary.
- Bring to the boil and simmer, uncovered, for 10 minutes.
- Add the halibut and mussels. Mix well and simmer, covered, for 5 minutes until the fish is opaque. Stir in the prawns and continue to simmer, covered, for a further 3 minutes until the prawns are cooked through.
- Discard any mussels that have not opened and season to taste. Serve hot.

Herbed cod one-pot

SERVES 4

INGREDIENTS:

2 tablespoons olive oil
4 potatoes (quartered)
1 large onion (chopped)
2 garlic cloves (chopped)
2 tablespoons chopped fresh parsley

Salt and pepper
4 cod fillets
225ml/8fl oz tomato sauce
175ml/6fl oz white wine

- Preheat the oven to 190°C/375°F/Gas mark 5.
- Pour the oil into a large pan. Lay the potatoes in the oil and cover with half the onion, garlic, parsley and seasoning.
- Lay the fish on top of the potatoes and top with the remaining onion, garlic, parsley and seasoning. Mix the tomato sauce and wine together and pour over the fish.
- Bake for 1¼ hours, uncovered, basting the fish occasionally with the sauce in the pan.

Rolled fillet of sole casserole

SERVES 6

INGREDIENTS:

50g/2oz Parmesan cheese (grated)
½ teaspoon ground black pepper
5 tablespoons chopped fresh parsley
6 sole fillets, about 175g/6oz each
½ teaspoon salt
2 tablespoons vegetable oil

25g/1oz plain flour
225ml/8fl oz chicken stock
100g/4oz Cheddar cheese (grated)
3 tablespoons dry sherry
3 tablespoons water

- Preheat the oven to 210°C/425°F/Gas mark 7.
- In a small bowl, mix the Parmesan, pepper and 2 tablespoons parsley. Sprinkle the sole with the salt and pat the parsley mixture on one side of each fillet. Then roll the fillets, parsley side in, and secure with a cocktail stock. Place the fillets, seam-side down, in a large, shallow casserole dish.

→

←

- In a large saucepan over a medium-high heat, heat the oil, then stir in the flour until blended and cook for 1 minute. With a wire whisk or fork, gradually stir in the stock, cheese, sherry and water. Cook, stirring constantly, until the mixture boils. Pour the cheese sauce over the fish.
- Bake, uncovered, for 20 minutes or until the sauce is hot and bubbly and the fish flakes easily when tested with a fork. To serve, sprinkle the fillets with the remaining parsley.

Cajun oyster & scallop stew

SERVES 8

INGREDIENTS:

75g/3oz butter
12 spring onions (chopped)
50g/2oz celery (chopped)
25g/1oz plain flour
1 tablespoon chopped fresh parsley
Salt and pepper
225ml/8fl oz hot water
½ teaspoon chopped basil

¼ teaspoon chopped thyme
½ teaspoon chopped oregano
½ teaspoon black pepper
1 garlic clove (minced)
1½ tablespoons Worcestershire sauce
36 oysters (shucked)
24 scallops
25g/1oz sherry

- Melt 50g/2oz butter in a saucepan. Add the spring onions and celery and sauté until slightly browned, then remove from the heat.
- In a separate pan, heat the remaining butter, reduce the heat and slowly stir in the flour. When it is blended well, add the remaining ingredients, except the sherry. Add the browned vegetables and simmer for 15 minutes, stirring frequently. Add the sherry and continue to simmer until the stew thickens.

Salmon casserole

SERVES 4

INGREDIENTS:

425g/15oz canned salmon
250g/9oz elbow macaroni
350g/12oz canned sweetcorn (drained)
150g/5oz canned chopped tomatoes
50g/2oz onion (chopped)

250g/9oz celery (sliced)
275g/10oz canned condensed cream of mushroom soup
2 tablespoons lemon juice
Salt and pepper

- Preheat the oven to 180°C/350°F/Gas mark 4.
- Drain the salmon, reserving the juices. Boil the macaroni in salted water, drain and transfer to a deep casserole dish. Mix in the salmon.
- In a bowl, mix together the sweetcorn, tomatoes, onion, celery, soup and lemon juice. Add salt and pepper to taste and pour over the salmon mixture. Bake in the oven for 30 minutes.

Tuna fish casserole

SERVES 4

INGREDIENTS:

200g/7oz thin egg noodles (boiled and drained)
275g/10oz canned tuna (drained)
275g/10oz canned condensed mushroom soup

125ml/4fl oz sour cream
150g/5oz mushrooms (chopped)
100g/4oz Cheddar cheese (grated)

- Preheat the oven to 180°C/350°F/Gas mark 4.
- Mix together the noodles, tuna, soup, sour cream and mushrooms in a large casserole dish. Sprinkle all over with the cheese.
- Bake in the oven for about 20 minutes, or until cooked through.

Chunky halibut casserole

SERVES 6

INGREDIENTS:

50g/2oz butter
2 large onions (sliced into rings)
1 red pepper (roughly chopped)
450g/1lb potatoes (cut into 2.5cm/1in cubes)
450g/1lb courgettes (thickly sliced)
25g/1oz plain flour
1 tablespoon paprika

2 teaspoons vegetable oil
300ml/½pt white wine
150ml/¼pt fish stock
400g/14oz canned chopped tomatoes
2 tablespoons chopped fresh basil
Salt and pepper
450g/1lb halibut fillet (skinned and cut into 2.5cm/1in cubes)

- Melt the butter in a large saucepan, add the onions and pepper and cook for 5 minutes, or until softened. Add the potatoes and courgettes and cook, stirring

→

←

frequently, for a further 2 to 3 minutes.

- Sprinkle the flour, paprika and vegetable oil into the saucepan and cook, stirring continuously, for 1 minute. Pour in 150ml/¼pt wine, the stock and the tomatoes and bring to the boil.
- Add the basil to the casserole and season to taste with salt and pepper. Cover and simmer for 15 minutes, then add the halibut and the remaining wine and simmer very gently for a further 5 to 7 minutes, or until the fish and vegetables are just tender. Serve immediately.

French seafood
& vegetable stew

SERVES 6

INGREDIENTS:

Pinch of saffron strands
600ml/1pt hot fish stock
1 tablespoon olive oil
25g/1oz butter
1 onion (sliced)
2 garlic cloves (chopped)
1 leek (sliced)
1 small fennel bulb (finely sliced)
450g/1lb potatoes (cut into chunks)

150ml/¼pt dry white wine
1 tablespoon fresh thyme leaves
2 bay leaves
4 tomatoes (peeled and chopped)
900g/2lb mixed fish, such as haddock, mackerel or hake (roughly chopped)
2 tablespoons chopped fresh parsley
Salt and pepper

- Using a pestle and mortar, crush the saffron and add to the stock. Stir and leave to infuse for at least 10 minutes.
- Heat the oil and butter together in a large saucepan over a low heat. Add the onion and cook gently for 4 to 5 minutes until softened. Add the garlic, leek, fennel and potatoes. Cover and cook for a further 10 to 15 minutes until the vegetables are softened.
- Add the wine and simmer rapidly for 3 to 4 minutes until reduced by half. Add the thyme, bay leaves and tomatoes and stir well. Add the stock and bring to the boil. Cover and simmer gently for 15 minutes until the vegetables are tender.
- Add the fish, return to the boil and simmer for a further 3 to 4 minutes until all the fish is tender. Add the parsley and season to taste with salt and pepper.
- Using a slotted spoon, remove the fish and vegetables and serve immediately.

Tuna noodle casserole

SERVES 6

INGREDIENTS:

225g/8oz medium egg noodles
1 garlic clove (minced)
200g/7oz green onions (finely chopped)
75g/3oz butter
50g/2oz plain flour
450ml/¼pt milk
400g/14oz canned tuna (drained and
flaked)

200g/7oz frozen peas and carrots
(thawed)
Salt and pepper
3 tablespoons breadcrumbs
2 teaspoons chopped fresh parsley

- Preheat the oven to 180°C/350°F/Gas mark 4.
- Cook the noodles in salted water, then drain and set aside.
- Sauté the onions and garlic in 25g/1oz butter until the onions are tender. Add the flour and blend until smooth. Add the milk and cook, stirring constantly, until thickened and smooth.
- Add the tuna, peas and carrots and seasoning to taste. Stir in the noodles.
- Transfer the tuna noodle mixture to a large casserole dish. Mix the breadcrumbs and parsley with the remaining melted butter and sprinkle over the top of the casserole dish. Bake in the oven for 15 to 20 minutes, or until heated through.

Scallop casserole

SERVES 2

INGREDIENTS:

100g/4oz celery (chopped)
100g/4oz onion (chopped)
150g/5oz green pepper (roughly
chopped)
200g/7oz broccoli (chopped)

350g/12oz scallops (chopped)
200g/7oz Cheddar cheese (grated)
1 teaspoon salt
3 eggs (beaten)

- Preheat the oven to 190°C/375°F/Gas mark 5.
- In a frying pan, sauté the celery, onions and green pepper for 3 to 4 minutes.
- Remove from the heat and drain. Cook the broccoli until tender.
- Add the scallops, vegetables, cheese salt and eggs to a casserole dish. Bake in the oven for about 35 to 40 minutes.

Okra stew with prawns

SERVES 4

INGREDIENTS:

1 tablespoon lime juice
450g/1lb shelled prawns
50g/2oz butter
6 tablespoons chopped spring onion
225g/8oz okra (topped, tailed and sliced)

225g/8oz canned sweetcorn
3 tomatoes (skinned and chopped)
2 red chillies (deseeded and sliced)
1 bay leaf
1 tablespoon tomato purée
Salt and pepper

- Mix the lime juice with the prawns and set aside. Heat the butter in a frying pan and sauté the onions for 3 minutes. Add all the remaining ingredients to the pan and simmer for 10 minutes.
- Add the prawns and bring to the boil, then simmer for 5 minutes. Remove the bay leaf before serving.

Chickpea, parsley & salt cod stew

SERVES 6

INGREDIENTS:

Salt and pepper
750g/1lb 11oz cod fillet
350g/12oz dried chickpeas
175g/6oz potatoes (chopped)
75ml/3fl oz olive oil

8 garlic cloves (finely chopped)
1 teaspoon dried chilli flakes
4 plum tomatoes (roughly chopped)
3 tablespoons chopped fresh parsley
300ml/½pt water

- To salt the cod, pour a thick layer of salt over the base of a plastic container, rest the cod on top and completely cover in another thick layer of salt. Cover and refrigerate overnight. Cover the chickpeas in plenty of water and leave to soak overnight.
- Drain the chickpeas, tip into a pan and pour over enough fresh water to cover. Bring to the boil, simmer for 1¼ hours or until tender. Add more boiling water, if necessary, to make sure they stay just covered. Then add the potatoes and cook for a further 15 to 20 minutes. Drain and set aside, saving the cooking liquid.

- Rinse the salted cod under cold water. Place in a pan of boiling water and simmer for 6 to 8 minutes until just cooked. Drain and flake into large pieces, discarding the skin and any bones.
- Heat the oil in a large pan and cook the garlic and chilli flakes for 2 minutes without browning. Add the tomatoes, chickpeas and potatoes.
- Add a little of the cooking liquid from the chickpeas and the water and simmer for 20 to 30 minutes until the stew has reduced and thickened a little.
- Gently fold in the salt cod and parsley and season to taste.

Squid casserole

SERVES 4

INGREDIENTS:

3 tablespoons olive oil
1 large onion (thinly sliced)
2 garlic cloves (crushed)
700g/1½lb squid rings
1 red pepper (sliced)
2 sprigs rosemary

150ml/¼pt dry white wine
250ml/9fl oz water
400g/14oz canned chopped tomatoes
2 tablespoons tomato purée
1 teaspoon paprika
Salt and pepper

- Heat the oil in a casserole dish and fry the onion and garlic until soft. Add the squid, increase the heat and continue to cook for about 10 minutes until sealed and beginning to colour. Add the pepper, rosemary, wine and water and bring to the boil. Cover and simmer gently for 45 minutes.
- Discard the rosemary, add the tomatoes, tomato purée, seasonings and paprika.
- Continue to simmer gently to 45 to 60 minutes, until tender. Serve hot.

Clam casserole

SERVES 4

INGREDIENTS:

425g/15oz canned minced clams
(drained)
4 large eggs (beaten)
50g/2oz butter (melted)
75ml/3fl oz milk

1 teaspoon salt
100g/4oz onion (finely chopped)
150g/5oz green pepper (chopped)
18 Jacob's cream crackers (crushed)

→

←

- Preheat the oven to 150°C/300°F/Gas mark 2.
- In a bowl, mix all ingredients together well. Pour into a large casserole dish, cover and cook in the oven for 3 hours, stirring occasionally. Alternatively, cook in a slow cooker on low for 4 to 5 hours.

Mussel casserole

SERVES 4

INGREDIENTS:

900g/2lb mussels
150ml/¼pt white wine
1 tablespoon olive oil
1 onion (finely chopped)

3 garlic cloves (finely chopped)
1 red chilli (finely chopped)
100g/4oz passata
1 tablespoon chopped fresh marjoram

- Scrub the mussels, remove the beards and rinse in clean water. Discard any mussels that do not close when they are tapped.
- Place the mussels in a large saucepan. Pour in the wine and cook for 5 minutes, shaking the pan occasionally until the shells open. Remove and discard any mussels that do not open.
- Remove the mussels from the saucepan with a slotted spoon. Strain the cooking liquid through a fine sieve set over a bowl, reserving the liquid.
- Heat the oil in a large frying pan. Add the onion, garlic and chilli and cook for 5 minutes or until just softened. Add the reserved cooking liquid to the pan and cook for 5 minutes or until reduced, stirring.
- Stir in the passata, marjoram and mussels and cook until hot, about 3 minutes.
- Serve hot.

Green chilli sole casserole

SERVES 4

INGREDIENTS:

450g/1lb mushrooms (thinly sliced)
25g/1oz butter
150g/5oz onion (chopped)
200g/7oz green chillies (chopped)
25g/1oz plain flour

175ml/6fl oz chicken stock
125ml/4fl oz sour cream
1 tablespoon lime juice
450g/1lb sole fillets
Salt and pepper

- Preheat the oven to 200°C/400°F/Gas mark 6.
- In a frying pan, fry the mushrooms in half the butter for about 5 minutes, until lightly browned. Spoon into a large, shallow casserole dish.
- Add the remaining butter and the onion and chillies to the pan. Stir for about 5 minutes over a high heat until the onion is soft. Add the flour, mix well and stir in the stock.
- Purée the mixture in a blender or food processor, then return to the pan. Add the sour cream and stir over a high heat until boiling. Remove from the heat and add the lime juice. Rinse the fish and arrange in an even layer over the mushrooms in the casserole dish, then cover with the sauce. Bake in the oven for 12 to 15 minutes, until the fish flakes when prodded. Season and serve.

Spicy monkfish stew

SERVES 6

INGREDIENTS:

1 tablespoon olive oil
1 onion (finely sliced)
1 tablespoon tom yum soup paste
450g/1lb potatoes (cut into 2.5cm/1in chunks)
400g/14oz canned chopped tomatoes

600ml/1pt fish stock
Salt and pepper
450g/1lb monkfish (cut into 2.5cm/1in chunks)
200g/7oz baby spinach

- Heat the oil in pan and fry the onion over a medium heat for 5 minutes until golden. Add the tom yum paste and potatoes and stir-fry for 1 minute. Add the tomatoes and hot stock, season well and cover. Bring to the boil then simmer, part-covered, for 15 minutes or until the potatoes are just tender.
- Add the monkfish to the pan and continue to simmer for 5 to 10 minutes or until the fish is cooked. Add the baby spinach and stir through until wilted.
- Serve immediately.

Artichoke stew with mussels, potatoes & saffron

SERVES 6

INGREDIENTS:

2 large lemons (halved)
5 medium prepared Jerusalem
artichokes (cut into wedges)
2.4 litres/4pt fish stock
2 tablespoons extra-virgin olive oil
1 bay leaf
12 small red potatoes
Salt and pepper

1 bay leaf
1 1/4 teaspoon mustard seeds
1/2 teaspoon celery seeds
1 teaspoon saffron
18 mussels (scrubbed and debearded)
200g/7oz shallots (chopped)
75g/3oz butter
2 spring onions (finely chopped)

- Squeeze the juice from 2 lemon halves into a large bowl, then add the lemon halves. Fill the bowl with water. Place the artichokes into the lemon water.
- Bring the stock, oil and bay leaf to the boil in a heavy-based casserole dish.
- Drain the artichokes and add to the pot. Return to the boil. Reduce the heat to medium-low and simmer for about 20 minutes until the artichokes are tender.
- Using a slotted spoon, transfer the artichokes to a medium-sized bowl. Reserve 225ml/8fl oz of the cooking liquid in a small bowl.
- Place the potatoes, salt, bay leaf, 1/2 teaspoon mustard seeds and the celery seeds in a large saucepan. Pour in enough cold water to generously cover the potatoes. Boil for about 20 minutes until the potatoes are tender. Drain, then cool for 15 minutes and peel.
- Stir the saffron in a heavy large pot over medium-low heat until fragrant, about 2 minutes. Add the reserved cooking liquid and bring to a simmer. Add the artichokes, potatoes, mussels, shallots, butter and remaining mustard seeds. Bring to the boil. Cover the pot and cook for about 8 minutes until the mussels open and the potatoes are golden. Mix in the spring onions. Season with salt and pepper.

Bream casserole

SERVES 4

INGREDIENTS:

40g/1½oz plain flour
Salt and pepper
700g/1½lb bream fillets (cut into large chunks)
25g/1oz butter

3 courgettes (cut into 2.5cm/1in slices)
4 tomatoes (quartered)
50ml/2fl oz water
3 tablespoons single cream
1 tablespoon lemon juice

- Place the flour, salt and pepper in a plastic bag and mix well. Add the bream and shake to coat. Remove the fish from the bag, shaking off any excess flour.
- Melt the butter in a large frying pan, add the fish and fry over a medium heat until golden brown, turning once. Add the courgette, tomatoes and water, cover and reduce the heat to very low and simmer for 15 minutes.
- Stir in the cream and lemon juice and cook, without boiling, for 2 to 3 minutes.
- Serve immediately.

Tuna & white bean casserole

SERVES 6

INGREDIENTS:

400g dried cannellini beans
50ml/2fl oz olive oil
2 red onions (chopped)
2 garlic cloves (crushed)
1 teaspoon ground coriander
1 teaspoon grated lemon zest
2 teaspoons chopped fresh thyme
500ml/18fl oz white wine
500ml/18fl oz fish stock
475g/1lb 1oz canned tuna in oil (drained)

50g/2oz basil leaves
4 large tomatoes (thickly sliced)

For the topping:
50g/2oz fresh breadcrumbs
1 garlic clove (crushed)
3 tablespoons chopped fresh parsley
25g/1oz butter (melted)

- Place the beans in a large bowl and cover with cold water, allowing room for the beans to expand. Soak for 8 hours. Rinse well, then drain.
- Heat the oil in a large frying pan, add the onion, garlic, coriander, lemon zest and thyme and cook over a medium heat for 10 minutes.

→

←

- Add the wine and stock and bring to the boil. Reduce the heat to low, cover and cook for 2 hours, or until the beans are tender.
- Preheat the oven to 210°C/425°F/Gas mark 7.
- Transfer the bean mixture to a large casserole dish. Top with the tuna and basil leaves. Overlap the tomato slices over the basil.
- For the topping, combine the breadcrumbs, garlic and parsley in a bowl and sprinkle over the tomato. Drizzle with the butter and bake for 30 minutes, or until the top is golden brown.

Haddock casserole

SERVES 2

INGREDIENTS:

450g/1lb frozen haddock fillets
(thawed)
Salt and pepper
1 teaspoon basil
550g/1lb 4oz canned chopped tomatoes
25g/1oz plain flour

1 onion (chopped)
2 celery sticks (finely chopped)
15g/½oz butter
1 egg (lightly beaten)
50ml/2fl oz single cream
1 teaspoon Worcestershire sauce

- Season the fillets with salt and pepper. Arrange them side-by-side in a microwave-safe dish.
- In a bowl, mix together the basil, tomatoes, flour, onion and celery.
- Melt the butter in the microwave on a high heat for 1 minute.
- Pour the butter into the tomato mixture, then pour over the fish. Cover the dish with a lid and microwave on medium-high for 10 minutes.
- Remove the fish with a slotted spoon on to a warm plate, leaving the tomato mixture in the dish.
- Beat together the egg and cream and mix in the Worcestershire sauce, then add to the tomato mixture. Microwave for 2 minutes on medium, stirring after 1 minute. Pour over the fish and serve.

Low-fat seafood stew

SERVES 3

INGREDIENTS:

400g/14oz canned chopped tomatoes
1 garlic clove
½ medium onion (chopped)
½ teaspoon thyme
1 bay leaf

Salt and pepper
100g/4oz cod (cubed)
100g/4oz scallops
100g/4oz raw prawns

- Combine the tomatoes, garlic, onion, thyme, bay leaf and seasoning in saucepan.
- Simmer for 10 minutes over a medium-high heat.
- Add the cod and simmer gently for 2 minutes, then add the scallops and simmer for 2 minutes. Add the prawns and simmer for 5 minutes, until the prawns turn pink. Serve hot.

Ratatouille & cod stew

SERVES 6

INGREDIENTS:

2 tablespoons olive oil
2 medium onions (sliced)
2 garlic cloves
1 large green pepper (chopped)
1 small aubergine (cut into 2.5cm/1in cubes)
1 medium courgette (chopped)

225ml/8fl oz fish stock
850g/1¾lb canned chopped tomatoes
50g/2oz fresh basil (chopped)
Salt and pepper
900g/2lb cod fillets (cut into 5cm/2in pieces)

- In a large casserole dish, heat the oil and sauté the onions, garlic, pepper, aubergine and courgette for 5 minutes, stirring frequently.
- Add the stock, tomatoes, basil, salt and pepper. Bring to the boil, lower the heat and simmer for 15 minutes. Add the fish and simmer for a further 8 minutes or until the fish flakes easily with a fork.

Brown fish stew

SERVES 4

INGREDIENTS:

900g/2lb red snapper fillets
Juice of 2 limes
2 tablespoons vegetable oil
2 tomatoes (chopped)
1 tablespoon pimento berries

1 garlic clove (chopped)
1/2 red chilli (chopped)
2 onions (sliced)
Salt and pepper
350ml/12fl oz water

- Clean the fish, then rub with the lime juice and pat dry with kitchen paper.
- Heat the oil in a frying pan until smoking. Add the fish and fry on both sides until crisp and brown. Drain the oil from the pan, leaving enough to coat the bottom, then add the tomatoes, pimento berries, garlic, chilli, onions and seasoning. Fry until the onion is soft, then add the water.
- Bring to the boil and reduce by half, then cover and simmer for 10 minutes.

Scallop stew

SERVES 4

INGREDIENTS:

600ml/1pt milk
2 bay leaves
1/2 onion (sliced)
3 sprigs parsley
50g/2oz celery (chopped)
1 teaspoon Tabasco sauce

40g/1 1/2oz butter
450g/1lb scallops
2 teaspoons chopped fresh tarragon
Salt and pepper
4 teaspoons finely chopped chives

- In a large saucepan, scald the milk with the bay leaves, onion and parsley. Cover and leave to stand for about 5 minutes. Strain out the bay leaf, parsley and onion and add the celery, Tabasco sauce and butter. Bring the liquid to a boil again, lower the heat, and simmer gently for about 5 minutes.
- Add the scallops, tarragon and seasoning. Simmer for 10 to 12 minutes. Sprinkle with the chives and serve.

Cod casserole

SERVES 5-6

INGREDIENTS:

900g/2lb smoked cod fillets (cut into chunks)
1 small bunch spring onions (chopped)
4 tomatoes (quartered)
1 red pepper (diced)
2 garlic cloves (chopped)

2 bay leaves (torn into pieces)
225ml/8fl oz dry white wine
1 tablespoon tomato purée
100g/4oz pitted black olives

- Place all the ingredients except the olives in a large casserole dish over a high heat. Cover and simmer gently for 30 minutes or until the fish is tender.
- Add the olives and heat through. Serve immediately.

Salmon Dijon casserole

SERVES 4

INGREDIENTS:

Vegetable oil for greasing
150g/5oz medium egg noodles
25g/1oz butter
25g/1oz flour
Salt and pepper
2 tablespoons Dijon mustard

450g/1lb frozen potatoes, peas and carrots (thawed)
425g/15oz canned salmon (drained, broken into chunks)
100g/4oz Cheddar cheese (grated)

- Preheat the oven to 180°C/350°F/Gas mark 4. Grease a large casserole dish with oil.
- Cook the noodles according to package instructions, then drain and cover to keep warm.
- Meanwhile, melt the butter in a saucepan over a medium heat. Stir in the flour, salt and pepper. Cook, adding water as needed, until the mixture is smooth and bubbly, stirring constantly.
- Cook until the mixture boils and thickens, stirring constantly.
- Stir in the mustard. In a large bowl, combine the noodles, sauce, vegetables and salmon. Spoon into the prepared casserole. Bake in the oven for 25 to 30 minutes until bubbly around the edges. Sprinkle with cheese. Serve immediately.

Hot prawn stew

SERVES 4

INGREDIENTS:

2.4 litres/4pt fish stock
4 medium potatoes (cubed)
1 large carrot (cubed)
1 large onion (sliced)
3 cloves
1 teaspoon ground mustard seeds

1 teaspoon granulated sugar
6 red chillies (deseeded and finely chopped)
2 tablespoons Worcestershire sauce
450g/1lb large prawns

- In a large casserole dish, bring the stock to the boil, then add the potatoes, carrot and onion and simmer for 5 minutes.
- Add the remaining ingredients except the prawns and simmer for 15 minutes, then add the prawns and simmer for a further 6 minutes. Serve immediately.

Smoked trout casserole

SERVES 4

INGREDIENTS:

250g/9oz spinach (cooked and drained)
15g/¹/₂oz butter (melted)
Salt and pepper
Pinch of nutmeg
2 tablespoons finely chopped onion
1 garlic clove (finely chopped)

1 tablespoon vegetable oil
25g/1oz plain flour
350ml/12fl oz milk
450g/1lb smoked trout
2 tablespoons sherry
100g/4oz Parmesan cheese (grated)

- Preheat the oven to 180°C/350°F/Gas mark 4.
- Place the spinach in a large baking dish and pour the butter over, followed by salt, pepper and nutmeg.
- Fry the onion and garlic in the oil until tender. Blend in the flour, stir, then gradually add the milk. Cook, stirring constantly, until smooth and thick.
- Break up and lightly mash the trout. Add it to the white sauce with the sherry, mix carefully and then pour over the spinach. Sprinkle with the cheese and bake, uncovered, for 20 to 25 minutes.

One-pot scallops

SERVES 6

INGREDIENTS:

4 rashers back bacon (chopped)
2 garlic cloves
700g/1½lb scallops
1 bunch spring onions (cut into
2.5cm/1in pieces)
225ml/8fl oz chicken stock

200g/7oz canned sweetcorn (drained)
1 tomato (chopped)
Salt and pepper
⅛ teaspoon dried thyme
Pinch of cayenne pepper
250g/9oz instant brown rice

- Cook the bacon and garlic in a frying pan over a medium heat for 6 minutes.
- Add the scallops and spring onions and sauté for 3 minutes.
- Add the remaining ingredients except the rice and cook for 3 minutes. Add the rice, cover and simmer for 8 to 10 minutes.

Smoked haddock casserole

SERVES 4

INGREDIENTS:

25g/1oz butter, plus extra for greasing
450g/1lb smoked haddock fillets (cut into 4 slices)
600ml/1pt milk
25g/1oz tablespoons plain flour
Salt and pepper

Pinch of freshly grated nutmeg
3 tablespoons double cream
1 tablespoon chopped fresh parsley
2 eggs (hard-boiled and mashed)
450g/1lb dried fusilli
1 tablespoon lemon juice

- Preheat the oven to 200°C/400°F/Gas mark 6. Grease a casserole dish with butter.
- Put the haddock into the casserole dish and pour the milk over. Bake in the oven for about 15 minutes, until tender.
- Pour the cooking liquid into a jug, leaving the fish in the casserole dish.
- Melt the butter in a small saucepan over a low heat. Stir in the flour, then gradually whisk in the reserved cooking liquid. Season to taste with salt, pepper and nutmeg. Stir in the cream, parsley and eggs and cook, stirring constantly, for 2 minutes.
- Meanwhile, bring a large saucepan of lightly salted water to the boil. Add the fusilli and lemon juice, bring back to the boil and cook for 8 to 10 minutes until tender.
- Drain the pasta and spoon it over the fish. Top with the egg sauce and return to the oven for 10 minutes. Serve hot.

Sauces, dressings & stocks

While you can usually buy ready-made sauces, dressings and stocks, if you have the time to make them yourself, it is preferable to use fresh ingredients where possible. This is especially true for salad dressings, which are quick and easy to make. In the case of stocks, while it is generally more convenient to use stock cubes as it cuts down on cooking time, a rich homemade stock with fresh ingredients has an edge over a shop-bought one.

White/Béchamel sauce

MAKES 450ml/³/₄pt

INGREDIENTS

450ml/³/₄pt milk
1 bay leaf
10 whole black peppercorns
1 slice onion (1cm/¹/₂in thick)

50g/2oz butter
25g/1oz plain flour
Salt and pepper

- Place the milk in a saucepan and add the bay leaf, peppercorns and onion. Cook over a low heat for approximately 5 minutes, letting it come slowly to simmering point. Remove the saucepan from the heat and strain the milk into a jug, discarding the flavourings.
- Melt the butter gently in a separate pan. As soon as the butter melts, add the flour and, over a medium heat, stir quite vigorously to make a smooth paste.
- Add the milk a little at a time, stirring vigorously between each addition. When about half the milk is in, switch to a whisk and start adding more milk at a time, whisking briskly, until all the milk has been added.
- Over a low heat, let the sauce simmer gently for 5 minutes, whisking occasionally. Season with salt and pepper.

Barbecue sauce

MAKES 600ml/1pt

INGREDIENTS

2 tablespoons vegetable oil
1 onion (finely chopped)
3 garlic cloves (minced)
225ml/8fl oz tomato ketchup or
tomato sauce

350ml/12fl oz cider vinegar
50ml/2fl oz Worcestershire sauce
75g/3oz sugar
1 teaspoon chilli powder
¹/₂ teaspoon cayenne pepper

- Heat the oil in a saucepan over a moderate heat and add the onion and garlic.
- Cook gently, stirring, for about 5 minutes. Add the ketchup, vinegar, Worcestershire sauce, sugar, chilli powder and cayenne.
- Reduce the heat and simmer, partially covered, for about 20 minutes, until the sauce has thickened slightly.

Tomato sauce

MAKES 600ml/1pt

INGREDIENTS

300ml/¹/₂pt white vinegar
1 teaspoon mixed spice
1.4kg/3lb ripe tomatoes (sliced)

25g/1oz salt
100g/4oz sugar

- Place the vinegar and the mixed spice in a saucepan, bring to the boil and remove from the heat. Cover and leave to infuse for 3 to 4 hours.
- Place the tomatoes in a heavy-based saucepan and simmer until pulpy.
- Rub the pulp through a sieve into a bowl.
- Clean the saucepan and add the strained pulp to it. Add the salt and cook gently until mixture begins to thicken
- Add the sugar and infused vinegar, stirring until fully dissolved.
- Continue simmering, stirring occasionally, until the mixture thickens to the consistency of whipped cream.

Creamed tomato sauce

MAKES 300ml/¹/₂pt

INGREDIENTS

6 medium ripe tomatoes
175ml/6fl oz water
125ml/4fl oz double cream

50ml/2fl oz plain yogurt
Salt and pepper

- Place the tomatoes in a bowl of just-boiled water for 30 seconds and skin. Then chop them finely.
- Place the tomatoes in a saucepan and add the water. Cover and simmer until the sauce is thick and creamy.
- Add the cream and yogurt.
- Season to taste with salt and pepper.

Mayonnaise

MAKES 300ml/¹/₂pt

INGREDIENTS

2 large egg yolks
1 teaspoon dry English mustard
powder
Pinch of salt

Ground black pepper
300ml/¹/₂pt groundnut oil or extra-
virgin olive oil
1 teaspoon white wine vinegar

- Put the egg yolks into a 900ml/1¹/₂ pt basin with a narrow base. Add the mustard powder. Season with the salt and pepper and mix well.
- Using an electric whisk, add the oil one drop at a time, whisking each drop in thoroughly before adding the next. When the mixture begins to thicken you can begin to add slightly more oil at a time.
- When about half the oil is in, add the vinegar. Pour in the rest of the oil in a steady trickle, whisking all the time.

Garlic mayonnaise

MAKES 300ml/¹/₂pt

INGREDIENTS

4 garlic cloves (minced)
2 large egg yolks
Pinch of salt

250ml/9fl oz olive oil
Juice of 1 small lemon
¹/₂ tablespoon boiling water

- Put the garlic, egg yolks and salt into a 900ml/1¹/₂pt basin with a narrow base. Mix well with a metal spoon.
- Using an electric whisk, add the oil one drop at a time, whisking each drop in thoroughly before adding the next.
- When about half the oil is in, start to add in drops of the lemon juice.
- When the mixture begins to thicken you can begin to add slightly more oil at a time. The mixture should become thick and well combined.
- Stir in the boiling water to prevent the mayonnaise from separating.

French vinaigrette

MAKES 150ml/¼pt

INGREDIENTS:

*2 tablespoons red or white
wine vinegar
125ml/4fl oz light olive oil
1 teaspoon Dijon mustard*

*1 garlic clove
Salt and pepper to taste
Pinch of sugar*

- Combine all the ingredients in a screw-top jar. Secure the lid and shake vigorously. Leave to infuse for 2 hours.
- Remove the garlic clove, then leave overnight before using.

Lemon vinaigrette

MAKES 150ml/¼pt

INGREDIENTS:

*1 teaspoon Dijon mustard
3 tablespoons fresh lemon juice*

*125ml/4fl oz extra-virgin olive oil
Salt and pepper*

- Whisk the mustard and lemon juice together.
- Whisking constantly, slowly drizzle in the olive oil.
- Season with salt and pepper.

Other variations

Note that other ingredients can be added to the French vinaigrette:
- Finely chopped fresh herbs such as parsley, basil, marjoram and mint.
- Capers, finely sliced gherkins or diced shallots.
- 1½ tablespoons roasting juices (with oil drained) may be added if the dressing is intended for a meat salad.

Chicken stock

MAKES 1.8 litres/3pt

INGREDIENTS:

1kg raw chicken carcass
3 litres/5pt water
100g/4oz carrot (coarsely chopped)
100g/4oz celery (coarsely chopped)

200g/7oz onion (coarsely chopped)
3 garlic cloves
1 teaspoon salt
1 bouquet garni

- Put the chicken carcass in a large stockpot and cover with the water. Add the remaining ingredients and bring to the boil over a high heat.
- Skim off any cloudy scum that has risen to the surface and, once the scum stops forming, reduce the heat to medium and simmer, uncovered, for 2 hours. If you wish to reduce the chicken stock, stir over a high heat until it has reduced to the required amount.
- Strain the stock through a fine-mesh sieve and leave to cool. Refrigerate for 8 hours or overnight, then remove any fat from the surface.

Vegetable stock

MAKES 500ml/18fl oz

INGREDIENTS:

1 tablespoon olive oil
2 leeks (roughly chopped)
2 carrots (chopped)
1 celery stick (chopped)
1 small russet potato (chopped)
2 garlic cloves (halved)
1.2 litres/2pt water

50g/2oz dried red lentils
1 bay leaf
½ teaspoon peppercorns
½ tablespoon soy sauce
1 pinch dried thyme
6 sprigs parsley

- Place the oil in a large casserole dish over a medium heat. Sauté the leeks, carrots, celery, potato and garlic until slightly browned. Add the water and the remaining ingredients.
- Bring to the boil, then reduce the heat and simmer uncovered for 1 hour.
- Strain the stock.

Beef stock

MAKES 1.8 litres/3pt

INGREDIENTS:

2.7kg/6lb beef bones
1 large onion (sliced)
3 large carrots (chopped)
2 celery sticks (chopped)
1 large tomato
100g/4oz parsnip (chopped)
100g/4oz potatoes (cubed)

8 whole black peppercorns
4 sprigs fresh parsley
1 bay leaf
1 tablespoon salt
2 teaspoons dried thyme
2 garlic cloves
3 litres/5pt water

- Preheat the oven to 230°C/450°F/Gas mark 8.
- Place the beef bones, onion, and carrots in a large shallow roasting pan. Roast, uncovered, for 30 minutes or until the bones are browned, turning occasionally.
- Drain off any fat. Place the browned bones, onion and carrots in a large soup pot. Pour 150ml/¼pt water into the roasting pan and rinse. Pour this liquid into the soup pot. Add the celery, tomato, parsnip, potato, peppercorns, parsley, bay leaf, salt, thyme and garlic. Add 2.8 litres/4¾pt water.
- Bring the mixture to the boil. Reduce the heat. Cover and simmer for 5 hours.
- Strain the stock. Discard the meat, vegetables and seasonings.

Fish stock

MAKES 1.8 litres/3pt

INGREDIENTS:

2.3kg/5lb fish trimmings
5 onions (quartered)
5 celery sticks, including leaves
(chopped)
5 sprigs of parsley

5 bay leaves
1 teaspoon dried thyme
Salt and freshly ground black pepper
750ml/1¼pt dry white wine
3 litres/5pt water

- Place all the ingredients in a large saucepan set over a high heat. Bring to boiling point and lower the heat.
- Simmer for about 40 minutes, without a lid, then strain.

Conversion tables
&
Index

Weights

Imperial	Approx. metric equivalent	Imperial	Approx. metric equivalent
$1/2$oz	15g	$1\,1/4$lb	600g
1oz	25g	$1\,1/2$lb	700g
$1\,1/2$oz	40g	$1\,3/4$lb	850g
2oz	50g	2lb	900g
$2\,1/2$oz	60g	$2\,1/2$lb	1.1kg
3oz	75g	3lb	1.4kg
4oz	100g	$3\,1/2$lb	1.6kg
5oz	150g	4lb	1.8kg
6oz	175g	$4\,1/2$lb	2kg
7oz	200g	5lb	2.3kg
8oz	225g	$5\,1/2$lb	2.5kg
9oz	250g	6lb	2.7kg
10oz	275g	$6\,1/2$lb	3kg
11oz	300g	7lb	3.2kg
12oz	350g	$7\,1/2$lb	3.4kg
13oz	375g	8lb	3.6kg
14oz	400g	$8\,1/2$lb	3.9kg
15oz	425g	9lb	4.1kg
16oz (1lb)	450g	$9\,1/2$lb	4.3kg
1lb 2oz	500g	10lb	4.5kg

The Imperial pound (lb), which is 16 ounces (oz), equals approximately 450 grams (g).

Oven temperatures

°C	°F	Gas mark	Temperature
130	250	$1/2$	Very cool
140	275	1	Very cool
150	300	2	Cool
160–170	325	3	Warm
180	350	4	Moderate
190	375	5	Fairly hot
200	400	6	Fairly hot
210–220	425	7	Hot
230	450	8	Very hot
240	475	9	Very hot

Fluid measures

Imperial	Approx. metric equivalent	Imperial	Approx. metric equivalent
1fl oz	25ml	9fl oz	250ml
2fl oz	50ml	10fl oz ($\frac{1}{2}$pt)	300ml
3fl oz	75ml	12fl oz	350ml
3$\frac{1}{2}$fl oz	100ml	15fl oz ($\frac{3}{4}$pt)	450ml
4fl oz	125ml	18 fl oz	500ml
5fl oz ($\frac{1}{4}$pt)	150ml	20fl oz (1pt)	600ml
6fl oz	175ml	30fl oz (1$\frac{1}{2}$pt)	900ml
7fl oz	200ml	35 fl oz (2pt)	1.2 litres
8fl oz	225ml	40 fl oz (2$\frac{1}{2}$pt)	1.5 litres

The Imperial pint (pt), which is 20 fluid ounces (fl oz), measures approximately 600 millilitres (ml).

Spoon measures

All the measurements given in the recipes are for levelled spoonfuls (British Imperial Standard)
1 teaspoon = 5ml
1 tablespoon = 15ml

The tablespoon measurements below are eqivalent to approximately 1oz (25g) of the following ingredients:

Breadcrumbs (dried)	3	Flour, unsifted	3
Breadcrumbs (fresh)	7	Rice (uncooked)	2
Butter/margarine/lard	2	Sugar (granulated, caster)	2
Cheese, grated (Cheddar)	3	Sugar (icing)	3
Cheese, grated (Parmesan)	4	Honey/syrup	1
Cocoa powder	4	Yeast (dried)	2
Cornflour/custard powder	2$\frac{1}{2}$		